The Dialectics of Music

The Dialectics of Music

Adorno, Benjamin, and Deleuze

Joseph M. Weiss

BLOOMSBURY ACADEMIC
LONDON • NEW YORK • OXFORD • NEW DELHI • SYDNEY

BLOOMSBURY ACADEMIC
Bloomsbury Publishing Plc
50 Bedford Square, London, WC1B 3DP, UK
1385 Broadway, New York, NY 10018, USA
29 Earlsfort Terrace, Dublin 2, Ireland

BLOOMSBURY, BLOOMSBURY ACADEMIC and the Diana logo
are trademarks of Bloomsbury Publishing Plc

First published in Great Britain 2021
This paperback edition published in 2023

Copyright © Joseph M. Weiss, 2021

Joseph M. Weiss has asserted his right under the Copyright,
Designs and Patents Act, 1988, to be identified as Author of this work.

Cover design by Charlotte Daniels
Cover images © iStock

All rights reserved. No part of this publication may be reproduced or transmitted
in any form or by any means, electronic or mechanical, including photocopying, recording,
or any information storage or retrieval system, without prior permission in writing
from the publishers.

Bloomsbury Publishing Plc does not have any control over, or responsibility for,
any third-party websites referred to or in this book. All internet addresses given in this
book were correct at the time of going to press. The author and publisher regret any
inconvenience caused if addresses have changed or sites have ceased to exist,
but can accept no responsibility for any such changes.

A catalogue record for this book is available from the British Library.

Library of Congress Cataloging-in-Publication Data

Names: Weiss, Joseph, author.
Title: The dialectics of music: Adorno, Benjamin, and Deleuze / Joseph Weiss.
Description: [1.] | New York: Bloomsbury Academic, 2021. |
Includes bibliographical references and index. |
Identifiers: LCCN 2020055533 (print) | LCCN 2020055534 (ebook) |
ISBN 9781350174962 (hardback) | ISBN 9781350174979 (ebook) |
ISBN 9781350174986 (epub)
Subjects: LCSH: Music–Philosophy and aesthetics. | Critical theory. |
Adorno, Theodor W., 1903-1969. | Benjamin, Walter, 1892-1940. |
Deleuze, Gilles, 1925-1995.
Classification: LCC ML3845.W44 2021 (print) | LCC ML3845 (ebook) |
DDC 781.1/7–dc23
LC record available at https://lccn.loc.gov/2020055533
LC ebook record available at https://lccn.loc.gov/2020055534

ISBN: HB: 978-1-3501-7496-2
PB: 978-1-3502-4407-8
ePDF: 978-1-3501-7497-9
eBook: 978-1-3501-7498-6

Typeset by Deanta Global Publishing Services, Chennai, India

To find out more about our authors and books visit
www.bloomsbury.com and sign up for our newsletters.

Contents

Prologue: On Presentation   vii

Introduction: Natural-History after the Brahmsian Mode   1

I   From the Lullaby to Electroacoustic Music   19
Gould, the Benjaminian—*Trauergesang*—Industrial Production and *The Ninth Symphony*—From Bird Song to Insect Noise—Reconciling Winds—Dynamic Contrast—Blurring the Human/Animal Distinction—The Spell of First and Second Nature—The Instrument Is the Animation—Tone Color—Informal Music—Regressive Consciousness and the Destruction of Memory—Humanism *Résumé*—Semblance, Praxis, and the Non-pulsed End of Dialectics—The Nonidentity of Nature and History—The Desecration of Silence—Critique of Pseudo-Praxis—The Mute Song of Justice

II   The Sorrow Song of Nature   53
Wreckage Universalized—Totality—Plugging the Sorrow Song into the *Trauergesang*—Anticipatory Echo—Stomping Out the Dialectic—Blind Myth—Silent Torture—*Was die Mode streng geteilt*—Dreambird—Forced Quantity—Scatting across Cultures—State of Nature—Fateful Improvisation—Weathering the Storm—Bury Me Deep—Transpositional Metaphysics—Advanced Decay—Fugitive Life—Technical Ecology—Decontextualization—Moon Satellite—Neutralization—Co-enactment—Stuffy Troubadour—Planned Spontaneity—Cruel Pragmatism—Deferred Improvisation—Variations from the Bottom

III **Music after Auschwitz**   **109**

Conatus—Ontologization—Infinite *Schuld*—*Der Ursprung des Übermenschen*—The Categorical Imperative of Music—Little Hans's Lullaby—The Most Advanced—Aeon and Chronos—Involuntary Reproduction—*Indifferenzpunkt*—Autumn Death—*Decasia*: Part 1—*Decasia*: Part 2—*Decasia*: Part 3—*Decasia*: Part 4—*Decasia*: Part 5—*Decasia*: Part 6

Bibliography   149
Index   170

Prologue

On Presentation

The argumentative form of philosophy blindly participates in the domination of nature. It, *a priori*, encumbers the task of the essay, which never aims to convince or interrogate but rather illuminate. As coercive as the abstract opposition between cause and effect in scholastic and modern metaphysics, its premises and conclusions are the ancient myth reiterated. Unsurprisingly, the jargon of the academic wing of the culture industry seldom veers from this rusty, self-satisfied form. *Disputatio* in renewed, class unconscious fashion, the jargon forgets, or willfully suppresses that, like the mute, nonintentionality of nature, language exceeds symbolic representation, the syllogism, and the characterological appearance (*Schein*) of identity. In the foreword to the *Ursprung des deutschen Trauerspiel*,[1] Walter Benjamin, by contrast, outlined a mode of dialectical presentation (*Darstellung*) that refuses to silence this nonintentional, expressionless moment, this multiplicity immanent to internal and external nature. While pointing to how phenomena are, in truth, constellated or how they, in truth, hang together (*zusammenhängen*), he showed that the movement of dialectics itself eventually shatters a language that would continue the self-preservative war of all against all by expelling its phantom adversary: the phonetics, rhythm, and overall musicality of language.[2] He, furthermore, showed that, in doing so, the dominant philosophy effectively effaces, *more geometrico*, the process by which an historically circumscribed context is decontextualized, by which each aesthetic moment in that original context is taken up, rearranged, stretched to its limit, and, mirroring a fleeting configuration of the stars, perhaps even transformed into an image of reconciliation (*Versöhnung*).

---

[1] Walter Benjamin, *The Origin of German Tragic Drama*, trans. John Osborne (New York: Verso, 1998); *Ursprung des deutschen Trauerspiels*, in *Gesammelte Schriften*, vol. 1, ed. Rolf Tiedemann and Hermann Scheppenhäuser (Frankfurt a.m.: Suhrkamp Verlag, 1974). Hereafter, all citations from Benjamin's *Gesammelte Schriften* will be abbreviated *GS*, followed by the volume number and the page number.

[2] For further consideration of the musicality of language, see, for example, the "Trauergesang" aphorism from Excursus I and the "Wreckage Universalized" aphorism from Excursus II.

In keeping with Benjamin's mode of presentation, the essays, aphorisms, or immanent planes that constitute the body of this work attempt to resist the natural-historical spell that, to this day, yokes the possibility of constellational transformation, of deterritorialization, to the ever same.[3] They do not assume the transformed, reconciled totality in advance. Nor do they claim the capacity to understand all, or even the majority, of the connections, to link all, or even the majority, of the virtual links to the real and the actual, without first sinking down into the movement of the matter at hand. Each fragment from the three excursus of this book, on the contrary, attempts to follow the tensions that constitute the limited nexus, the gravitational center, around which the concepts, that is, the moving "stars," cluster.[4] The assumption is that the fragments, the *membra disjecta*, whose ownmost need is to avoid being extorted into step-by-step progressions, hasty conclusions, or an overzealous, puffed-up pragmatics, have already been blasted apart by the natural-historical dialectic of enlightenment.[5] A thousand zigzagging lines—shards of incomplete and damaged networks—comprise the movement of the whole. The essay as form can only gesture to their deferred fulfillment negatively, it can only point to the missed chances by not pointing to them, or it can only practice philosophy from the "standpoint of redemption" by renouncing the possibility of achieving that redemption without a concomitant transformation in the organization of social labor.[6]

If Gilles Deleuze is, in contrast to T.W. Adorno and Benjamin, too quick to assert the immediate pragmatics of philosophical and literary texts,[7] or if he

---

[3] The natural-historical spell (*Bann*) is an essential concept throughout this work. See Adorno, *Negative Dialectics*, trans. E. B. Ashton (New York: Continuum, 1973), 344–9; *Negativ Dialektik*, in *Gesammelte Schriften*, vol. 6, ed. Rolf Tiedemann (Frankfurt a.m.: Suhrkamp Verlag, 1972), 339–43. See, also, the Introduction and the aphorism, "The Spell of First and Second Nature," from Excursus I. Hereafter, all citations from Adorno's *Gesammelte Schriften* will be abbreviated *GS*, followed by the volume number and the page number.

[4] To force philosophical language to defend itself, to prove itself "right" before the tribunal of reason, by abstractly separating its thesis from its argument is to perpetuate the ancient taboo against the *episteme* of music. It is, moreover, to miss the substance of the object itself, which can only be gleaned by gleaning the lost or buried associations, the drowned-out resonance, or the past labor that is congealed in every word. For more on the illogic of abstractly separating the thesis statement from both its argument and its "multiplicitous components," that is, following the straight line and successiveness of *prima philosophia*, instead of the simultaneity of the constellation or assemblage, see, for example, T. W. Adorno, *Minima Moralia: Reflections from Damaged Life*, trans. Edmund Jephcott (New York: Verso, 2002), 70–1; *Minima Moralia: Reflexionen aus dem beschädigten Leben*, in *Gesammelte Schriften*, vol. 4, ed. Rolf Tiedemann (Frankfurt a.m.: Suhrkamp Verlag, 1972), 77–8. See, also, Gilles Deleuze and Félix Guattari, *What Is Philosophy?* trans. Hugh Tomlinson and Graham Burchell (New York: Columbia University Press, 1996), 15–34.

[5] T. W. Adorno and Max Horkheimer, *Dialectic of Enlightenment: Philosophical Fragments*, trans. Edmund Jephcott (Stanford, CA: Stanford University Press, 2002); *Dialektik der Aufklärung: Philosophische Fragmente*, in *Gesammelte Schriften*, vol. 3, ed. Rolf Tiedemann (Frankfurt a.m.: Suhrkamp Verlag, 1972).

[6] Adorno, *Minima Moralia*, 247/ *GS*4, 281.

[7] For more on this immediate pragmatics or this prioritization of answering the question of whether the text "works," see, for example, Deleuze, *Proust and Signs*, trans. Richard Howard (Minneapolis:

maintains that the text is merely a set of forces in an assemblage of forces that can be activated or dissipated, connected or rechanneled to other machines and circuits, so that representation of reality is far from their primary end, he does so, in part, because he also rightly detects the narrowness of the argumentative form, the traditional *ratio*. This brings the three philosophical figures of this book into closer proximity than might initially be expected. Adorno's well-known claim that every object of the paratactical essay is "equally close to the center" prefigures rhizomatics.[8] The immanent critique of the Frankfurt School parallels the post-structuralist imperative to remain on the plane of consistency, despite the fact that it might take you down a dizzying, chaotic path.[9] "These difficulties consist," Adorno clarifies, in the fact "that a book's almost ineluctable movement from antecedent to consequence prove[s] so incompatible with the content that for this reason any organization in the traditional sense [. . .] prove[s] impracticable. The book must, so to speak, be written in equally weighted, paratactical parts that are arranged around a midpoint that they express through their constellation."[10] There is no denying that what Deleuze once described as the open character of *A Thousand Plateaus* or what Brian Massumi characterized as finding the cut of the album that suits you, regardless of its connection to the other cuts,[11] seems to resemble Adorno's Benjaminian point of departure. Each thinker appears to abandon what Adorno called the "higher level essentiality" of first philosophy,[12] which, in Deleuze's terms, is maintained by the arborescent pretense of Western metaphysics.[13] If, as Adorno and Benjamin similarly claim, the philosophical form of presentation must mimetically resemble its object or become similar to it in order to know it in empathy, this imperative is likewise embodied by Deleuze

University of Minnesota Press, 2000), 94.

[8] T. W. Adorno, "Essay as Form," in *Notes to Literature*, vol. 1, ed. Rolf Tiedemann, trans. Shierry Weber Nicholsen (New York: Columbia University Press, 1992), 19; "Der Essay als Form," in *Gesammelte Schriften*, vol. 11, ed. Rolf Tiedemann (Frankfurt a.m.: Suhrkamp Verlag, 1972), 28. This is an important similarity between these theorists, even if, as Deleuze shows, the center is itself moving, becoming decentered, or proliferating. See Gilles Deleuze, *Cinema 2: The Time-Image*, trans. Hugh Tomlinson and Robert Galeta (Minneapolis: University of Minnesota Press, 1991), 139–40.

[9] For an examination that, anticipating some of the themes in this work, links the Frankfurt School to the post-structuralist tradition, see Deborah Cook, *Adorno, Foucault and the Critique of the West* (New York: Verso, 2018).

[10] Cited from Robert Hullot-Kentor, "Editor's Afterward," in T. W. Adorno, *Aesthetic Theory*, trans. Robert Hullot-Kentor (Minneapolis: University of Minnesota Press, 1997), 364; *Äesthetische Theorie*, in *Gesammelte Schriften*, vol. 7, ed. Rolf Tiedemann (Frankfurt a.m.: Suhrkamp Verlag, 1972).

[11] Brian Massumi, "Translator's Foreword," in Gilles Deleuze and Félix Guattari, *A Thousand Plateaus: Capitalism and Schizophrenia*, trans. Brian Massumi (London: Continuum, 2004), xiii–xiv.

[12] T. W. Adorno, *Metaphysics: Concept and Problems*, trans. Edmund Jephcott (Stanford, CA: Stanford University Press, 2001), 4; *Metaphysik: Begriff und Probleme* in *Nachgelassene Schriften, Abteilung IV*, vol. 14 (Frankfurt am Main: Verlag, 1998), 14. Hereafter, all citations from the *Nachgelassene Schriften* will be abbreviated *NS*, followed by the volume number and page number.

[13] Deleuze and Guattari, *A Thousand Plateaus*, 3–25.

and Guattari's form of presentation, which, to be sure, mirrors the rhizomatic horizontality of nature they seek to unveil and, more importantly, set in motion. Inasmuch as the ancient *topos* of like knowing like holds as a universal truth, philosophy is ultimately compelled to reactivate a mimetic language, on the one hand, and take seriously, on the other, the prospect of a becoming-other that would, at last, break out of the identitarian semblance, the image of thought, which so insidiously rules over the predominant philosophical language.

At the same time, from *Nietzsche and Philosophy* on, dialectics is often conceived as the greatest of dangers for Deleuze.[14] Indeed, for Deleuze, the becoming-reactive thesis, which is nothing short of a characterization of the nihilistic trajectory of Western civilization, reaches its apex with Hegelian dialectics. The reactionary spirit concerning the greatest embarrassment precedes and resonates well beyond the discovery of the truly abominable *Schwarze Hefte*. Even if, as the following pages intend to show, there are scarcely three better examples of continental philosophers reflecting the movement of music, that is, where it has been and where it is going, how it might be deterritorialized, critically grasped, and how the ongoing mediation between nature and technology might still prefigure a transformation that could one day alter the political terrain, there is no escaping the fact that the philosophy of difference seems to be fundamentally at odds with dialectics. After all, from the perspective of the latter, the former threatens to overstep the dialectical truth-content (*Wahrheitsgehalt*) of natural-history, or it at least borders on hypostatizing difference on the basis of a false, all-too-pervasive, ontological need.[15] Becoming and life are, in the final analysis, abstractions. They do not become or live without becoming *something* and living in *some way*, and it is foreseeable that, given an historically determinate context, their alleged *élan vital* could be completely extinguished.[16]

When this work thus violates Deleuze's demand to remain on his own plane of consistency and, instead, aims to unveil the dialectic in the non-dialectical thinker, this is not done in order to smoothly subsume, without remainder, the differences in the identity of a positive dialectics. The irreconcilability between these thinkers is itself a moment in the movement of negative dialectics. Perhaps a circuit-jamming that can only result in feedback and dissonance is what is needed in order to amplify just how much both sides, which do not add up

---

[14] Gilles Deleuze, *Nietzsche and Philosophy*, trans. Hugh Tomlinson (New York: Columbia University Press, 1983), 156–63.
[15] Adorno, *Negative Dialectics*, 92–3; *GS6*, 99–100.
[16] Compare Gilles Deleuze, *Bergsonism*, trans. Barbara Habberjam (New York: Zone Books, 2006) to Adorno's understanding of Bergson in *Negative Dialectics*, 8/ *GS6*: "[t]he dialectical salt was washed away in an undifferentiated tide of life."

when pieced together, are expressions of the false totality. The persistent need for multiplicity without identity is a real need, if a false one. One cannot explain it away. When "second reflection"[17] eventually forswears the abstract subsumption of difference through which "first reflection" has long functioned, and that same stubborn need to be done with the subject nonetheless persists in philosophical discourse,[18] this is evidence of the fact that the exchange principle through which ancient anxiety is perpetuated still haunts every epistemology. Dialectics is the "ontology of the wrong condition,"[19] but thinking undialectically is a socially necessary moment in the process of preserving this contradictory condition. The subject has, of course, been nothing other than the agent of domination heretofore. But this is not grounds for assuming that it must go on being such an agent or that it is, *a priori*, consigned to such blindness, as if that were its ontological essence.

As Adorno maintained in the context of his study on Beckett, "[i]t is only in opposition to identity, and thus falling within its concept, that dissociation as such is possible; otherwise it would be pure, unpolemical, innocent multiplicity."[20] Chaos is inextricably tethered to unity, to the concept. The one can be neither posited nor recognized without the other. It is difficult to imagine a statement more intractably opposed to Deleuze's schizoanalysis than this. Yet, a situation that, on Adorno's account, is enough to make the schizoid persona of Beckett's plays farcical and hallucinatory accurately characterizes the historical crisis of the individual as such. Subject has indeed reversed into object, into an inert and stubborn body, devoid of the self-reflective capacity through which the idea of emancipation first glimmers. If, along these lines, Deleuze and Guattari's call for schizoanalysis does not mean that the schizophrenic is the vanguard, but rather the one who reveals the missed links, the unplugged circuits, which constitute the desiring production of all of us, human and nonhuman alike, then their mode of philosophizing, in reality, converges with Benjamin's and Adorno's in an incontestable manner. Recall that, for Adorno, it is "solely in pathogenic

---

[17] For more on this concept of "second reflection" (*zweite Reflexion*), see T. W. Adorno, "On Subject and Object," in *Critical Models: Interventions and Catchwords*, trans. Henry W. Pickford (New York: Columbia University Press, 2005), 246; "Zu Subjekt und Objekt," in *GS10.2*, ed. Rolf Tiedemann (Frankfurt a.m.: Suhrkamp Verlag, 1972), 742. See, also, Adorno, *Negative Dialectics*, 44/*GS6*: 54.

[18] For a look at how this asubjective need has been exceedingly influential for the so-called speculative turn of "realist" philosophy, see, for example, Levi Bryant et al. "Towards a Speculative Philosophy," in *The Speculative Turn: Continental Materialism and Realism* (Melbourne: re.press, 2011), 1–18.

[19] Adorno, *Negative Dialectics*, 11 (translation modified)/*GS6*, 22.

[20] T. W. Adorno, "Trying to Understand *Endgame*," in *Notes to Literature*, vol. 1, trans. Shierry Weber Nicholsen (New York: Columbia University Press, 1992), 257; "Versuch, das Endspiel zu verstehen," in *Gesammelte Schriften*, vol. 11, ed. Rolf Tiedemann (Frankfurt a.m.: Suhrkamp Verlag, 1972), 300.

conditions that consciousness learns about its unfree side."²¹ When he, in a parallel way, attempts to assess the gapless web of ideology and claims that "semblance [*Schein*] has become so concentrated," under the current system, "that to see through it objectively assumes the character of hallucination,"²² he once again anticipates Deleuze and Guattari's goal of disrupting narratives of the truth in and through the powers of the false,²³ in and through the "sickness." This is, of course, not to mention just how much each of these theoretical orientations seeks to stretch the Marxist critique of political economy, as well as the psychoanalytic understanding of the ego, to their outermost limits. Without, in the end, playing the infantile game of determining who is right and who is wrong, or who is more equipped to grasp the matter itself, the reader has grounds for believing that deploying the conceptual schemata of each of these theorist, that is, setting them into dialectical tension with one another, might well reveal something about the limits and possibilities of experience that philosophy continues to overlook.

The philosophical task could, in this respect, be framed as the attempt to grasp with the most advanced theoretical resources the determinate character of the present moment, whether it starts from musical, sociopolitical, or even metaphysical phenomena. Part and parcel of the same immanent totality, the same composition of capital, these phenomena, in fact, penetrate one another or are formed by the same cluster of concepts and the same blocked or jammed schiz-flows. Wherever the accent of analysis rests, the point is that critique cannot be adequately approximated without reading the past off of the sonorous and optical image of the present. Addressed in Excursus I, this more specifically requires illuminating the variations that comprise the movement from the "first" state of emergency, namely the lullaby song, to the "last" state of emergency, namely the experiments of electroacoustic and so-called cosmological music. Addressed in Excursus II, it similarly requires rescuing something of the unanswered sorrow (*Trauer*) that has, from the mythical origin to the mythical culmination, constituted the movement of nature as a whole. For, at virtually every interval, this voiceless sorrow breaks through the form and expression of, for example, the blues and jazz, as well as the post-tonal experimentations of the twenty-first-century avant-garde.

A philosophy of music that, moreover, fails to come to terms with the infinite debt and guilt-context (*Schuldzusammenhang*) of both the Middle Passage and Auschwitz is all but guaranteed to mischaracterize the limits and

---

[21] Adorno, *Negative Dialectics*, 222 (translation modified)/*GS6*, 221.
[22] Adorno and Horkheimer, *Dialectic of Enlightenment*, 170/*GS3*, 231.
[23] Deleuze, *Cinema 2*, 126–55.

possibilities of a *praxis* in whose name it speaks.[24] As Kant argued long ago, this mischaracterization—the semblance (*Schein*) of reason itself—reduces philosophy to the repetition compulsion of tautological statements. In thus renouncing comparative philosophy, the far more urgent task of this work might also, in the spirit of the German philosophical tradition, be described as the attempt to grasp the concrete without lapsing into the pseudo-concrete. This work seeks, in other words, to avoid the navel-gazing platitudes that allegedly attest to one's lived experience of the so-called popular.[25] Stupefied by the appearance of simple exchange, C-M-C, philosophical convention unwittingly preserves the real movement of expanded reproduction, M-C-M'. Resistance to and expropriation of that process is forfeited through an analysis that, all too frequently, parallels the false immediacy of *Lebensphilosophie*.[26] Blind to the objective illusion of the *camera obscura*, the vaunted, affective variations appear upside down so long as they are not traced back to the accumulated labor—collective *Schuld*—and the crisis of reproduction from which they, in reality, unfold.

Against this fetishization of theory, the critical theory of music insists that following the dialectic of the extremes, that is, the contrast between the omnipresent standardizations of the culture industry and the outermost experimentations of autonomous music, is the precondition of rescuing the truth-content of music and the still deferred politics that it prefigures from the territorializing spell of domination. Hence, the relationship between, for instance, Du Bois's concept of the "sorrow song" and the dialectical compositions of Michael Gordon, respectively addressed in Excursus II and III, appears at first glance to be one of indifference. But the proper juxtaposition of their divergent lines of flight illustrates a shared, escape-train longing, a *universal* diaspora, which yearns to finally break free of the escape-and-capture, guilt-and-atonement logic of the capitalist axiomatic. Something similar could be said of the relationship between blues and jazz improvisation and the involuntary release of overtones from post-minimalist composition. Apparently existing on

---

[24] This attempt constitutes the guiding theme of Excursus III. It is also intermittently thematized in Excursus II in relationship to the sorrow and play of the blues.
[25] Cf. Agnès Gayraud, *Dialectic of Pop*, trans. Robin Mackay et al. (Windsor Quarry: Urbanomic Media, 2019).
[26] Adorno and Deleuze share a similar suspicion regarding the false immediacy or conventional territorializations of phenomenology and its "lived-experience." See, for example, T. W. Adorno, *Against Epistemology: A Metacritique*, trans. Willis Domingo (Malden, MA: Polity Press, 2013), 45–7; *Zur Metakritik der Erkenntnistheorie*, in *Gesammelte Schriften*, vol. 5, ed. Rolf Tiedemann (Frankfurt a.m.: Suhrkamp Verlag, 1972), 52–4; Gilles Deleuze, *The Logic of Sense*, trans. Mark Lester (New York: Columbia University Press, 1990), 102.

wholly different planes, the right presentational placement—"exact fantasy"[27]—reveals that an underlying *need*, a fugitive (*flüchtig*) and nomadic desire,[28] to liberate living-labor from the strictures of dead-labor continues to constitute both the "popular" and "autonomous" iterations of music.

The choice between which side to emphasize, paralleling the stale debate between Benjaminian and Adornian aesthetics, is thus revealed to be a false choice. It is conceived on the basis of an undialetical relation that blocks comprehension of the whole. The compartmentalization of spirit appears as preference, as mere taste, for which there is either no accounting or class reductionist and identitarian explanations. Truth-content, the refracted light of redemption that shines forth from the unreconciled object itself, is thereby conflated with an hypostatized political content.[29] Reified consciousness forgets that the autonomous works of the European tradition, which form the subject matter of Excursus I and III and are Adorno and Deleuze's primary concern, are threatened with the same commodification, that is, the same logic of the exchange principle, that besets both the popular and autonomous works of Black music, which form the bulk of the subject matter of Excursus II. This suggests that, despite the different points of departure and the different features of concretization, the theory and practice of Afro-modernism and Euro-modernism have several points of convergence.[30] It also suggests that these traditions reciprocally constitute one another, just as the commodity form from which the experimental work tries to differentiate itself chains it, via negation, to its popular counterpart.[31]

---

[27] T. W. Adorno, "The Actuality of Philosophy," trans. Benjamin Snow, *Telos* 31 (Spring 1977): 120–33, 131; "Aktualität der Philosophie," in *Gesammelte Schriften*, vol. 1, ed. Rolf Tiedemann (Frankfurt a.m.: Suhrkamp Verlag, 1972), 325–44, 342.

[28] See, for instance, the "Fugitive Life" aphorism from Excursus II.

[29] In trying to avoid this conflation, I share Michael Gallope's assessment that the dichotomy between the so-called cultural history of sound studies and the alleged philosophical formalism of musicology is, in reality, a false dichotomy. In a study that compares and contrasts the music theory of Bloch, Adorno, Jankélévitch, and Deleuze and Guattari, Gallope convincingly argues that a dialectic exists between these fields of analysis. More specifically, the ineffability of music is the, as it were, productive motor that generates the movement between, in Gallope's terms, the sensory immediacy of an embodied culture and the formal coherence of a linguistic or conceptual system. See Gallope, *Deep Refrains: Music, Philosophy, and the Ineffable* (Chicago: University of Chicago Press, 2017), 15–16.

[30] As a major refrain in the following aphorisms, this affinity is especially poignant in a context where the memory destroying terror of the transatlantic slave trade eventually turns back, as Aimé Césaire famously argued, against the European victor. The need for a recollective aesthetics, embodied in the Frankfurt School and elements of Euro-modernism, is in dialectical tension with the need for an aesthetics that, embodied in Deleuze and Afrofuturism, attempts to part ways with recollection altogether.

[31] In illuminating some of the disjunctive, conjunctive, and associative moments of the history of music, this book hopes to resonate with an internationalist tendency that has, for instance, tried to link Marxist social theory to the anti-racist struggle for decolonization, but discovered what Frantz Fanon, on the verge of collapse, once discovered vis-à-vis Sartre's conception of universal history: the impossibility of a transformation that would leave intact the material contradiction. Frantz

It is this antinomic problematic, then, that crystalizes the effort to break decisively with the positivist spirit of the contemporary world. In flouting critique, such a spirit necessarily misrecognizes the stores of energy that, in the digital era of technical reproduction, are now at the producer's disposal. If these stores of energy were expropriated and rechanneled, they could, as the three figures of this study persistently maintained, be used to burst the narrow passageways through which they are currently flowing. The variational dynamism between the unamplified voice and its "machining,"[32] between the profane and the sacred,[33] or between the infinitesimally small flutters and infinitely large echoes, could still, in short, be widened. Any approach that refuses to follow this dialectic between forces and relations of production is tantamount to resignation before domination.[34] The presupposition of this work is that the possibilities opened up by music itself, and reflected in critico-philosophical presentation, are an index of the still unrealized nonidentity of nature. Dialectics is the self-consciousness of this blocked realization.

Fanon, *Black Skin, White Masks*, trans. Charles Lam Markmann (New York: Grove Press, 1967), 140. For a further look at how this Afro-modernist tendency has unfolded in relationship to the internationalist features of jazz, see John Lowney, *Jazz Internationalism: Literary Afro-modernism and the Cultural Politics of Black Music* (Urbana: University of Illinois Press, 2017).

[32] Deleuze and Guattari, *A Thousand Plateaus*, 303.

[33] Unlike the predominant aesthetic theory, Benjamin insists upon following the dialectic between the profane and the sacred, between the "dream kitsch" of the everyday street song (*Gassenhauer*) and the utopian longing for the new. See Walter Benjamin, "Surrealism: The Last Snapshot of the European Intelligentsia," in *Selected Writings*, vol. 2.1, ed. Michael W. Jennings (Cambridge, MA: Harvard University Press, 2003), 207–21, 210; "Der Sürrealismus: Die letzte Momentaufnahme der europäischen Intelligenz," in *Gesammelte Schriften*, vol. 2, ed. Rolf Tiedemann and Hermann Scheppenhäuser (Frankfurt a.m.: Suhrkamp Verlag, 1974), 295–310, 300.

[34] In Benjamin's terms, this means that both the theorist and the musician have given up on the need to rescue the unfulfilled sorrow of the past and eventually fulfill or complete (*vollenden*) it, via critique, on a higher plane. Walter Benjamin, "The Concept of Criticism in German Romanticism," in *Selected Writings*, vol. 1, ed. Michael W. Jennings (Cambridge, MA: Harvard University Press, 2003), 159; "Der Begriff der Kunstkritik in der deutschen Romantik," in *Gesammelte Schriften*, vol. 1, ed. Rolf Tiedemann and Hermann Scheppenhäuser (Frankfurt a.m.: Suhrkamp Verlag, 1974), 78.

Introduction
Natural-History after the Brahmsian Mode

In one of the anecdotes that intermittently punctuate the melancholic science of *Minima Moralia*, T.W. Adorno recalls that, as a child, he completely misunderstood the text to Johannes Brahms's famous *Lullaby*.[1] As opposed to hearing the *Näglein* that adorn the cradle as coronations, the young Adorno heard the diminutive "*lein*" as modifying the German word for nails (*Nägel*). His description of this "misunderstanding," which at first glance appears to be a mere idiosyncrasy, is striking for the manner in which it anticipates a philosophical problematic that would, without exaggeration, guide the whole of Gilles Deleuze's thought, namely the natural-historical potential for deterritorialization or, in the case of human beings, the material possibility of breaking free, at last, from the imitative game of the Oedipal triangle. Are not these little nails, "with which the curtain round the cot [. . .] was thickly studded, so that the child, shielded from every chink of light, could sleep in an unending peace without fear," the perfect visual complement to the echo of the mother's voice, which is to say, the promise of happiness at play in this first iteration of song, this first oath of security?[2] Resonating with and against the sharp edges of the metal, with and against the flowers on the chain of history,[3] does not this image of the lullaby comprise every child's initial attempt at territorialization, at marking out a terrain via sound, so that the fright of impending departure, of the dark, fairytale night, can be borne in solace? "How much the flowers fell short of the tenderness [*Zärtlichkeit*] of those curtains," writes Adorno, insisting upon the shelter and safety (*Geborgenheit*) that this originary language affords.[4]

---

[1] Adorno, *Minima Moralia*, 199/*GS*4, 224–5. The lullaby reads as follows in the German: "Guten Abend, gute Nacht / mit Rosen bedacht / mit Näglein besteckt / schlupf' unter die Deck! / Morgen früh, wenn Gott will / wirst du wieder geweckt."
[2] Ibid., 199/*GS*4, 224–5.
[3] Karl Marx, "Contribution to the Critique of Hegel's *Philosophy of Law*. Introduction," in *Collected Works*, vol. 3, ed. James S. Allen et al. (New York: International Publishers, 1975), 176.
[4] Adorno, *Minima Moralia*, 199/*GS*4, 225. This understanding of language as having an originary connection to song is derived from Walter Benjamin's analysis of C.G. Jochmann's work. See Benjamin, "'The Regression of Poetry,' by Carl Gustav Jochmann," in *Selected Writings*, vol. 4, ed. Michael W. Jennings (Cambridge, MA: Harvard University Press, 2003), 356–80, 364; "Die

The degree to which the lullaby is, as will become evident in the following excursus, essential not only to the developmental course of music but also to the natural-historical potential for transformation becomes more intelligible when one observes that Deleuze and Guattari explicitly juxtapose this form of song to other forms of protective self-preservation.[5] "[T]he Lullaby that territorializes the child's slumber" needs, in their view, to be thought alongside "the Lover's Refrain that territorializes the sexuality of the loved one, the Professional Refrain that territorializes trades and occupations, [and] the Merchant Refrain that territorializes distribution and products."[6] Add to this list of coercive, stabilizing forces the song of birds, a slew of acoustically based mating rituals, even the "composition" of the stars, and the seasonal patterns that reflect them. Human and extra-human nature is, to state it simply, part of a cosmological and elemental refrain. In the case of humans and other animals, the above-mentioned tenderness (*Zärtlichkeit*) and safety (*Geborgenheit*) may, in a certain sense, be constitutive of the "success" of the phylogenetic refrain, but, as Adorno's description makes clear, so too is the impulse to expel the beggar, the alleged predator, or those who threaten to steal one's precious possessions in the terror of the amorphous night.[7]

The difficulty that will, accordingly, guide this work concerns whether or not these ambivalent repetitions within the larger cycle of "natural" *ritornelli* can ever, in reality, be freed from what Adorno provocatively calls the "spell" (*Bann*) of natural-history (*Naturgeschichte*). If they can be, one must provisionally assume that something of this sheltering tenderness will have to return, softened, after the delicate touch has, paradoxically, hardened in a ruthless struggle for survival. Like Walter Benjamin's mimetic similarities, one must, in other words, assume that acoustic refrains constitute nature. But whether or not they will ever be genuinely "laid hold of" (*emparer*) in the process of *becoming-music*, the process of *lulling* the war of all against all, or escaping the state of emergency, remains an unresolved question.[8] What are the conditions of an actual deterritorialization

---

Rückschritte der Poesie von Carl Gustav Jochmann," in *GS*1.2, ed. Rolf Tiedemann and Hermann Scheppenhäuser (Frankfurt a.m.: Suhrkamp Verlag, 1974), 572–98, 594.

[5] For further consideration of this concept of transformation, especially as it is distinguished from an imitation or a mere simulation that stops short of breaching the social hierarchy, that is, the social prohibitions on transformation, see Elias Canetti, *Crowds and Power*, trans. Carol Stewart (New York: Farrar, Straus and Giroux, 1984), 369–84.

[6] Deleuze and Guattari, *A Thousand Plateaus*, 327.

[7] Adorno makes this clear when, as he continues the previous passage on Brahms, he describes Taubert's lullaby as containing the ambivalent desire to both end all persecution and perpetuate it in a violence against the weak. Adorno, *Minima Moralia*, 199–200/*GS*4, 225–6.

[8] Deleuze and Guattari, *A Thousand Plateaus*, 327. It goes without saying that a strict adherence to the letter of their work would not allow Deleuze and Guattari to accept the conception of peace implied here.

of the current *milieu*? How might we finally break free from the terrestrial, pass into the cosmological sphere on which all electroacoustic music is modeled, and thus release ourselves from the history of domination that has heretofore plagued all life?[9]

Adorno, with notorious pessimism, cautions against what might be called pseudo-becomings and the pseudo-praxis that allegedly brings them into being.[10] In his words, the "spell and ideology are one and the same. The fatality [*Fatalität*] of ideology is that it dates back to biology. Self-preservation, the Spinozist *sese conservare*, is truly the natural law of all living things [*Naturgesetz alles Lebendigen*]."[11] Deterritorializations doubtless occur in tandem with reterritorializations, as Deleuze, the anti-dialectician, dialectically reminds his reader.[12] This suggests, however, that the changing appearance or surface phenomenon—in a word, the superstructural image—often gives the impression that previous limits have been overcome, when, in actuality, the static element of nature remains just that: undisturbed, tucked away, as it were, or preserved amid the semblance (*Schein*) of change.[13] In short, even when one specifies, with Adorno, à la Deleuze, that "ideology" is not "superimposed as a detachable layer on the being of society" but rather "dwells [*wohnt*] in that being,"[14] the spell of not having escaped the law of self-preservation continues to haunt all of the alleged deterritorializations in social and biological reality.[15] To Adorno's Marxian insight that the veil of the social is as old as political philosophy, one must, therefore, append the proviso that as far as "humans" are concerned, the veil of the social is also as old as the biological.[16] History and prehistory remain chained to one another. Social construction was never merely construction

---

[9] For more on the concept of domination as the organizing principle through which Adorno understands natural history, see Adorno and Horkheimer, *Dialectic of Enlightenment*, 1–34/GS3, 19–60.

[10] T. W. Adorno, "Marginalia to Theory and Praxis," in *Critical Models: Interventions and Catchwords*, trans. Henry W. Pickford (New York: Columbia University Press, 2005), 259; "Marginalien zur Theorie und Praxis," in *Gesammelte Schriften*, vol. 10.2, ed. Rolf Tiedemann (Frankfurt a.m.: Suhrkamp Verlag, 1972), 259. Cf. Ernst Bloch, *The Principle of Hope*, vol. 1 (Cambridge, MA: MIT Press, 1995), 272. Both Adorno and Bloch notably employ the German term *Scheinpraxis* to describe this phenomenon.

[11] Adorno, *Negative Dialectics*, 349 (translation modified)/GS6, 342. Cf. Gilles Deleuze, *Spinoza: Practical Philosophy*, trans. Robert Hurley (San Francisco: City Light Books, 1988).

[12] Deleuze and Guattari, *A Thousand Plateaus*, 327.

[13] For an exceptional analysis of Adorno's concept of semblance (*Schein*), especially as it appears in the face of Auschwitz, see Henry W. Pickford, *The Sense of Semblance: Philosophical Analyses of Holocaust Art* (New York: Fordham University Press, 2013).

[14] Adorno, *Negative Dialectics*, 354 (translation modified)/GS6, 348.

[15] For a further examination of the dialectical understanding of self-preservation in Adorno's thought, see Deborah Cook, *Adorno on Nature* (New York: Routledge, 2014), 17–35.

[16] T.W. Adorno and Max Horkheimer, "Society," in *German Sociology*, ed. Uta Gerhhardt (New York: Continuum, 1988), 151.

ex nihilo; it was always, rather, a natural outgrowth (*Naturwüchsigkeit*) of, or autochthonous to, its predecessor.[17]

It might, with this problematic in view, come as a surprise that Johannes Brahms should stand at the point of departure for a dialectical conception of the natural-history of music. Even if the lullaby is the first moment of security for music, and Brahms is justifiably called the master of the lullaby, suspicion toward a composer who is often characterized as "neo-classical" likely lurks. Can a composer of this kind embody anything other than a kind of *revanchism*, that is, the very territorializing and reterritorializing play of forces that have just been equated with the conservative turning-in-circles of the spell? One's misgivings diminish, however, when one begins to reflect upon the manner in which the lullaby and songlike character of Brahms's music extends far beyond his famous, small-scale nursery rhyme.

Anyone fortunate to have learned Brahms in their childhood is likely familiar with the first movement of the *Symphony No. 2 in D*. Nowhere is Goethe's dictum that one receives in adulthood what one wishes for in one's youth more applicable. In this work, after a brief rumbling in the timpani and horns that opens up a turbulent exposition, a melody virtually identical to that of the cradle song is suddenly introduced. With the warmth of pizzicato basses and cellos grounding it, this theme now figures as a kind of gravitational center holding together the entire movement. Undergoing harmonic and rhythmic variations throughout, the child learns that the cradle theme is never too far away. The journey to come, the departure from the maternal voice, is not, therefore, to be feared.

The oft-cited idyllic landscape of this movement comes into even sharper relief when one situates Brahms's music within the constellational totality of Western art-music. Twenty-one years of seemingly unending compositional toil preceded his long-awaited *Symphony No. 1 in C minor*, which was rightly hailed as the "Tenth Symphony" after its 1876 premiere, a mere five years subsequent to the Paris Commune. By the time of the *Symphony No. 2*, however, the tragic and storm-ridden features of Brahms's first large-scale, orchestral work had, on the whole, subsided or *lulled*, giving way to a calm, spring-like repose that, despite being bourgeois in origin, is essentially antithetical to the bombastic features of so much so-called Romantic music. The singularity of the cuddling protection evoked here, the lullaby rocking that floats and sways as if upon a wave (*Sur l'eau*),[18] echoes with Brahms's extraordinary *String Quartet No. 2 in A*

---

[17] Adorno, *Negative Dialectics*, 354–8/GS6, 347–50.
[18] Guy de Maupassant, *Aflout*, trans. Douglas Parmée (New York: NYRB Classics, 2008).

minor. There too, in the first movement, the cello's pizzicato repetition holds the child's hand, only this time the tempo is faster, and the downbeat is syncopated, albeit in a no less stabilizing fashion. Each pluck is a little kiss on the forehead, a reminder that gives courage for departure, since it is now contrasted with an unparalleled lyrical expressivity in the higher register, a stretching outward, *troisième arabesque*, in the viola and violin's rhapsodic duet.

This songlike, lover's lament, whose literary analogue is Proust's remembrance of his mother, now sings—confident beyond measure—like no human voice can sing. It reaches its apex in Brahms's *Violin Concerto in D*. It should be noted that Brahms composed this work in collaboration with Joseph Joachim, the virtuoso who, of Jewish decent, was under the protection of the Esterhazy family in late nineteenth-century Hungary.[19] What might seem like an insignificant biographical detail becomes arresting when the formal and material content of the work itself is examined. It has seldom, if ever, been observed, but this work for violin is fundamentally structured by the refrain of a little, secondary melody that bears a remarkable similarity to the three-syllable Passover song "Day-en-u." Many know this tune as a light bagatelle of sorts, a celebratory frolic. But in Brahms's and Joachim's hands it is slowed down and transformed into a melancholy as deep as the deepest river, into the sweetest sorrow that the world has perhaps ever known.[20] There it is, making its way on the scene in the early bars: not only in the flutes and bassoons from the orchestral exposition, or the high and low strings that precede the recapitulation, but, above all, in Joachim's own virtuosity and later his own cadenza. Alone and surrounded, finally, by silence, the trembling, inward sigh of this most lyrical of all instruments threatens to rip apart altogether, threatens to break up the solidarity of the four voices sung on the four strings. Will a broken cry be the last words for the soloist as he collapses to the ground (*untergehen*), hair and bow in tatters? It is as though this aural protest could, like the vibrato phrasing of every great, Jewish virtuoso, no longer withstand the tonal constraints of Western expression. And yet, there its memory is once more, threadbare, in a call and response with the clarinet and bassoons, after the storm has *lulled*. It will even make its way, slowly but surely, into the second movement and beyond.

---

[19] Just how much this collaboration was essential to the construction of this work can be seen in Boris Schwarz, "Joseph Joachim and the Genesis of Brahms's Violin Concerto," *The Musical Quarterly* LXIX, no. 4 (October 1983): 503–26.

[20] Cf. Langston Hughes, "The Negro Speaks of Rivers," in *The Collected Poems of Langston Hughes*, ed. Arnold Rampersad and David Roessell (New York: Vincatage Classics—Random House, 1995), 23; Paul Allen Anderson, *Deep River: Music and Memory in Harlem Renaissance Thought* (Durham, NC: Duke University Press, 2001).

Vinteuil's phrase was not Swann's alone.[21] For Brahms has given us the ever-recurring phrase of the Jewish diaspora itself, only now that diaspora is recognized for what it always was: the *universal* diaspora, the homesickness that torments every last creature living under the reign of the spell.[22] The truth of this ostensibly hyperbolic claim is sensed all the more when one remembers the historical lineage of the thousand-year-old Passover song. Yes, the uncertain convulsions have waned or, playing on the contested and admittedly dubious Hebrew etymology of the lullaby (*Lilith-abi*), the demon of the night has been cast out. Yes, Brahms's lullaby is often sung to the blessings of Jacob, who defies the property relation and is left with a stone for a pillow in the Hebrew Bible. But, most importantly, the combination of "day" (enough) and "enu" (to us) roughly translates into "it would have been sufficient," or "it would have been enough." This, then, is a song of gratitude (*Dankgesang*), of a "second harvest" that springs from abundance.[23] The journey into foreign lands, into the dark forest of uncharted territory and, above all, through the unspeakable torture of slavery, is no more.[24] The return, *morgen früh*, is here. Gifts proliferate, when just one—deliverance—would surely have been enough.

Far from being an idiosyncrasy, the essence of historical materialism is secretly ensconced in this redemptive music. Adorno gives voice to its muteness when he says of happiness that "the same applies to [it] as to truth: one does not have it, but is in it. Indeed, happiness is nothing other than being encompassed, an after-image of the original shelter within the mother [*Nachbild der Geborgenheit in der Mutter*]. But for this reason no-one who is happy can know that he is so." "He who says he is happy," Adorno continues, "lies, and in invoking happiness sins against it. He alone keeps faith who says: I was happy. The only relation of consciousness to happiness is gratitude: in which lies its incomparable dignity."[25] The great theorist of the metaphysical consequences of life after Auschwitz is, as early as 1945, well aware of the dissolution of the bourgeois concept of dignity.[26]

---

[21] Deleuze and Guattari, *What Is Philosophy?*, 189. Deleuze and Guattari's point is that every theme and variation is already a variation on the "great Refrain" or the "song of the universe."

[22] As the reader will observe in Excursus II, this Jewish diaspora is fundamentally entwined with the African diaspora, as well as the creaturely diaspora of all animal life. See Paul Gilroy, *The Black Atlantic: Modernity and Double Consciousness* (Cambridge, MA: Harvard University Press, 1993), 187–223.

[23] Adorno, *Minima Moralia*, 109–13/GS4, 121–6.

[24] It is not incidental that this escape from Egypt, or better, this retelling of the West's relation to Egyptian mythos, helps to constitute various threads of Afrofuturist music, in particular that of Sun Ra's. See Kodwo Eshun, *More Brilliant than the Sun* (London: Quartet Books Limited, 1998), 156–61.

[25] Adorno, *Minima Moralia*, 112/GS4, 124.

[26] Cf. Jean Améry, "Torture," in *At the Mind's Limits*, trans. Sidney Rosenfeld and Stella P. Rosenfeld (Bloomington: Indiana University Press, 1980), 27–8; Giorgio Agamben, *Remnants of Auschwitz: The Witness and the Archive*, trans. Daniel Heller-Roazen (New York: Zone Books, 1999), 47.

The historical basis of that dissolution is detected in the trajectory articulated here. Life in the camp has become practically total, which is to say, the crack in the proverbial door, under which the faint light of hope, the promise of an abundance of gifts pouring forth on holiday morning, has not only been closed, it has been, with Kafka, virtually bolted shut.[27] Happiness and a gratitude that would retrospectively preserve it, transformed in "second reflection,"[28] *dans la recherche*; that would, stated simply, retain the memory of this ephemeral and anticipatory hope, is blocked before the horrors of natural law (*vor dem Naturgesetz*). Proust heads the fragments on damaged life because he was the last gasp of air. The memory trace is all but effaced. Nothing escapes the *Schuldzusammenhang*, the guilt-nexus, of the living.[29] Real security was never won via historical practice and so the catastrophic storm that, for Benjamin, is blowing from paradise was never calmed.[30] The promise that the wind, as in every sober (*nüchtern*) work of art, would instead "blow cool like [...] a coming dawn,"[31] or instead interrupt the frantic "progress" of history, is not to be.[32] A music that neglects to reflect and incorporate this *objective*, world-historical betrayal, or a song that glibly chooses affirmation in face of it, truly does become what Adorno once controversially said of poetry: barbarism.[33] For it makes common cause with the domination of nature, "asserting that what was inflicted on [it]," whether conscious or unconscious, "was all for the good."[34] Brahms, then, is impossible today, but this does not eliminate the preponderant need to live up to the *promesse du bonheur* contained in his music. Just as little does it eliminate the need to stay true to the idea of art by continuing to gesture to the conditions under which true thankfulness, that is, metaphysical meaning, could

---

[27] T.W. Adorno, "Introduction to Benjamin's *Schriften*," in *Notes to Literature*, vol. 2, trans. Shierry Weber Nicholsen (New York: Columbia University Press, 1992), 232; "Einleitung zu Benjamins Schriften," in *Gesammelte Schriften*, vol. 11, ed. Rolf Tiedemann (Frankfurt a.m.: Suhrkamp Verlag, 1972), 582.

[28] Adorno, "On Subject and Object," 246/GS10.2, 742.

[29] Walter Benjamin, "Fate and Character," in *Selected Writings*, vol. 1, ed. Michael W. Jennings (Cambridge, MA: Harvard University Press, 2003), 201–6, 204; "Schicksal und Charakter," in GS2.1, ed. Rolf Tiedemann and Hermann Scheppenhäuser (Frankfurt a.m.: Suhrkamp Verlag, 1974), 171–9, 175.

[30] Walter Benjamin, "On the Concept of History," in *Selected Writings*, vol. 4, ed. Michael W. Jennings (Cambridge, MA: Harvard University Press, 2003), 389–400, 392; "Über den Begriff der Geschichte," in GS1.2, ed. Rolf Tiedemann and Hermann Scheppenhäuser (Frankfurt a.m.: Suhrkamp Verlag, 1974), 691–706, 697–8.

[31] Walter Benjamin, *The Arcades Project*, trans. Howard Eiland and Kevin McLaughlin (Cambridge, MA: Harvard University Press, 1999), 474 [N9a,7]; *Passagenwerk*, in *Gesammelte Schriften*, vol. 5.1, ed. Rolf Tiedemann and Hermann Scheppenhäuser (Frankfurt a.m.: Suhrkamp Verlag, 1974), 593 [N9a,7].

[32] Benjamin, paralipomena to "On the Concept of History," 402/GS1.2, 1232.

[33] T. W. Adorno, "Cultural Criticism and Society," in *Prisms*, trans. Samuel Weber and Shierry Weber Nicholsen (Cambridge, MA: MIT Press, 1984), 34; "Kulturkritik und Gesellschaft," in GS10.1, 30.

[34] Adorno, *Aesthetic Theory*, 160/GS7, 240.

return: gratitude in the face of death, self-relinquishment without fear, not the triumphal song of individuation.³⁵

Take the lyrical expression of Brahms's violin again. When coupled with his womb-like, even aquatic, remembrance of the mother's protection, Brahms's astonishing and, ultimately, indispensable construction of the musical coda comes into view. In, for instance, the conclusion to the *Symphony No. 3 in F*, when the first movement's original theme returns, like the fleeting sent of blossoming flowers or the transitory taste of Proust's madeleine, the becoming-child of music fearlessly sinks back into the void, into the *gute Nacht*, embraced once again by both the gentle plucking of the bass and the now-hovering, soft, fairytale bliss of high-pitched, pulseless whole notes from the woodwinds. Similarly, but perhaps even more profoundly, in the concluding moments to the *String Quartet No. 3 in B-flat*, an unmistakable interlude on a lullaby theme emerges, *tout à coup*, from nowhere. This is one last memory, one last hush or sigh, in the break, the gap, before the mechanical rigidity, the expressionless, smoke-stack industrialization from the first movement returns to swallow it up or perhaps rob it of the solace of the past, when one *was* happy. Moments like these are, Adorno maintains, bound up with "Brahms['s] [. . .] splendid *resignation*." "[I]n principle," he says, Brahms's "best final movements go back to the *Lied*, as if music were returning to the land of childhood."³⁶ Can you resist singing along with him, holding those same notes, smiling, skipping, tears of gratitude in your eyes?

Even if it has grown austere for having lost that encompassing, pre-reflective feeling, virtually all of Brahms's best works conclude by returning to this innocence. In other words, these works construct the *Abgesang*, the farewell or swan song, gracefully, with composure, fully confident and sheltered, in spite of the inescapable relation to death or the downfall (*Untergang*). That sweet passing that no longer fears, and is thus thankful for the protection it received, is the transitory downfall, the fleeting cipher to be read, in the moment of danger. Here the nonidentity between nature and history appears.³⁷ Marx called this moment *praxis*: the revolutionary chance that history might actually begin for

---

³⁵ For an excellent analysis of the importance of self-relinquishment in Adorno's thinking, see Kathy Kiloh, "Towards an Ethical Politics: T.W. Adorno and Aesthetic Self-relinquishment," *Philosophy and Social Criticism* 43, no. 6 (2017): 571–98.

³⁶ T. W. Adorno, *Beethoven: The Philosophy of Music*, ed. Rolf Tiedemann (Stanford, CA: Stanford University Press, 1998), 74; *Beethoven: Philosophie der Musik*, in *Nachgelassene Schriften, Abteilung I*, vol. 1, ed. Rolf Tiedemann (Frankfurt am Main: Verlag, 1994), 115.

³⁷ This Benjaminian and Adornian conception of the moment of danger, of the fleeting chance to escape the reproduction of prehistorical trauma that is signaled in the cipher, is remarkably close to Deleuze and Guattari's conception of the cipher as the nomad's numbering that is and is not subsumed, is and is not coded, by the state apparatus. See Deleuze and Guattari, *A Thousand Plateaus*, 390–1.

the first time.³⁸ Benjamin articulated this same phenomenon with incomparable sensitivity in both his work on *Trauerspiel* and, later, the *Arcades Project*. Seizing the moment of undifferentiatedness (*Indifferenz*) in its temporary pause may, as the reader will learn, require incorporating the electroacoustic current, not only because the promise of happiness at play in the old technology (*Technik*) was catastrophically broken but because, after the industrialization and rationalization of life, which Wittgenstein rightly said he could already hear in Brahms,³⁹ the parting, farewell echo has become a panicked, inconsolable shriek, the reverberation of which now ricochets off heights and subterranean depths never before thought possible. The visual compliment to this historical anxiety is Stanislaw Lem's description of one human moment, in which a field, not of mountains and rivers but of the corpses of history, flashes up through the murk of a stormy, lighting-filled night.⁴⁰ Electrical power is the precondition of this vision of the totality laid bare for a fraction of a second. Its impression, the after image of now-time (*Jetztzeit*), lingers negatively along with the crackling texture, the vastness of which stretches to all horizons, east to west, infinite to infinitesimal. There are loops within loops, temporalities within temporalities, vibrating the strings of the cosmos. Will the trickster who dupes Zeus become more than the beautiful semblance (*schöner Schein*) when this electrical current is finally expropriated?⁴¹

One need only think of the drone hum of highways in the distance or the white flashing of radio tower lights that, uniform like the time signature of late capitalism, tick their silent tock before mountainous horizons. Today, in an infernal reversal of the moral universe, the "cosmic interior of the steel helmet" stands guard over the inner sense, while "the moral law above" drowns out the starry heavens.⁴² Hence, today, after Auschwitz, this hum, which accompanies every child as they fall asleep on automobile and high-speed rail travel to

---

³⁸ Cf. T.W. Adorno, "Progress," in *Critical Models: Interventions and Catchwords*, trans. Henry W. Pickford (New York: Columbia University Press, 2005), 150; "Fortschritt," in *GS*10.2, 625: "The progress, which the eternal invariant brought forth, is that finally progress can begin, at any moment."

³⁹ The gathering bassoons and timpani of the third movement to the *Violin Concerto* or, similarly, the expressionless repetition of the main theme from the first movement to the *String Quartet No. 3 in B-flat*, come to mind in reference to Wittgenstein's claim about the coming industrialization in Brahms. Brahms, allegedly a Romantic composer, is hardly Romantic in these moments, just as his technical innovations, far from being regressions, point beyond neo-classicism.

⁴⁰ Stanislaw Lem, *One Human Minute*, trans. Catherine S. Leach (New York: Harvest Book, 1986), 8.

⁴¹ Cf. Günther Anders, "On Promethean Shame," in *Prometheanism: Technology, Digital Culture, and Human Obsolescence*, ed. Christopher John Müller (New York: Rowman & Littlefield, 2016).

⁴² Walter Benjamin, "Theories of German Fascism," in *Selected Writings*, vol. 2.1 (Cambridge, MA: Harvard University Press, 2003), 312–21, 319; "Theorien des deutschen Faschismus," in *GS*3, 238–50, 247.

faraway lands, echoes the horror and unrest of airplane bombardment, not the tender caress and rhythm of horse-drawn carriage, which was, to be sure, the basis of the music from Brahms's era. Will this drone, and this static, electrical surge, be rescued one day as their acoustic similarity to the calm, undulating ocean is finally, in peace, recognized? Will the becoming-other of music become *like* or *with* the "hardened and alienated"?[43] Will it sink down and empathize with the noise, with the commodity, "strok[ing] the hair of the helpless, giv[ing] sustenance to the destroyed mouth, and watch[ing] over the sleep of those who will never again awake," instead of perpetuating the territorializing expulsion that, in revelry, banishes the victims that it itself produces? If so, it might, in a sudden reversal (*Umschlag*), still be capable of generating a critical distance from that which is merely the case.[44] It might remember and act in the service of the hidden truth that nature and history are not, in the last analysis, identical to one another, that "what is possible," as Adorno once said regarding Mahler's *Kindertotenlieder*, "has not yet been."[45]

Marx provides the key to understanding how this broken promise of reconciliation, of the end of war, determines both the acoustic and political horizon.[46] A hard and fast alternative between either the fascist or communist, reactionary or emancipatory, subject comes to the fore. "The proletariat revolution," he asserts, grappling with the manipulative tactics of the *ancien régime* "will obtain that chorus without which its solo song becomes a swan song [*Sterbelied*] in all peasant nations."[47] One now, of course, knows that such a chorus never emerged. The *people* who, in transforming themselves, deterritorializing all hitherto existing class relations, were to sing the revolutionary hymn, never came into being. The requiem or death-song, which did emerge and has never once stopped blaring its deafening *oratio pro aris et focis*, signifies that the grace of departure, of the fulfilled *adieu*, has fallen to the ground in tatters as well. The asphyxiated victims of civilization twitch in their last moments. The composure needed to bring theory and practice together, to capture, in a flash, the fleeting

---

[43] Adorno, *Aesthetic Theory*, 21/GS7, 39.

[44] For a critique of what Adorno takes to be Wittgenstein's obedience to the positivist spirit of the age, especially the dictum from the *Tractatus* in which what is simply the case (*der Fall sei*) is simply the case, see Adorno, *Aesthetic Theory*, 45, 205/GS7, 73, 305. For an analysis that, against this verdict, illustrates an affinity between these two thinkers, see Roger Foster, *The Recovery of Experience* (Albany: State University of New York Press, 2007).

[45] T. W. Adorno, "Marginalia on Mahler," in *Essays on Music*, ed. Richard Leppert (Los Angeles: University of California Press, 2002), 612; "Marginalien zu Mahler," in GS18, 235–40, 235.

[46] For an analysis that attempts to stay attuned to the ever-shifting developments in the "acoustics" of the sociopolitical landscape, that is, that aims to show how "noise" and "dissonance" are themselves ultimately incorporated into the productive resiliency of neo-liberal capitalism, see Robin James, *Resilience and Melancholy: Pop Music, Feminism, Neoliberalism* (Winchester: Zero Books, 2015).

[47] Karl Marx, "The Eighteenth Brumaire of Louis Bonaparte," in *Collected Works*, vol. 11, ed. James S. Allen et al. (New York: International Publishers, 1975), 193.

moment of danger, the dialectic at a standstill, before it slips from our grip, is all but gone. Failing to live up to the hopes of our forebears, rationality and the mimetic impulse, thought and becoming, do not finally unite to break the ancient taboo.[48]

If, in keeping with this logic of betrayal, the individualism of the unamplified solo song necessarily passes over into a confrontation with collectivization, the chorus, and the accumulated store of energy implicit in instrumentation, then song—itself a repetition of the originary plaintive cry—will be faintly preserved even in the midst of its passing (*Vergänglichkeit*), even in the midst of its radical, technical transformation. In the same way as the *promesse du bonheur* persists amid the upheavals of the twentieth century, so the task of fulfilling the lullaby, of staying true to the reconciliation (*Versöhnung*) immanent to all song, persists. This is what Brahms, the last of the great classicists, teaches. This is also what Adorno means by the return to the land of childhood, to the *Lied*, and what Deleuze and Guattari mean by the becoming-child of music, as well as the contemporary need to finally lay hold of the "multiple-cry."[49] Together they might, as Adorno says, harkening to Maupassant, keep faith with the pledge that the dialectic will one day return to its origin, that adults will learn to become, as Nietzsche said, children again and thus, "lying on water [. . .], looking peacefully at the sky, without any further determination and fulfillment,"[50] finally renounce the restless movement of contradiction and resolution, of flow interrupted by flow, of organ-machine plugged into power-source, for what purpose?—not a single soul knows.

What concrete determinations, then, can one attribute to the memory of song after music has come into a confrontation with this practical block? Or, returning to the previous terminology, namely the territorializing refrain and the aporia of the natural-historical spell (*Bann*): What can a music attempting to break out of natural law actually achieve?[51] What sonic qualities must it embody, what technique (*Technik*) must it use, if it is to differentiate itself from the endless array of goods on the market, wherein "value" appears to this day as nature?[52]

---

[48] Adorno, *Aesthetic Theory*, 53–6/GS7, 86–90.
[49] Deleuze and Guattari, *A Thousand Plateaus*, 342.
[50] Adorno, *Minima Moralia*, 157 (translation modified)/GS4, 177.
[51] This task of breaking out of the "natural law" of value should be thought in connection with Benjamin's critique of violence, where the oscillation between law-positing (*rechtsetzend*) and law-preserving (*rechtserhaltend*) violence gives the impression of progress but in truth maintains the ancient order, the spell, of prehistorical might. Walter Benjamin, "Critique of Violence," in *Selected Writings*, vol. 1, ed. Michael W. Jennings (Cambridge, MA: Harvard University Press, 2003), 236–52, 243; "Zur Kritik der Gewalt," in GS2.1, ed. Rolf Tiedemann and Hermann Scheppenhäuser (Frankfurt a.m.: Suhrkamp Verlag, 1974), 179–203, 190.
[52] Adorno, *Negative Dialectics*, 354–5/GS6, 347–8: "The law is natural because of its inevitable character under the prevailing conditions of production. Ideology is not superimposed as a detachable layer on the being of society; it dwells [*wohnt*] in that being. It rests upon abstraction, which is of the

Two approaches will guide the present attempt to answer these questions, and two conceptions of natural-history will, moreover, undergird them. Whether they can form a block or be set to work in the joint task of critically understanding both the truth-content of advanced music and the natural-historical developments with which it has always struggled remains for the reader to decide.[53]

On the one hand, positing an identity between nature and history seems necessary, insofar as it is precisely the arrogance of the subject, or its feigned separation from nature, that unwittingly repeats the self-enclosed trap from which it longs to escape.[54] This, in part, grounds the well-known polemic from Deleuze and Guattari's *Anti-Oedipus*. There one recalls the claim that, against the orthodox conception of ideology, which, for them, is synonymous with idealism, theory must begin considering the manner in which "Nature = Industry" or "Nature = History."[55] As a tactical maneuver, collapsing the two terms of the traditional base-superstructure model appears to avoid that which, already in *Difference and Repetition*, would ceaselessly trouble Deleuze.[56] Rather than passively inheriting philosophy's rigid dichotomy between the artificial and the natural, between machinic and so-called organic processes, the point was

---

essence of the exchange process [*Tauschvorgang*]. Without disregard for living human beings there would be no exchange. What this implies in the real progress of life to this day is the necessity of social semblance [*Schein*]. Its core is value as a thing-in-itself, value as "nature." The natural outgrowth [*Naturwüchsigkeit*] of capitalist society is real, and at the same time it is that semblance" (translation modified).

[53] For one of the few attempts to think the music theory of Adorno and Deleuze alongside one another, see Nick Nesbitt, "Deleuze, Adorno, and the Composition of Musical Multiplicity," in *Deleuze and Music*, ed. Ian Buchanan and Marcel Swiboda (Edinburgh: Edinburgh University Press, 2004). I share Nesbitt's conclusion that, as opposed to "abandon[ing] each [thinker] to his proper plane of immanence," combining these thinkers into a new block may reveal something previously hidden from thought or may even give voice to previously unamplified or unchanneled forces. For more on the entwined dialectic between natural beauty (*Naturschöne*) and art beauty (*Kunstschöne*), see Adorno, *Aesthetic Theory*, 61–99/GS7, 97–153.

[54] Adorno plays on this non-reconciling or, as it were, territorializing echo of the natural law of myth and punishment, in Adorno, "Kierkegaard Once More," *Telos* 174 (Spring 2016): 57–74, 70; "Kierkegaard noch einmal," in *GS2*, 239–58, 254: "[The mythical layer of Kierkegaard's language] is one of intentional and cryptic repetition. Its archetype [*Urbild*], beyond the dialectic, is the echo, which unites the authority of the determinate sound with illusion, because it is nothing other than the very voice of the interrogator" (translation modified).

[55] Gilles Deleuze and Félix Guattari, *Anti-Oedipus: Capitalism and Schizophrenia*, trans. Robert Hurley (New York: Penguin Books, 1977), 25. See, also, Deleuze and Guattari, *Thousand Plateaus*, 4, where they, in my view, purposefully exaggerate the claim that there has never been such a thing as "ideology." This exaggeration is, as I understand it, designed to dispel precisely the common notion that ideology is merely a "detachable layer," as opposed to being a real, immanent force whose real semblance plays an essential role in driving forward natural-historical developments. The point, then, is to grasp just how much "ideology" is not simply a residue or echo of those "material" developments. Although such a claim is arguably a tactical attempt to move discourse away from an apparent stalemate, this collapsing of two traditionally bifurcated terms resembles Jason Moore's more recent attempt to think the "double internality" or simultaneity of nature and society. Moore, *Capitalism in the Web of Life* (New York: Verso, 2015).

[56] Gilles Deleuze, *Difference and Repetition*, trans. Paul Patton (New York: Continuum, 1997), xx.

to explode the bad, metaphysical binary and the concept of "mediation" that supports it.[57] Instead of a "historical history,"[58] that is, a history that happens *for* the subject, *for* the categories that humans employ, "natural-history" was meant, for Deleuze, as a concept that helps philosophy grasp those processes that cannot be subsumed by the subject and its representations, that cannot simply be added on or supplemented to a static recipient, whose essence somehow remains unchanged in the midst of the great transformations of modernity. The spirit of critique, of resisting what is simply the case, is certainly, on the face of it, at play in this approach, or this fidelity to the silent and the mute, to the nonhuman forces that propel "history." The advent of technically reproduced music is thus, on this model, hardly different from the advent of the film screen. Both must be understood as evolutionary metamorphoses, as deterritorializations taking place within a broader assemblage. And both apparently upset or fundamentally transform the human condition.[59]

On the other hand, there is Adorno's dialectical conception of natural-history, which cannot, as should now be obvious, be plugged into Deleuze's conception without generating a considerable degree of dissonance or static. For, recalling the above analysis of the fleeting *Abgesang*, or the afore-mentioned task of bringing dialectics to a standstill, the point for Adorno was to avoid what might be called the positivist effacement of the nonidentity between the two terms.[60] Rather than rigidly separating history and nature in a crude, hypostatized dualism, this approach suggests that one should attempt to see in "pure" nature the allegory of history and to see in "pure" history the allegory of nature.[61] Mediation, in the Hegelian sense, is thus the watchword of this approach. Lest one lapse into either a false, unmediated, spiritualism or vitalism,[62] in the first place, or a false, unmediated absolutism and ontology, in the second, such an "anthropomorphic" conception, that is, such a consideration of the material force of subjectivity as it intervenes in and is mediated by objectivity, is actually,

---

[57] Deleuze and Guattari, *Anti-Oedipus*, 5.
[58] Gilles Deleuze, *Negotiations*, trans. Martin Joughin (New York: Columbia University Press, 1995), 49.
[59] For more on this notion of an evolutionary leap that attends these metamorphoses in the technical forces of production, see Claire Colebrook, *Deleuze: A Guide for the Perplexed* (New York: Continuum, 2006), 9.
[60] Cf. Gayatri Spivak, "Can the Subaltern Speak?" in *Marxism and the Interpretation of Culture*, ed. Cary Nelson and Lawrence Grossberg (Chicago: University of Illinois Press, 1988), 275.
[61] For further consideration of this attempt to think against or to dynamize a Spinozian dualism, see Adrian Johnston, "For a Thoughtful Ontology: Hegel's Immanent Critique of Spinoza," in *Adventures in Transcendental Materialism* (Edinburgh: Edinburgh University Press, 2014), 23–50.
[62] For further consideration of this critique of Deleuze's alleged vitalism, see Alain Badiou, *Deleuze: The Clamor of Being*, trans. Louise Burchill (Minneapolis: University of Minnesota Press, 1999).

in spite of the popular outcry, the desired path.[63] "[T]o comprehend [*zu begreifen*] historical being in its most extreme historical determinacy, where it is most historical, as natural being," writes Adorno, in one of his more concise formulations of this dialectical task, "or if it were possible to comprehend nature as an historical being where it seems to persist most deeply in itself as nature."[64] Taken as a tactical approach, not, it must be emphasized, as an ontological claim, Deleuze's collapsing of the two terms is not so much to be avoided, as held onto, tarried with to the extreme, followed into the deepest recesses, until suddenly, without anticipation, the difference internal to repetition, the blind spot or silence internal to subjectivity, breaks open into a still, rippleless gesture of the body without organs.[65] A temporality beyond the "ontology of the wrong condition," that is, beyond dialectics, would presumably emerge on the basis of precisely this surrender to the matter at hand, where nature and history appear, if only briefly, to be identical and nonidentical to one another simultaneously.[66]

Two passages in particular are especially germane to understanding the critical tension between Adorno's and Deleuze's respective theories. Letting them hover here, at the beginning, should set the stage, as it were, for addressing the significance of the following foray into the dialectics of music.

---

[63] See, for example, Quentin Meillassoux, *After Finitude: An Essay on the Necessity of Contingency*, trans. Ray Brassier (New York: Continuum, 2008). Donna Haraway's conception of a multispecies becoming-with might provide an alternative to this so-called object orientated or "realist" turn. A likeness between "human" and "animal" or, in a word, anthropomorphism, is in her view and Adorno's the basis of stopping the domination of nature, not perpetuating it. This suggests that a similarity exists that is neither subsumptive nor coercive but rather mimetic. One might also add that against Heidegger, who learned his conception of "world" (*Umwelt*) from Jakob von Uexküll, the most striking element of the latter's conception of interspecies language or epistemology, the perception-mark (*Merkmal*) through which communication occurs, is that the subject, or "machine operator," communicates *with* the object. In other words, the mimetic similarity between receptors and operators produces a translation or an attunement between subject and object, not a hierarchical relationship, in which poor is distinguished from rich. The muteness (*Stummheit*) or nonidentity is not, therefore, as certain threads of Levinasian ethics have maintained and, still worse, as the present "anti-correlationist" fashion is maintaining, the result of failing to appreciate absolute otherness, radical alterity, or "mind independence," it rather emerges because of the taboo on anthropomorphism itself, on mimetic similarity, or the refrain between different species. Haraway, *Staying with the Trouble: Making Kin in the Chthulucene* (Durham, NC: Duke University Press, 2016); Uexküll, *A Foray into the Worlds of Animals and Humans*, trans. Joseph D. O'Neil (Minneapolis: University of Minnesota Press, 2010).

[64] T. W. Adorno, "The Idea of Natural History," trans. Robert Hullot-Kentor, *Telos* 60 (Summer 1984), 117 (translation modified); "Die Idee der Naturgeschichte," in *Gesammelte Schriften*, vol. 1, ed. Rolf Tiedemann (Frankfurt a.m.: Suhrkamp Verlag, 1972), 354–5.

[65] Deleuze and Guattari, *Anti-Oedipus*, 9–16. For further analysis of the (dissonant) connections between this Deleuzean conception of difference and Adorno's negative dialectics, see Nick Nesbitt, "The Expulsion of the Negative: Deleuze, Adorno, and the Ethics of Internal Difference," *SubStance* 34, no. 107 (2005): 75–97.

[66] Adorno, *Negative Dialectics*, 11 (translation modified)/*GS6*, 22. This Adornian refrain concerning the need to surrender to the matter at hand, or follow it immanently in a fully immersive experience, runs parallel to what Deleuze and Guattari imply regarding the "following" that occurs in nomadic science. See Deleuze and Guattari, *A Thousand Plateaus*, 369, 409.

After working through the relationship between bird and insect song, through the technical advancements that "machine" or instrumentalize the voice, and that, in so doing, point to the possibility of laying hold of the "full song" and "multiple cry" of nature for the first time, Deleuze and Guattari conclude the "becoming-music" section of a *Thousand Plateaus* by contending the following: "through becomings-woman, -child, -animal, or -molecular, nature opposes its power, and the power of music, to the machines of human beings, the roar of factories and bombers."[67] At the precise moment when, in these words, one fears that the old logic of territorialization is about to rear its ugly head again, is about to "oppose" or turn away from the "hardened and alienated," away from the acoustic echo of industrialization and modern warfare, instead of sinking down to their level and rescuing their "noise," one also discovers, in the next breath, that a subtle temporality, perhaps even a transitional cadence, is at play. Is this the same passing or transitoriness (*Vergänglichkeit*) that must be seized in a snapshot, like the terrain illuminated from Lem's lighting flash? Is this turning-away that then turns back the natural-historical rhythm that points the way to real transformation, to the potential for breaking the mythical spell of the dialectic of enlightenment? One thing is certain: banishment and flight will no longer suffice. Thus, without losing their momentum, Deleuze and Guattari pick up from this initially jarring sentence, and now insist, citing Henry Miller, that

> it is necessary to reach that point, it is necessary for the nonmusical sound of the human being [i.e., the factories and bombers] to form a block with the becoming-music of sound, for them to confront and embrace each other like two wrestlers who can no longer break free from each other's grasp, and slide down a sloping line: "Let the choirs represent the survivors. . . Faintly one hears the sound of cicadas. Then the notes of a lark, followed by the mockingbird. Someone laughs. . . A woman sobs . . . From a male a great shout: WE ARE LOST! A woman's voice: WE ARE SAVED! Staccato cries: Lost! Saved! Lost! Saved!"[68]

Here the horizon of advanced music begins to appear. Despite and because of the fact that the lyrical or melodious character of song can no longer be employed without regressing into bourgeois, and eventually, fascist grandeur, the warm resonance of Brahms's pizzicato accompaniment becomes the cold staccato of an abbreviated and expressionless voice.[69] Chained, in this way, to the whipping

---

[67] Deleuze and Guattari, *A Thousand Plateaus*, 309.
[68] Ibid.
[69] For further analysis of this transformation in the pathos of song, or this emotive emphasis that either speaks by restraining itself or lapses into bourgeois kitsch, see Roland Barthe, "The Bourgeois Art of

post of history, the lullaby's muffled rhyme might still, in the concluding moments, flicker up, only to pass away instantaneously, but this ambivalent call and response, this variation on the only theme of security that ever was,[70] is now cocooned in an electroacoustic dissonance or a micro-tonal coloring that can no longer abide the conventional harmony and fulsome sentimentality of yesteryear. Reflecting the outermost consequences, that is, the historical and technical mediations between the nonmusical and the musical, the "once upon a time" of storytelling is cancelled and preserved in this new choir of nature-sounds.[71] Sewing machines and air-conditioners, subway stations and power grids, no less than cicadas, crickets, and bird calls, are stores of nature's past labor, echoes of the cosmic refrain, are they not? Don't they, ask Deleuze and Guattari, carry a hope for the hopeless ones as well, for a nature that, as the music of Maryanne Amacher demonstrates, is still unfulfilled, still mute, and thus still waiting to be taken up, rechanneled and, in that way, emancipated from the terrestrial limits of all previously existing music?

Similarly, but perhaps, to repeat, in irresolvable tension with Deleuze, Adorno sets to work on his Benjaminian conception of natural-history in an early essay from 1933 entitled "The Natural-History of Theatre."[72] With the Alte Oper of Frankfurt am Main as the archetype for his dialectical images, Adorno is already, at this early stage, attuned to the task of the historical materialist. These dialectical images, which bring the dialectical tumult to a momentary stop or give us a momentary sense of the "smooth" space of the body without organs, require exact placement, critical juxtaposition.[73] As Adorno would later articulate it, they are "constellations between alienated things and incoming meaning, pausing in the moment of undifferentiatedness [*Indifferenz*] between death and meaning." "While things in appearance [*Schein*] are awakened to what is newest," that is to say, while they enter on the scene, professing the purposiveness of the commodity form, "death," or the approaching *Abgesang*, "transforms the[ir] meanings into what is most ancient."[74] Thus, in this text, the virtuoso of the stage and the clapping audience are seen for what they are: echoes of prehistorical sacrifice, of animal slaughter offered up by priests for the

---

Song," in *Mythologies*, trans. Richard Howard and Annette Lavers (New York: Hill and Wang, 2012), 190–2.

[70] Deleuze and Guattari, *What Is Philosophy?*, 189.
[71] Ibid., 191.
[72] T. W. Adorno, "The Natural History of the Theatre," in *Quasi Una Fantasia: Essays on Modern Music*, trans. Rodney Livingstone (New York: Verso, 1998); "Naturgeschichte des Theaters," in *GS*16.
[73] Deleuze and Guattari, *A Thousand Plateaus*, 474–8.
[74] Cited from Benjamin, *The Arcades Project*, 466 [N5, 2] (translation modified)/*GS*5.1, 582.

sake of the community's atonement.⁷⁵ Thus the sounds from the foyer are heard for what they are: the static electricity of the harmony of the spheres, which demands prattle from the patrons in order to recover, in the *interregnum*, from the earsplitting silence of that same stage.⁷⁶ And thus each of the new ceremonial features of the theater, from the conspicuous consumption of the boxes to the pomp and circumstance of the stalls and gallery, carry a remnant of the ancient spell, of a prehistory that, faced with death or faced with the fleeting moment of undifferentiatedness between nature and history, cries for metaphysical meaning, for redemption, in the exact moment when that meaning falls away. Are not the inhabitants of the boxes ghosts of the nobility who inherit their privilege from forces they fail to understand?⁷⁷ Is not the upper circle the site of the middle class who, from time immemorial, has paid for its acoustic advantage with the incapacity to see the real producer's skills?⁷⁸ Adorno gives a resounding answer to this Sisyphean play between the old and the new when he contemplates the dome as finale (*Kuppel als Schlußstück*):

> By rising above the theatre like a crowning piece, the dome completes the form which began enigmatically with the cumbersome stage of tragedy and now fades away gently, floating down from on high. For the sorrow [*Trauer*] of all those images rising up from the plaintive word [*klagenden Wort*] to the edge of the space they would like, as sung tone [*als gesungener Ton*], to burst asunder, is not shattered by this barrier, but rather finds there its way home. Having reached the pinnacle of the dome [*Kuppelhöhe*] it is transformed into solace [*Trost*]. The imprisoned sound of the creature [*gefangene Laut der Kreatur*], which rose up as song and is not shattered, but returns in the echo to meet its origins, reverberates the hope that no creature is lost that was once able to sing. Thus the dome, which is what separates our closed theatres most clearly from the open amphitheaters of antiquity, contains the promise that whatever happens here will not be forgotten, but will be preserved, so that one day it will return as an echo, subtly transformed, and will welcome us in the sphere of this finite cosmos [*im Rund des endlichen Weltraums*]. *Non confundar*; that is the resounding assurance which the dome bestows to the cloudy, fallible, impure song [*trüben, fehlbaren, unreinen Gesang*]. One day, so it appears [*so scheint es*], the sphere of the dome wants to draw the entire theatre into itself. The theatre will then become a sphere which has ceased to know the direction of historical time, something which our theatre had yearned to master. In the imagined

---

[75] Adorno, "The Natural History of the Theatre," 66/*GS*16, 309–10.
[76] Ibid., 75/*GS*16, 318.
[77] Ibid., 70/*GS*16, 314.
[78] Ibid., 74/*GS*16, 317.

spherical theatre the past becomes present and not just as our best costume play. Thanks to the transitoriness [*Vergänglichkeit*] with which it transparently makes its entrance on the stage and then its exit, the present is made eternal. Here lies the justification of theatrical illusion. . . . But the song whose melody traces the outlines of the dome which earlier had formed it is not vouchsafed to the mute [*Stummen*] in vain. Singers will join in [*einstimmen*] and the sequence of song [*Nacheinander von Gesang*], restatement and echo, will release itself in the simultaneity of the hovering [*schwebend*], fulfilled space, whose tranquility trembles in itself.[79]

In 1944, the Alte Oper was bombed to the ground.

The allegory of nature, which always hoped that illusion would one day dissolve into reality, appears to have imploded along with it. Who and what, then, will sing the song of redemption today? Who and what, moreover, will sing the song of gratitude (*Dankgesang*), the convalescents' hymn, after catastrophe appears as the fate of natural-history, after the memory of all those who have sung under the reign of the spell appears to have been extinguished?

---

[79] Ibid., 76–7 (translation modified)/*GS*16, 320.

Excursus I

From the Lullaby to Electroacoustic Music

The wolf will live with the lamb; the leopard will lie down with the young goat. The calf and the lion will graze together, and a little child will lead them.

—Isaiah 11:6

Echo reconciles.

—Adorno, Aesthetic Theory

Gould, the Benjaminian

Well known for the technical and expressive mastery of his interpretation of Bach's piano works, Glenn Gould is also, of course, famous for his apparent eccentricity, in particular the idiosyncratic humming or crooning that, in the lower, bass register of his singing voice, accompanies his live performances and recordings. Less well known is a tale told by his father that, as a child, when under duress, and thus expected to cry like the other children, the young Gould would respond with precisely this same humming. "A child in the dark, gripped with fear," write Deleuze and Guattari, beginning an old refrain, "comforts himself by singing under his breath. He walks and halts to his song. Lost, he takes shelter or orients himself with his little song as best he can. The song is like a rough sketch of a calming and stabilizing, calm and stable, center in the heart of chaos."[1] Is this merely the early stage of a territorialization process? Is the child, as Ernst Bloch says, alone, and thus merely hearing himself?[2] Is he merely warding off intruders, alien forces, in defense, in the *fort-da* production of an illusory self? If one effaces the similarity between Gould's stance on the superiority of the music studio to the live performance and Walter Benjamin's

---

[1] Deleuze and Guattari, *A Thousand Plateaus*, 311.
[2] Ernst Bloch, *The Spirit of Utopia*, trans. Anthony A. Nassar (Stanford, CA: Stanford University Press, 2000), 34.

thesis on technical reproduction,[3] one might be inclined to answer in the affirmative. For, as if scurrying off into seclusion, Gould did, indeed, all but retire from public performances at an early age. Yet, if one listens with more subtlety, one might also discover that both his humming and his departure from the *theatrum mundi* form a kind of cryptogram, as it were, of natural-historical truth, not unlike Benjamin's characterization of Karl Kraus's own humming, which is said to relate to the messianic word as his smile relates to the joke, the mute underside relates to *pathos*, or the peaceful crater lake relates to the monstrous crags and cinders of nature.[4] A cursory look at many of the virtuosi of the music world will show a tendency to "mouth" or silently "voice" the identical notes they play on their instrument, their *organon*. Such an imitative doubling or lip-syncing, to be sure, indicates something fundamental about all music making, namely, the task of "machining the voice,"[5] running it through the circuits of technology in order to fulfill it, as well as its inverse, namely, the drive to part with the instrument and thereby return to pure, unmediated song, to the language of things.[6] The uniqueness of Gould consists, however, in the fact that, for him, this faint gesture is not always monophonic with the lead melody. For him, the accompanying voice is frequently uttered contrapuntally, that is, as a separate line, a third voice, distinct from the main musical material that he plays with his two hands. It therefore forms a separate, enfeebled, or barely discernable harmony that is absent from the original, graphic notation. One might say, then, that this Schopenhauerian *Grundbass*, this deep, echoing *Lied von der Erde*, which, as few have noted, precedes and, in reality, subtends the oculocentric mirror stage, is an anticipatory hope of sorts, a concrete utopia, that waits for an answer, waits to come out of itself and, at last, join the unwritten song of nature.[7] Where, asks Gould, will you enter into this cosmological work?

---

[3] Walter Benjamin, "The Work of Art in the Age of Its Technological Reproducibility: Third Version," in *Selected Writings*, vol. 4, ed. Michael W. Jennings (Cambridge, MA: Harvard University Press, 2003), 251–83; "Das Kunstwerk im Zeitalter seiner technischen Reproduzierbarkeit: Dritte Fassung," in *Gesammelte Schriften*, vol. 1.2, ed. Rolf Tiedemann and Hermann Scheppenhäuser (Frankfurt a.m.: Suhrkamp Verlag, 1974); Glenn Gould, "The Prospects of Recording," in *Audio Culture*, ed. Christoph Cox and Daniel Warner (New York: Continuum, 2010), 115–26.

[4] Walter Benjamin, "Karl Kraus," trans. Edmund Jephcott, in *Selected Writings*, vol. 2.2 (Cambridge, MA: Harvard University Press, 2003), 433–58, 450–1; "Karl Kraus," in *Gesammelte Schriften*, vol. 2.1, ed. Rolf Tiedemann and Hermann Scheppenhäuser (Frankfurt a.m.: Suhrkamp Verlag, 1974), 334–67, 356–7.

[5] Deleuze and Guattari, *A Thousand Plateaus*, 303.

[6] See Walter Benjamin, "On Language as Such and on the Language of Man," in *Selected Writings*, vol. 1, ed. Michael W. Jennings (Cambridge, MA: Harvard University Press, 2003), 62–74; "Über Sprache überhaupt und über die Sprache des Menschen," in *Gesammelte Schriften*, vol. 2.1, ed. Rolf Tiedemann and Hermann Scheppenhäuser (Frankfurt a.m.: Suhrkamp Verlag, 1974), 140–57.

[7] For more on this conception of the "echo-stage" that precedes the "mirror-stage," see Mladen Dolar, *A Voice and Nothing More* (Cambridge, MA: MIT Press, 2006).

At which interval? And how, moreover—with what technique (*Technik*), if today the in-between, the "break,"[8] has opened up in untold ways or been shrunk down to an infinitesimally small, molecular, or microtonal moment? Does your fluttering voice, resounding in and off your body, not stand in as the link—the "smallest link"—in the natural-historical constellation?[9] Against the so-called harmony of the spheres, to which Bach's reactionary devotees still cling,[10] do you not occupy a moment in the process of deterritorialization, of breaking out of the policed borders by beginning to form or, at least, plant the seeds of a *people* who are still lacking, since this opening onto the cosmos, this "full song" of nature is, in Deleuze and Guattari's understanding, also still lacking?[11]

Trauergesang

The unfulfilled need at work in this blocked opening onto the world could account for why, especially after catastrophe or especially in the face of the present ecological crisis, inquiries into the experience of song are often compelled to take measure of the significance of so-called nature-songs or nature-sounds (*Naturlauten*). The bad conscience of human arrogance is a potentially deterritorializing force or at least a humbling one that, like the critique of the conventions upholding the noise/music distinction,[12] eventually calls into question the human/animal distinction. Not incidentally, both Adorno and Deleuze spent considerable time probing the musical significance of bird song. Tracing the affinity and difference in their understanding of this natural phenomenon, in fact, helps to chart a line of development leading from the lullaby to the music that both thinkers would ultimately champion: experimental electroacoustic music. This line, or better, this rupture from the stand-alone virtuosity of bird song to the prioritization of the more collective "chirring and rustling" of insects,[13] to what Nietzsche called the song of *Grillen*, might be best

---

[8] Fred Moten, *In the Break: The Aesthetics of the Black Radical Tradition* (Minneapolis: University of Minnesota Press, 2003).
[9] T. W. Adorno, *Alban Berg: Master of the Smallest Link*, trans. Christopher Hailey and Juliane Brand (Cambridge: Cambridge University Press, 1994); *Berg: Der Meister des kleinsten Übergangs*, in *Gesammelte Schriften*, vol. 13, ed. Rolf Tiedemann (Frankfurt a.m.: Suhrkamp Verlag, 1972).
[10] T. W. Adorno, "Bach Defended against His Devotees," in *Prisms*, trans. Samuel Weber and Shierry Weber (Cambridge, MA: MIT Press, 1984); "Bach gegen seine Liebhaber verteidigt," in *Gesammelte Schriften*, vol. 10.1, ed. Rolf Tiedemann (Frankfurt a.m.: Suhrkamp Verlag, 1972).
[11] Deleuze and Guattari, *A Thousand Plateaus*, 333. See, also, Jacques Rancière, *Aesthetics and Its Discontents*, trans. Steven Corcoran (Malden, MA: Polity, 2009), 25–6.
[12] See Jacques Attali, *Noise: The Political Economy of Music*, trans. Brian Massumi (Minneapolis: University of Minnesota Press, 1985).
[13] Deleuze and Guattari, *A Thousand Plateaus*, 308.

summed up by Benjamin's articulation of the dynamic movement of *Trauerspiel*. After all, such "play for the sorrowful" surfaces, in modernity, amid a "blocking" (*Hemmung*) moment or expressive *incapacity* revealed to be at the heart of all human language. This is the path, in Benjamin's conceptualization, "from nature-sound (*Naturlaut*) via lament to music,"[14] the process of melancholic recognition in which the faith in meaning (*Bedeutung*), in communication, is shattered and, therefore, induced to take up the "multiple-cry," or the deterritorialization of the sovereign king's solo song.[15] Once again, the "machining of the voice" or, in Adorno's more Hegelian terms, the spiritualization of nature-sound, of the suffering, incommunicable object, is at issue. On the one hand, the musician is now, vis-à-vis modern alienation, charged with the task of maintaining what Adorno calls music's "purity from the dominance of nature," its resistance or recalcitrance to the projections of a self-preservative, intentional subject.[16] But, on the other hand, the musician increasingly senses that the path to liberation, that is, the path of instrumentalization or rationalization, of giving voice (*ertönen lassen*) to this mute, nonintentional suffering, dictates that one must first *pass through* the meaning-forming apparatus, through the subject or the symbolic realm, in order to remain faithful to the object. Hence, the emancipatory effort appears to be inextricably bound to precisely this history of domination, to the irresistible (*unwiderstehlich*) advance in the technical mastery over nature that humanity, in the same breath, longs to escape. Addressing something of this guilt-ridden *aporia*, Adorno accordingly writes in his fragments on *Beethoven* that "Benjamin speaks of song, which may possibly rescue the language of birds as visual art rescues that of things. But this seems to me the achievement of instruments much rather than of song; for instruments are far more like the voice of birds than are human voices. The instrument *is* animation."[17] "[T]he vocal," he continues, insisting that life lives only insofar as it is at once taken up and transformed by the forces of production,

> is inalienably *preserved* in all instrumental music. Here we should not think only of the 'vocal' flow of the instrumental melody, which in turn determines the vocal flow in the *Lied*, but of something more primitive, almost anthropological. For the imagination of all music, and especially of instrumental music, is vocal.

---

[14] Walter Benjamin, "The Role of Language in *Trauerspiel* and Tragedy," in *Selected Writings*, vol. 1, ed. Michael W. Jennings (Cambridge, MA: Harvard University Press, 2003), 59–61, 60; "Die Bedeutung der Sprache in Trauerspiel und Tragödie," in *Gesammelte Schriften*, vol. 2.1, ed. Rolf Tiedemann and Hermann Scheppenhäuser (Frankfurt a.m.: Suhrkamp Verlag, 1974), 137–40, 138.
[15] Deleuze and Guattari, *A Thousand Plateaus*, 342.
[16] Adorno, *Beethoven*, 172/*NS1*, 248.
[17] Ibid., 173/*NS1*, 249.

To imagine music is always to sing it inwardly: imagining is inseparable from the physical sensation of vocal cords, and composers take account of the 'vocal limit.' Only angels could make music freely. These ideas must be related to Beethoven. In musical terms, humanity [*Humanität*] means: the permeation of the instrumental with spirit, reconciliation of the alienated means with the end [*Zweck*], the subject, within the process, instead of mere humane immediacy. That is one of the innermost dialectical moments in Beethoven. The cult of the vocal against the instrumental today points precisely to the *end* [*Ende*] of humanity in music.[18]

One could add that, in addition to angels, beings who, at a certain point in the history of accumulation, have concentrated virtually the entire "labor of creation" into a productive, electric flow that is now at their push-bottom command also have this "free" capacity.[19] The hour of the General Intellect is, in other words, at hand.[20] The technical means of overcoming bourgeois humanism and all of the puffed-up heroism, atomization, and false immediacy that thwarts our reconciliation with technology cannot be denied any longer. The end (*Zweck*) of humanity, that is, its self-overcoming, goal, or *telos* fulfilled, is just as much expressed, albeit refractedly, in the reactionary cult of pure, unamplified song, as it is in the advanced, electroacoustic work. Both are marked by the irreversible features of the new terrain. Today, then, the human is either fulfilled in a technical sublation (*Aufhebung*) or destroyed in a regression to the monstrous. There is no middle ground, and certainly no "back to," even if pastiche seems, at present, to be all that remains,[21] or even if—following Michael Gordon's technique—minute alternations in tempo and volume, rather than the production of new forms, appear to comprise, as Deleuze and Guattari observe, the last remaining phase in music.[22] The *ritornelli* made available, firstly, by the analogue slicing of the magnetic tape and, then, by the infinite sustain of digital recording and editing technology are approximations, in the realm of music, of a perpetual motion machine. They augur nothing other than this end (*Zweck*). As natural-historical outgrowths (*Naturwüchsigkeit*),[23] they furthermore point, already in

---

[18] Ibid., 173/*NS1*, 249.
[19] Deleuze and Guattari, *A Thousand Plateaus*, 350.
[20] Karl Marx, *Grundrisse: Foundation of the Critique of Political Economy*, trans. Martin Nicolaus (New York: Penguin Books, 1973), 706.
[21] Fredric Jameson, *Postmodernism, or, the Cultural Logic of Late Capitalism* (Durham, NC: Duke University Press, 1991), 24–9.
[22] For example, see Deleuze and Guattari, *A Thousand Plateaus*, 267, 309.
[23] Adorno, *Negative Dialectics*, 358/*GS6*, 351. The relationship between this Adornian concept of a natural-historical "outgrowth" (*Naturwüchsigkeit*) and Marx's famous conception of the state as a "parasitic excrescence" (*Schmarotzerauswuchs*) should be analyzed in detail.

Adorno's lifetime, to a mode of (aesthetic) production that—beyond the capacity to stretch, augment, or diminish vocal lamentation (*Klagen*) via, say, the lyrical power of the violin or cello—no longer needs to either catch its breath or gather itself during the rest, the pause. Deleuze and Guattari's tale about the runner whose breath is double the tempo of other humans has been realized by the machine.[24] The expansion and contraction of the diaphragm has been exceeded by the collective power stored up in the technical means of reproduction. That internalized, vocal, and, above all, anthropological limit, the hum or auratic breath from which even the instrumentation of the voice was derived, prior to electronification, no longer constrains the imagination or the *durée* of the notes themselves. One finger, not three, plays a triad immediately. One touch holds a note indefinitely.

Industrial Production and *The Ninth Symphony*

Industrial production is, in truth, the decisive break. The railway train of a burgeoning system of international trade, powered on the dead-labor, the fossil-fuel, of human and nonhuman organisms, already enlarges the echo of the farewell song, the *Abgesang*, already signals the infinite sustain of computerization, which is the antithesis to the infinite debt (*Schuld*) of modernity.[25] Its slowly approaching bass and long descending retreat anticipate a natural-historical development that would, in due course, overwhelm the individual, reducing her to a fungible object, a mere point, in the reproduction of the machine.[26] But this breach in the local rhythms or short-lived, gentle caresses of pre-capitalist *Handwerk* also promises a different, perhaps grander epic than the epics of the past, one that stretches to the furthest distance, beyond the human, to the depths of the earth and the heights of the heavens, before it resoundingly returns or calmly comes to a halt. The limits of human strength are no longer an obstacle. As the epoch of manufacture ends, machines begin to make machines, which are designed to make even more gargantuan machines.[27] Can the appendages be more than appendages when all of the forces of the past, of the prehuman, of prehistory, are tapped? It has seldom been said, but this movement between

---

[24] Deleuze and Guattari, *A Thousand Plateaus*, 305.
[25] Deleuze and Guattari, *Anti-Oedipus*, 197.
[26] Cf. Haraway, *Staying with the Trouble*, 46.
[27] Karl Marx, *Capital: A Critique of Political Economy*, vol. 1, trans. Ben Fowkes (New York: Vintage Books, 1977), 493–564.

our human and angelic capacity, this dialectic of the post-human and the monstrous, arguably reaches its pinnacle, its aesthetic turnabout (*Umschwung*),[28] in Beethoven's *Ninth Symphony*.[29] In the culminating moments to the apotheosis of song, after the famous "Freude" from the celebratory Ode, but before the accelerated coda beckoned by the cymbal and flutes, Schiller, in homage to Kant's supersensible and cosmopolitan hope, commands: "Seek him above the starry canopy / Above the stars he must live [*Such' ihn über'm Sternenzelt! / über Sternen muss er wohnen*]." Do not these words, articulated alongside the floating chorus and rising woodwinds, anticipate Deleuze and Guattari's hovering, "non-pulsed" music of the future?[30] The last, blissful notes of the choir and orchestra are held and want to vibrate eternally in now-time (*Jetztzeit*), together, but when they subside, as they inevitably must, the listener is left with one form in particular: the fugue. That most human, all-too-human of well-tempered constructions interrupts or takes over the sustained choir's collective voice, which wanted to hover, angelically, forever. The fact that the music breaks off into the fugue, that the silence is ever-so fleeting, that it is, in the end, desecrated by cloudy, fallible song, cannot help but conjure up disappointment or prove, in Adorno's terms, the "insolubility" of the problem of the *Ninth*, which is the problem of bourgeois society as such. In this sense, the beautiful semblance (*Schein*) of the *Ninth*, its promise of happiness, of utopia, is threatened with betrayal by the mere semblance at play in the earlier narration of the expulsion of the criminal or vagabond. Despite the immanent drive to transcend humanity, Schiller's "Ode to Joy" still insists that "he who has [no love], [must] steal away weeping from our company [*wer's nie gekonnt, der stehle Weinend sich aus diesem Bund*]."[31] As if with a guilty conscience, Beethoven knows to play this line with a softer, *pianissimo* accent, but the fragmented, broken cry of the oppressed, the lament of those who are left outside the gates of Elysium, "*nicht umschlungen*," is poignantly felt at the

---

[28] Benjamin, *Origin of German Tragic Drama*, 232/GS1.1, 406: "Allegory [...] loses everything that was most peculiar to it: the secret, privileged knowledge [*Wissen*], the arbitrary rule [*Willkürherrschaft*] in the realm of dead things [*Dinge*], the supposed infinity of a world without hope. All this vanishes with the *one* about-turn [*Umschwung*], in which the immersion [*Versenkung*] of allegory has to clear away the final phantasmagoria of the objective and, left entirely to its own devices, re-discovers itself, no longer playfully in the earthly world of things [*spielarisch in erdhafter Dingwelt*], but seriously [*ernsthaft*] under the eyes of heaven."

[29] For an exception, see Slavoj Žižek, "Against the Populist Temptation," *Critical Inquiry* 32, no. 3 (Spring 2006): 551–74. The difference between Žižek's analysis and my own is that after he locates the regressive, populist urge of the *Ninth*, he still insists on finding a "new" melody. As the above analysis implies, the problem of the melody, of the single line, in contrast to the multiple-cry of nature-sounds, is altogether problematic at this historical conjuncture.

[30] Deleuze and Guattari, *A Thousand Plateaus*, 267.

[31] Adorno, *Beethoven*, 33/NS1, 60. For a look at how this "steal away" trope makes its way into the sorrow song and the blues, see the aphorism "Fateful Improvisation" from Excursus II.

most triumphant moment in the history of bourgeois culture, the moment when the human voice can neither continue its sustained, upward ascent, nor fulfill its unity, its reconciliation, with the instrument. Resonating with the failure of the *Große Fuge*, which shatters into pieces or catastrophically breaks into fragments when the tonal constraints of Western chromaticism are no longer satisfactory,[32] when anthropological song begins its descent into the farcical, the unwieldly entrance of the fugue after the momentary silence to Beethoven's choral climax unveils the *Ninth* as a work more akin to *Trauerspiel* than Romanticism.[33] Thus Adorno, addressing both Schiller's texts and Beethoven's music, asserts that "[i]nherent in the bad collective is the image of the solitary, and joy desires to see him weep. Moreover, the rhyme word in German, *stehle* [steal], points rightly to the property relationship. We can understand why the 'problem of the Ninth Symphony' was insoluble. In the fairytale Utopia, too, the stepmother who must dance in burning shoes or is stuffed into a barrel spike with nails is an inseparable part of the glorious wedding. The loneliness punished by Schiller, however, is no other than that produced by his revelers' community itself. In such a company, what is to become of old maids, not to speak of the souls of the dead?"[34] Until the fairytale song of the first lullaby becomes the song of the people reconciled with nature *in* technology, not even the dead are safe.

From Bird Song to Insect Noise

The attempt at superseding the rhythm and pause of human breath gives rise, of necessity, to a new problematic, a new line of flight, in the history of music. It is, in reality, already nascent in the "sweet suffering," the standstill, of the third movement to the *Ninth*. As Deleuze and Guattari tacitly note, this new development would guide Wagner from *Tristan* onward. And yet, as they also note, this blending of the tonal spectrum, this rise in the importance of overtones, of textures weaved inside of textures, remained, in Wagner's case, limited in scope, given that his was the pre-amplified era of the industrial transition. The sheer quantity that would soon be harnessed and rechanneled by

---

[32] Adorno, "Beethoven's Late Style," in *Can One Live after Auschwitz*, ed. Rolf Tiedemann (Stanford, CA: Stanford University Press, 2003), 298; "Spatstil Beethovens," in *GS17*, 16–17.

[33] Benjamin highlights this asymmetry or brokenness of *Trauerspiel* when he observes that, unlike ancient Greek drama, they generally consist of four parts. They are essentially opposed to the three-part work that finds a resolution to the syllogistic contradiction. Benjamin, *Origin of German Tragic Drama*, 131; *GS1.1*, 314.

[34] Adorno, *Beethoven*, 33/*NS1*, 60.

the synthesizer had not yet recoiled (*umschlagen*) dialectically into a new set of qualities. Although in part heralding the innovations of, for example, Karlheinz Stockhausen and György Ligeti, the stand-alone virtuosity of what Deleuze and Guattari call *becoming-bird* endured as a dominant feature of Wagner's music. In other words, the male/female dichotomy persisted, the soloist still stood over and against the orchestra, alighting on a, so to speak, branch, the stage.[35] Unlike Schumann, who allegedly first begins to bring the voice of the singer down to the tonal plane of the piano,[36] who presages Gould's "mouthing" gesture at blending voice and instrument, nature and technology, in a complete, selfless immersion, Wagner and Verdi gave one last gasp to the hard and fast separation of each instrument from each instrument, of each voice from each voice, the shortcomings of which the members of the *Studio für elektronische Musik des Westdeutschen Rundfunks* would finally make self-evident roughly fifty years later. This late nineteenth-century composition, therefore, betrays the confines of a production process that has not yet gleaned the implications of Marx's conception of social labor. Its epistemology, like each of its instruments, is still, at bottom, akin to the Robinsonade hero. It deludes itself about its autonomy and its differentiation from the tonal spectrum or non-instrumental noise continuum that, in truth, constitutes it.[37] "Dissonance is," as Adorno says, "the truth of harmony."[38] Parallel to the movement of molecules in physics, a process of reverse diffusion is underway. As Sun Ra would later reveal in, for example, *Astro Black*, the lines between the high-pitched cries of the trumpet, the surging electroacoustic current of the Moog synthesizer, the brake-horn of a bus in a traffic jam, and the outright screeching of human agony have now been fundamentally blurred.[39] Music wants, in empathy, to merge with the suffering object. Without a hint of esoterism implied, it wants to nestle up (*sich anschmiegen*) in a kind of astral projection with that which has been repressed or abjected from the realm of music.[40] This suggests that there is a point of convergence between two contrasting lines, namely the immanent movement of European modernism and,

---

[35] Deleuze and Guattari, *A Thousand Plateaus*, 307.
[36] Ibid., 307–8.
[37] For further consideration of how "undesired circumstantial noises and blemishes" have been incorporated into music production, in contrast to the desire for a pristine recording or reproduction, see Edward Campbell, *Music after Deleuze* (New York: Bloomsbury, 2013), 47–8. See, also, Eshun, *More Brilliant than the Sun*, 187, where Eshun problematizes the political efficacy of the decline of the aura thesis via the aura creating force of the dubplate. "Noises" appear to be, in the era of mass-produced vinyl, becoming music all the time, in real time.
[38] Adorno, *Aesthetic Theory*, 110 (translation modified)/*GS7*, 168.
[39] Eshun, *More Brilliant than the Sun*, 162.
[40] Cf. Julia Kristeva, *Powers of Horror: An Essay on Abjection*, trans. Leon S. Roudiez (New York: Columbia University Press, 1982).

following Sun Ra, the radical repudiation of that "white" tradition, including its very cosmology, in Afro-modernism and Afro-futurism. In both cases, despite the different motivations, the rebellion of technology awaits its musical ally.[41] In both cases, intentionality gives way to the neediness (*Bedürftigkeit*) of the object. The musical material itself demands a different course.

Reconciling Winds

Even in, for instance, works such as Terry Riley's magnificent *Harp of New Albion*, which is not composed with electronic instruments, a sensitivity for this blurring of the line, this mimetic absorption in one's environment or this erotic connection to previously tabooed acoustic fields, is clearly at play. No music, especially unamplified music performed with traditional instruments, can escape the new lines of flight or the new "distributions of the sensible"[42] that, from Pierre Schaeffer's *musique concrète* to the tonal experiments of Alvin Lucier, Sun Ra, and Brian Eno, have been opened up by technical reproduction. The latter developments retroactively act back upon the former, traditional methods, at once revealing their truth-content (*Wahrheitsgehalt*) and the limits to their expressive capacity. This likely forms the basis of Riley's cross-cultural influence. In the repetitive pounding of his minimalist piano, the piano itself begins to melt, as it were, or *bend* and *stretch toward* the atonal sound of a freight train's distant horn. In the "mis-tuned" emphasis that violates all previous boundaries, that, in and through repetition, hearkens to acoustic memories as diverse as the just intonation of La Monte Young's Imperial Bösendorfer, the flattened, toy-like resonance of Cage's prepared piano, and the "dim-dada" of Beethoven's late *Sonata in C minor*,[43] overtones in particular start to take on a life of their own. Now they eclipse the distinct notes that, before electricity, used to obey the equally spaced system of the semitone. It is as if these overtones were always there, hidden, waiting to burst at the seams or break out of the bottlenecked ambit of conventional tonality. Now they come into the foreground. Now it is their trajectory that matters. The tradition of European art-music, which was once seemingly located on an entirely separate plane, suddenly merges with the longing of the Black expressive tradition, which, in the spiritual, the blues, jazz,

---

[41] Benjamin, "The Work of Art in the Age of Its Technological Reproducibility," 270/*GS*1.2, 507.
[42] Rancière, *Aesthetics and Its Discontents*, 25.
[43] Thomas Mann, *Doctor Faustus: The Life of the German Composer Adrian Leverkühn as Told by a Friend*, trans. H. T. Lowe-Porter (New York: Vintage Books, 1948).

and rock-and-roll, coalesces with the rhythm of the train on which the promised escape from capture, from slavery, is fashioned.[44] Will you sing the tone within the tone, asks Riley and his contemporaries, the silent harmony, as it tenderly departs with a passing, distant horn, as it resounds *in and off* the rhythm of a slave labor that has never once, in either the factory or the office, broken the link to the plantation? Will you, like Benjamin's children who, with mimetic genius, imitate windmills and trains, not shopkeepers and teachers,[45] sing the triad of the train horn, the ragtime piano, and the harmonica, as their tonal similarity is unchained from the shackles that have heretofore muted this suspended, breathy halo? Will the *onward* march, the skipping gallop of the horse, the harrowing repetition of the plow, and the *flanged* wheels of the locomotive combine to become your song, meld to become your acoustic vaccine, in tribute to the vanquished, to the *universal* diaspora? And will you thereby resume the appointment (*Verabredung*) between past and present generations, the struggle to redeem what was foretold long ago: the end of forced labor?[46] Anyone with an ear plugged into the *currents* of music, in contrast to its trends and facts, is doubtless tempted to answer yes.[47] But only so long as the tones emanating from this rhythm finally get their share. Only when they, the silenced, mechanical voices, are laid hold of (*emparer*), distilled, recombined, and collectivized by the low, becoming-frog clavinet, by the latest, jaw-dropping wah-wah pedals, octave-shifters, and tremolo-oscillator effects. The teeth-gnashing grimace of distortion, materialized in Hendrix, Allman, and Anastasio, is the physiognomy of the present. Again and again,

---

[44] It should be noted that highlighting this similarity between these different music traditions is not an attempt to collapse the one into the other, to efface their differences, or worse, assert that the Black expressive tradition is devoid of content until it is subsumed under or appropriated by a set of European norms and techniques. I also do not intend to imply that hybridization is the only viable option for advanced music. As Excursus II will hopefully make more evident, a multiplicity of musical trajectories constitute the at once similar and different, contiguous and divergent, needs of what I call, following Paul Gilroy's suggestion, the universal diaspora. For more on this nonidentical need that unites without subsuming, see the aphorism "Fugitive Life" subsequently.

[45] Walter Benjamin, "On the Mimetic Faculty," in *Selected Writings*, vol. 2.2, ed. Michael W. Jennings (Cambridge, MA: Harvard University Press, 2003), 720; "Über das mimetische Vermögen," in *Gesammelte Schriften*, vol. 2.1, ed. Rolf Tiedemann and Hermann Scheppenhäuser (Frankfurt a.m.: Suhrkamp Verlag, 1974), 210.

[46] When juxtaposed to Eshun's understanding of the white, Eurocentric appeal to redemption and the corresponding need to flout its lineage via alternative practices of musical memory, this Benjaminian and Adornian approach to the past brings several contemporary problems, that is, still unresolved tensions, in political and musical reality to the fore. Eshun, *More Brilliant than the Sun*, -002. Compare, also, this apparent conflict between a Deleuzean and Adornian music theory to Campbell, *Music after Deleuze*, 149–54. Concentrating in particular on musical theory and practice of Helmut Lachenmann, Campbell attempts to highlight the similarities between Deleuze and the Frankfurt School.

[47] T. W. Adorno, *Current of Music: Elements of a Radio Theory*, trans. Robert Hullot-Kentor (Malden, MA: Polity Press, 2009). For a further look at the contrast between the "current" or "currents" of music and its positivist, experience-destroying "trends" and "facts," see Adorno, *Negative Dialectic*, 300–3/GS6, 295–7.

morning after morning, a similar refrain hammers away. Sunday is always too little Sunday when work looms.[48] Then, suddenly, unexpectedly, an old theme somehow becomes dissimilar, until the musical analogue to the left-over ash and soot, the billowing miasma of industry, floats upward, evaporating into air along with all that has been profaned.[49] Colors unforeseen are all that remain. The trilling tone of an industrial generator is now as eloquent as the quavering texture of the river. An atmosphere fluctuating like vaporous weather grows calm in remembrance of the forgotten aura, as the wind, which "hounds" the unhappy man "from shallow sleep and violent dreams," is transformed into a "song of his protectedness [*Geborgenseins*]: its furious howling [. . .] no longer ha[ving] any power over him."[50]

Dynamic Contrast

Imagine a stroll through a forest on a star-filled evening. Capturing the content that flits past in relation to a nearly infinite set of elemental and cosmological phenomena is akin to the natural-historical truth-content that dialectics aims to capture in a snapshot. The contrasting velocities between that stroll and, say, a run, or the differential content that fleetingly opens up between these moving elements and the faster, circling route of Proust's motorcar, suggest that the attempt to understand the limits and possibilities of nature, the critical openings and closing of the relationality, requires precise, philosophical determination. The Archimedean point is moving. The rising and subsiding, twisting and turning dance of the castle and sea around the foliage of Beaumont is at once relative and objective, individual and collective.[51] Think, along these lines, of the widening divergence between the play of natural phenomena and the individuated monad when the ever-moving, aural and optical relations are gleaned from the supersonic speeds of jet airplanes and high-speed rail. The "mechanical rhythm [of military instruments] completely determines the human relation to the war,"[52] asserts Adorno, well aware that the trick is to see this mechanical warfare at work in every aspect of life, even the seemingly most mundane or innocuous.[53]

---

[48] Adorno, *Minima Moralia*, 175/GS4, 197.
[49] Cf. Toni Morrison, *Song of Solomon* (New York: Vintage, 1977), 337.
[50] Adorno, *Minima Moralia*, 29 (translation modified)/GS4, 54.
[51] Marcel Proust, *Remembrance of Things Past*, vol. 2, trans. C. K. Scott Moncrieff (London: Wordworth Editions, 2006), 343–4.
[52] Adorno, *Minima Moralia*, 54/GS4, 60.
[53] Benjamin, "Theories of German Fascism," 321/GS3, 250.

It achieves this complete control, he continues, "not only in the disproportion between individual bodily strength and the energy of machines, but in the most hidden cells of experience."[54] Catching up, as it were, with this rhythm, or expropriating it so that it—the General Intellect—no longer annihilates the capacity to organize diffuse experiences, may require the rehabituations that are rehearsed in the refuge spaces of advanced musical production. The immediate view from within a high-speed train is a blur. All the colors blend, no objects can be differentiated. But a mere turn of the gaze to the distant horizon brings the static moments of the totality into view. For, unlike the immediately passing, blurred objects, the mountain on the horizon and Venus in the heavens remain unmoved.[55] Everything up close passes away at lightning speed, but the mountain and planets calmly abide in their stillness. Slow the tempo only slightly, and suddenly the objects reemerge into distinctness. Increase the tempo once more and, within an instant, they pass back into an ephemerality that unfolds in relation to the previous constancy. Technically reproduced music is hardly different from this fossil-fuel-powered mode of transportation. Its acceleration and deceleration are but the mixing board, the effects rig, and a refined, multi-generational congealment of compositional and improvisational technique. Glenn Gould learned, for example, the truth of Bach by practicing his keyboard works in tempi that were exaggeratingly too fast or too slow in relationship to the written score.[56] The strength of the studio, in which editing unleashes the full range of the dynamic contrast between each of the parts, is as latent in this pre-digital rehearsal method as the aura-destroying and politically revolutionary photograph is latent, on Benjamin's account, in ancient Greek coinage and Gutenberg's printing press.[57] The assault on living-labor by dead-labor could still be reversed. Sovereignty over the past—true *Herrschaft*—is still the goal.

Blurring the Human/Animal Distinction

If becoming-animal, -molecular, or -woman is not to be taken literally, as Deleuze and Guattari maintain;[58] and if what is meant, on the contrary, is the possibility that so-called humans could undergo *real* transformation, breaking free of our

---

[54] Adorno, *Minima Moralia*, 54/GS4, 60.
[55] William Ross Kemperman first alerted me to this dialectical image of the train.
[56] Cited from Fred Moten, *Black and Blur: Consent Not to Be a Single Being* (Durham, NC: Duke University Press, 2017), 58.
[57] Benjamin, "The Work of Art in the Age of Its Technological Reproducibility," 252/GS1, 474.
[58] Deleuze and Guattari, *A Thousand Plateaus*, 275.

natural-historical inheritance, instead of remaining in thrall to the masked-play, the Oedipal triangle, of *mere* imitation, then the experiments rehearsed in music do, indeed, anticipate, in Jacques Attali's formulation, a different future, a new, non-bourgeois mode of being.[59] More specifically, Deleuze and Guattari's disconcerting and seldom addressed claim that the sounds of insects must, in the era of the synthesizer, supplant, or at least complicate, the song of birds becomes more and more comprehensible. In the final analysis, this claim simply means that the de-differentiation of humans from nature, of man from woman, and of the sound of the musical instrument from the "noise" of the environment are all finally, at this late hour, gathering steam.[60] Resembling *Klangfarbenmelodie* in which no single instrument, no single voice, completes the melodic line alone, each of us is, in truth, the wave.[61] Each of us is caught up in a flow that rises and subsides, that pulsates, gathers momentum, and drops without anticipation. We are like the cicadas that, following Elias Canetti's conception of crowd-formation, expand and contract without calculation, that ebb and flow, buzzing and whirring, without the aid of foresight.[62] An increase or decrease in mere volume transforms the entire textural web. No one as yet knows if this will lead to absolute terror or absolute emancipation. But one thing cannot be denied: this newly recognized resemblance, this becoming-insect modeled on and echoing with the vibrating, tanpura drone of industrial production, with the churning and squealing of a perpetual motor, is neither grounded in nor constrained by our transhistorical "nature." After the downfall (*Untergang*) of the ideology of the organic and, with it, the alleged harmony and purposiveness on which all natural-historical "progress" was founded, leaning in to that metallic hum, becoming-with the noise of dead-labor, the jagged edges and bass murmurs (*Rauschen*) of helicopters and airplanes, waterfalls and static electricity, became an increasingly pressing need for advanced music. Each of us is like the crickets (*Grillen*), then, not simply because the individual has regressed to the "dividual."[63]

---

[59] For a critique of Attali, in particular his conception of "repetition," see Robin James, "Neoliberal Noise: Attali, Foucault, and the Biopolitics of the Uncool," *Culture, Theory and Critique* 55, no. 2 (2014): 138–58.

[60] For more on this decentering process that disrupts the previous basis of the human/animal distinction, see Mathew Calarco, *Thinking Through Animals: Identity, Difference, Indistinction* (Stanford, CA: Stanford University Press, 2015), 33–43.

[61] Deleuze and Guattari, *A Thousand Plateaus*, 252. For an analysis that troubles the commonsensical conception of the noise/signal binary by illuminating how it follows Deleuze's critique of the image of thought, see Sean Higgins, "A Deleuzian Noise/Excavating the Body of Abstract Sound," in *Sounding the Virtual: Gilles Deleuze and the Theory and Philosophy of Music*, ed. Brian Hulse and Nick Nesbitt (Burlington, VT: Ashgate, 2010), 51–76.

[62] Canetti, *Crowds and Power*, 15–16.

[63] Gilles Deleuze, "Postscript on the Societies of Control," *October* 59 (Winter, 1992): 3–7.

Each of us resembles them because we are, today more than ever, cyborgs linked to a cybernetic network, to the colossal flows of the multinational markets, whose electrically powered channels and circuits are themselves outgrowths of nature (*Naturwüchsigkeit*) and thus a part of nature's spell (*Bann*), a part of a natural-historical process that cannot yet, strictly speaking, be called historical, since it only masquerades as if it has escaped the reign of Sisyphean passivity that surges through all differentially modified organisms.[64]

The Spell of First and Second Nature

Every last creature on earth is imprisoned by this mythical fate. As Schubert knew well before Deleuze and Guattari would naively declare the opposite,[65] the impossibility of joyous music is, in reality, constitutive of music, since music— "the enemy of fate"[66]—wants to be realized in the world, not confined, as always, by the neutralized realm of the beautiful illusion (*Schein*) or the hitherto existing relations of natural-historical *praxis*. A nature that, in short, remains blind-compulsion—"woe speaks: go"[67]—and, therefore, trapped, as always, like art, in a mirror-play of recognition with the very forces it wishes to escape, cannot avoid mourning its predicament in the release, in the lament that, coming out of itself, aims to redeem sorrow (*Trauer*) in song. Anthropomorphism is, in this sense, unavoidable.[68] As Alfred Döblin taught, trying to escape it without transforming the material reality from which it, as an epistemological reflex, is first posited is the oldest navel-gazing trick in the idealist repertoire.[69] Since, however, we live in the era of the amplified and technically reproduced instrument, since every

---

[64] For a further look at this differential modification that never gives rise to individuation or divisibility, see Deleuze, *Cinema 1: The Movement-Image*, trans. Hugh Tomlinson and Barbara Habberjam (Minneapolis: University of Minnesota Press, 1986), 14.

[65] T. W. Adorno, *Introduction to the Sociology of Music*, trans. E. B. Ashton (New York: Continuum, 1976), 43; *Einleitung in die Musiksoziologie*, in GS14, 223; Deleuze and Guattari, *A Thousand Plateaus*, 299. This naiveté should be understood in the sense that Deleuze meant it when he responded to Foucault's suggestion that the twentieth century might be the century of Deleuze. It, in other words, connotes something of the Schillerian sense of the term, an element of which may well be required for any responsible politics after catastrophe. See, also, Paul Patton and John Protevi et al. *Between Deleuze and Derrida* (New York: Continuum, 2003), 6.

[66] T. W. Adorno, *Philosophy of New Music*, trans. Robert Hullot-Kentor (Minneapolis: University of Minnesota Press, 2006), 180; *Philosophie der neuen Musik*, in *Gesammelte Schriften*, vol. 12, ed. Rolf Tiedemann (Frankfurt a.m.: Suhrkamp Verlag, 1972), 67: "Musik ist der Feind des Schicksals."

[67] Adorno, *Negative Dialectics*, 203/GS6, 203: "Weh spricht: vergeh."

[68] For a similar view on the impossibility of avoiding anthropomorphism, see Brian Massumi, *What Animals Teach Us about Politics* (Durham, NC: Duke University Press, 2014), 50–1.

[69] Alfred Döblin, "Materialism, A Fable," in *Bright Magic: Stories*, trans. Damion Searls (New York: New York Review Books, 2016), 156–203.

human and nonhuman plaintive cry on the way to both song and, ultimately, instrumental recuperation is, with the advent of analogue-to-digital-MIDI-technology, immediately convertible or transposable, like Gould's Bachian dream, to any other instrument or sound-effect, any other voice or object on any other tonal spectrum, one cannot deny that this hyper-real conjuncture produces a set of world-historical possibilities. They are perhaps best characterized as expressions of a crisis that, as Deleuze and Guattari continually repeat, could unfold toward either the fascists liquidation of the subject or its communist fulfillment.[70] For this level of accumulation, congealed as technology, as a "second nature," opens up the first material chance to break the spell of "first nature" under which all natural organisms, *all beasts of burden*, remain unhappily cast. The new and the old, convention and expression, are just that dialectical.[71] Toil, imposed from the outside, hardened into the dead-labor of a genetic code, is the static moment to the dynamic appearance (*Schein*) of change.

The Instrument Is the Animation

"Already Wagner was reproached for the 'elementary' character of his music, for its aquaticism, or its 'atomization' of the motif, 'a subdivision into infinitely small units,'" remark the authors of *A Thousand Plateaus*, highlighting the dialectic of the old and the new that, especially in *Der Ring*, recapitulates the heaviness of amniotic fluid, the spirit of gravity, or echo-stage, from which every amniote emerges.[72] "This becomes even clearer," they continue, aware of the dangers of commodification, of the mass production schema at work in the easily identifiable *Leitmotiv*,

> if we think of becoming-animal: birds are still just as important, yet the reign of birds seems to have been replaced by the age of insects, with its much more molecular vibrations, chirring, rustling, buzzing, clicking, scratching, and scraping. Birds are vocal, but insects are instrumental: drums and violins, guitars and cymbals. A becoming-insect has replaced becoming-bird, or forms a block with it. The insect is closer, better able to make audible the truth that all becomings are molecular (cf. Martenot's waves, electronic music). The molecular has the capacity to make the *elementary* communicate with the *cosmic*: precisely

---

[70] Deleuze and Guattari, *A Thousand Plateaus*, 348.
[71] Benjamin, *Origin of German Tragic Drama*, 175/ GS1.1, 351.
[72] Cf. Vladimir Safatle, "Mirrors Without Images: Mimesis and Recognition in Lacan and Adorno," *Radical Philosophy* 139 (2006): 9–19.

because it effects a dissolution of form that connects the most diverse longitudes and latitudes, the most varied speeds and slownesses, which guarantees a continuum by stretching variation far beyond its formal limits.[73]

Here Deleuze and Guattari come remarkably close to Adorno, inasmuch as here the instrument *is* the animation for them as well, or appears to be superior, today, at eliciting the truth of the possibility of metamorphosis, of becoming something other than what we are. For all three thinkers, then, the voice must unite with technology in order to fulfill or, at least, transform nature, in order to stop the history of domination, connect the cosmic to the elementary and, in so doing, begin to establish a *people* who have hitherto disavowed precisely these connections. Each previously individuated tone must be taken up afresh and transformed by the rhizomatic or constellational effects-board.[74] This, however, is only possible by heeding the advancements in technique, by passing through the Anthropos, on the way to *musique informelle*,[75] not discarding it in one stroke, as the pseudo-realists and neo-ontologists of the present imply in precritical fashion.[76] Or, to paraphrase Adorno: despite the metaphysical truth that subject is object while object is not subject, one still has no choice but to attempt to glean the object through the subject. Now the circuit-jamming potential or "schiz-flow" that was, in truth, always immanent to the previous channeling mechanism, the previous territorial, formal, or conventional limits, finally makes its, so to speak, return, or it is finally discharged, instead of being suppressed and drowned out in the never-ending spectacle of the beautiful.[77] A wide, humming, spectral range engulfs all space before the socket is plugged in. This range abruptly narrows, concentrates, when the electric circuits meet. The reverberating contact of metal against metal, the feedback that surges upon touch, upon compression, cannot be forgotten anymore. Before even Varèse's siren, noise music had already emerged with the Italian futurist, Luigi Russolo. Skipping, crashing, distorting, loops within loops—a latent "glitch" aesthetic was already at work. And so, without anyone noticing, the need to maintain the individuation of each soloist, of each instrument from each instrument, to

---

[73] Deleuze and Guattari, *A Thousand Plateaus*, 309 (my emphasis).
[74] For a more thorough look at the social, political, and metaphysical implications of the latest developments in the technology of the effects-board, see my essay, Joseph Weiss, "The Composer as Producer," in *The Aesthetic Ground of Critical Theory*, ed. Nathan Ross (New York: Roman and Littlefield, 2015).
[75] T. W. Adorno, "Vers une musique informelle," in *Quasi una Fantasia: Essays on Modern Music*, trans. Rodney Livingstone (New York: Verso, 1998); "Vers une musique informelle," in GS16.
[76] Cf. Alastair Morgan, "A Preponderance of Objects: Critical Theory and the Turn to the Object," *Adorno Studies* 1, no. 1 (2017): 13–30.
[77] Deleuze and Guattari, *Anti-Oedipus*, 240–1.

declare heroically and romantically one's refined taste and style in the era of the regression of style to a brand,[78] likewise became progressively less tenable. In reality, this need was already revealed, in Nietzsche's time by Baudelaire, as the false one par excellence. In light of the molecular or microtonal vibrations, the "most varied speeds and slownesses," which the technology of the electric flow has made audible, it is downright impossible to turn away from the previously silenced, but now amplified and reassembled "vibrations, chirring, rustling, buzzing, clicking, scratching, and scraping" that constitute the acoustic field.[79] One can no longer deny that gnawing dissonance, that piercing edge of the clipping moment that—now but a turn-of-the-knob away—approaches absolute noise. Echoing from within and without, in the throat, and in one's guts, off the clouds, and off the arena dome, the new spaces of advanced musical production upset the line between the cityscape and the naturescape like never before. Were they ever that far apart? Were nature and history, Murray Schafer and Francisco López, ever-so separate?[80] The transformative potency at work in connecting the "most diverse longitudes and latitudes" was simply out of reach before or could not be seized by the reproductive mechanism of the "human" ear. The abstract, mechanical schema of serialism and, later, Xenakis's computerization fell short too. In effect, the theory of the passage from the lullaby to electroacoustic music says nothing more than that, prior to industrial production, prior to the automatized and automatizing machine, we could not hear the connections between the smallest and the largest, the fractal refrain between the microcosm and macrocosm. "Nature," as Benjamin once put it, "produces similarities."[81] But we were deaf to them. We were deaf, that is, to the mimetic interplay between the elementary and the cosmic and, therefore, could not gather the "waves or flows of sonic energy irradiating the entire universe" into an emancipatory, technically mediated project produced for and by the *people*.[82] Imagine running all of the sound bites, gestures, mass produced, phatic twitching, filler-laughter, and character masks of the culture industry through an effects-board. They are scarcely different from the spell under which insects mechanically toil. Then imagine altering their tempo, first infinitesimally slow, then infinitely fast. Now

---

[78] Adorno, *Aesthetic Theory*, 230/GS7, 305–6.
[79] Deleuze and Guattari, *A Thousand Plateaus*, 308. To better understand this irreversibility in the movement of the dialectic, especially as it relates to post-tonal music, see Slavoj Žižek, *Less than Nothing: Hegel and the Shadow of Dialectical Materialism* (New York: Verso, 2012), 193–4.
[80] R. Murray Schafer, *The Soundscape: Our Sonic Environment and the Tuning of the World* (Rochester, VT: Destiny Books, 1994); Francisco López, "Profound Listening and Environmental Sound Matter," in *Audio Culture*, ed. Christoph Cox and Daniel Warner (New York: Continuum, 2010).
[81] Benjamin, "On the Mimetic Faculty," 720/GS2.1, 210.
[82] Deleuze and Guattari, *A Thousand Plateaus*, 309.

distill these speechless stirrings, this dead-labor, down to blocks of individuated sound and, amplifying the minute din of each machinic quivering, make them tick to precisely the meter of "homogenous, empty time."[83] Now let them pass, clicking and ticking, through the assembly line of eternity in a ruined cityscape bereft of inhabitants. Now the silence off of which they are differentiated reverberates all the more as it rises to the stars under which the hallowed-out skyscrapers gently rest. There they are, alone, devoid at last of the purposiveness (*Zweckmäßigkeit*) that the bustle of capitalist life feigned for so long. Benjamin's dialectical image becomes auditory. Historical time is negated, not by fleeing the scene but by sinking down to the cold, lifeless level of the mundane, playing it its own tune.

Tone Color

Another way to describe the equally fascist and communist potency, the implicit attempt to fulfill the promise of the lullaby, is to say that, in the age of electroacoustic reproduction, music threatens to pull away from song altogether, to drift away and never come back from both the steady familiarity of the down beat and the easily recognizable instrument that the soloist plays. *Tempted* by space, by the dispossession of the death drive, as Roger Caillois once said regarding the mimetic comportment of all natural organisms,[84] not even the "atonality" of Schoenberg's twelve-tone technique goes far enough in breaking with the rhythmic and metrical conventions of the Western tradition. The tonal derivatives of symmetry, that is, "the predominance of an abstractly maintained pulse," insists Adorno, in an almost word-for-word prefiguration of Deleuze and Guattari's conception, "the strong beat, and its negative retention in syncopation," must, at some point, be resisted.[85] For they are still too "human," despite their "atonality," still too caught up in the sublime pretensions of old that pull us back, once more, to "human" song and breath, back to the rounded arc, or the familiar territory of a familiar time signature, both of which continue to close us off to that ever-elusive "opening onto the world." This shortcoming is a prevalent feature in so much of so-called new music, despite the fact that, as Adorno already saw, anticipating Kodwo Eshun's observation about the polyrhythmic openings unleashed by the new technology, "[i]nformal music could augment

---

[83] Benjamin, "On the Concept of History," 395/*GS*1.2, 701.
[84] Roger Caillois, "Mimicry and Legendary Psychasthenia," *October* 31 (Winter, 1984): 16–32.
[85] Adorno, "Vers une musique informelle," 321–2/*GS*16, 540.

rhythmic flexibility to a degree as yet undreamed of."[86] The so-called soar, the organizing principle of most Techno and EDM, is hardly what he had in mind. Even if the new tonal possibilities are, beyond those early attempts at the *Studio für elektronische Musik*, sometimes hinted at in electronic genres—especially in recent ambient and film music like Jóhann Jóhannsson's, Stephan Mathieu's, and Richard Skelton's, and before them, in Miles Davis's and George Russell's experiments[87]—these genres still adhere, on the whole, to predigested, formal patterns, most of which confirm the semblance of a subjectivity modeled on historical time, on capitalist circulation, instead of renouncing it. New possibilities in timbre, texture, or musical color are no doubt squandered by the narrowness of this tie to the formal or schematic other, but so too is the potential for incorporating noise, for the *becoming-music of noise*.

Informal Music

When musicians begin to embody the critique and rescue of the past, which is not incidentally Adorno's concise definition of *musique informelle*,[88] this dialectic of form and content, of rhythm and color, music and noise, arguably comes into its own. An unrecognized rift with the natural-historical basis of capitalist temporality secretly takes place: the mammal's heartbeat need not order the transitional or developmental unfolding of music any longer. The tonal transformations of the past—even, to repeat, those of Schoenberg, Webern, and Berg—were not, in this respect, as radical as was once thought. So long as they remained rigidly fixed to the temporal dimension of music, that is, to the rhythmic conventions that give rise, as Deleuze and Guattari highlight, to metrical conformism, they unwittingly assist in the production of an illusory, all-too-human identity. In Stockhausen and Pierre Boulez and, more recently,

---

[86] Ibid., 322/*GS*16, 540; Eshun, *More Brilliant than the Sun*, 78–9. As early as *Difference and Repetition*, 21, Deleuze was also addressing the manner in which polyrhythmic possibilities are, despite appearances, immanent to music production or, in his terms, how the rhythmic element proceeds symmetry and order and is more aligned with chaos or actual repetition. For a discussion of how this seeming immediacy of rhythm or this "sensation in itself" is, on the one hand, in dialectical tension with Adorno's conception of the mediation of musical form and, on the other, perhaps a basis for Deleuze's less stringent criterion of successful musical resistance, see Gallope, *Deep Refrains*, 243–58.

[87] For more on the relation between Deleuze's music theory and the cosmological element in Davis's musical practice, see Marcel Swiboda, "Cosmic Strategies: The Electric Experiments of Miles Davis," in *Deleuze and Music*, ed. Ian Buchanan and Marcel Swiboda (Edinburgh: Edinburgh University Press, 2004).

[88] Adorno, "Vers une musique informelle," 305/*GS*16, 525.

composers such as Pauline Oliveros, John Adams, and Kaija Saariaho, advanced music reveals a compulsion to resemble expressionist painting, or, in Adorno's language, it is driven to *spatialize temporality*, reversing the long-standing prioritization of form over matter, or identity over difference, so that form is finally recognized for what it always was: sedimented material.[89] Once again prefiguring in striking detail the task that Deleuze and Guattari would, following Boulez,[90] set for music, Adorno, as early as 1965, argues that

> [this painterly procedure] expresses itself most clearly in electronics, but can also be observed in the realm of music that makes use of more or less traditional methods of sound production. Composers are operating with individual tones the way painters operate with individual color values; although as a rule the tones may no longer be separated from each other, like dots, but may be more densely layered, still they represent almost the entirety of the composition. The integration of total planning and the atomization into tones correspond. The unit of construction is reduced to the relations among these tones. The form of this kind of music is thoroughly homophonic; it is composed, as people like to say nowadays, of "blocks." The concept of line is not applicable to it, any more than it knows true polyphony; in its place, the sounds, in their simultaneity, have become extraordinarily nuanced and differentiated in themselves, exploiting discoveries made by the early Stravinsky, among others. The things that in traditional music, including Schoenberg, Berg, and Webern, apply specifically to the temporal dimension—the entire art of development and thematic transition—become irrelevant to the composers; at best, tone progressions in the sense of the newly available continuum still retain something of that art. The most recent musical production is so uniform, where these characteristics are concerned, that one is almost tempted to suspect some objective compulsion [*objektiven Zwang*], although one cannot help hearing a certain impoverishment, the withering away of numerous musical elements in favor of the manipulation of the overvalued tones. In general, in the most recent development, an extreme measure of differentiation, of sophistication in the use of means, goes hand in hand with primitivism, a kind of forgetting of what has been achieved [*Erworbene*]. The apologetic argument that in the history of music one dimension has always been developed at the expense of the others falls flat. History had transcended

---

[89] Adorno, *Aesthetic Theory*, 144/GS7, 217. It should be noted that Deleuze and Guattari suggest that maintaining a separation between the comportment of painting and music is necessary. Deleuze and Guattari, *A Thousand Plateaus*, 303. This critique of the primacy of form is also the basis of Deleuze and Guattari's claim in Ibid., 364, that for nomadic art and science the terms of production, that is, the preconditions of movement, are "material-forces," in contrast to the alleged abstractness of the content-form or form-matter dualism.

[90] For more on the link between Deleuze's conception of non-pulsed or smooth time and Boulez's own musicology, see Campbell, *Music after Deleuze*, 99–107.

precisely this particularity and was getting ready to begin a profound, all-sided development of all its elements [*allseitigen Durchbildung aller Elemente*], and it is hard to believe that this would be abandoned. Otherwise the idea of integral composition would literally merge into disintegration. The convergence of music and painting also opens up the possibility of crass infantilism, at least in music; it is able to spellbind [*bannen*] this element only to the extent that it reflects it within itself, as an expression of decay [*Zerrüttung*], and composes it out, so to speak.[91]

The breakdown of the traditional temporal organization of music mirrors the destruction of experience and the memory on which its cohesion was based. Blocks of sensation temporarily assembled together slowly but surely become the content of music itself. In Deleuze and Guattari's view, these disconnected blocks seem to have always constituted virtual experience, regardless of the historical period. In their view, prioritizing them does not, therefore, seem to be the *result* of artists grappling with historical devastation or the trauma of having the totality, the machinery of permanent war, crush life into "a timeless succession of shocks, interspersed with empty, paralyzed intervals."[92] Primitivism and infantilism really do threaten here, not only because the subject, who needs a past, who needs the long practice of non-alienated labor, of storytelling, to unify and weave together experiences,[93] is threatened with complete liquidation, but also because total integration and an increasing sophistication in the technical means of organizing sound reverse into total disintegration: the rule of intentionless chaos. Whatever the real basis is, then, of this disunity, on the one hand, and this prioritization of space over time, of simultaneity over successiveness, on the other, there is no escaping the implications of, for example, the color compositions of Mark Rothko and Morton Feldman or the single-pitched constructions of Giacinto Scelsi. A considerable segment of musical production has, not unjustifiably, abandoned that which used to signify the most advanced consciousness, namely polyphonic construction. From Bach to Schoenberg polyphony stood for the

---

[91] T. W. Adorno, "On some Relationships between Music and Painting," *The Musical Quarterly* 79, no. 1 (Spring, 1995): 66–79, 68 (translation modified); "Über einige Relationen zwischen Musik und Malerei," in *GS*16, 630–1. For more on what Adorno calls the "erosion" of the traditional taboo on miscegenation between the different arts, the social preconditions of which seem to escape Deleuze, see Adorno, "Art and the Arts," in *Can One Live after Auschwitz?*, ed. Rolf Tiedemann (Stanford, CA: Stanford University Press, 2003), 370; "Die Kunst und die Künste," in *Gesammelte Schriften*, vol. 11.1, ed. Rolf Tiedemann (Frankfurt a.m.: Suhrkamp Verlag, 1972), 434.

[92] Adorno, *Minima Moralia*, 54/*GS*4, 60.

[93] Walter Benjamin, "The Storyteller: Observations on the Works of Nikolai Leskov," in *Selected Writings*, vol. 3, ed. Michael W. Jennings (Cambridge, MA: Harvard University Press, 2003), 143–66; "Der Erzähler: Betrachtungen zum Werke Nikolai Leskows," in *GS*2.2, ed. Rolf Tiedemann and Hermann Scheppenhäuser (Frankfurt a.m.: Suhrkamp Verlag, 1974), 438–65.

most progressive step in the attempt to unify multiple voices or, in Deleuze and Guattari's terms, to harmonize the "multiple-cry," the chorus of nature. Yet today one observes that the immanent tensions of the musical material have shifted to such a degree that this previous "inclusiveness" of voices often sounds too much like a narrow, anthropocentric projection. Hearing only itself, it seems in fact to suppress the voice of nature and the language of things, instead of beginning to emancipate them. Lacking solidarity with difference, and thus failing to embody the new, "plunderphonic" spirit or predatory "remixology" that,[94] in its best moments, sees through the limits of private property on which anthropocentric song is based, so much of the music from the past—to say nothing of contemporary light music (*Leichtmusik*)—now rings hallow as a kind of tragic affectation. "Castrated" and "eunuchlike" adaptations to domination, masochistic coping mechanisms for the fact that one's body is not, in reality, one's own, abound.[95]

Regressive Consciousness and the Destruction of Memory

Those "scribb[lings] effacing all lines," the "fuzzy aggregates" that side too easily with the reterritorializations of the child, the madman, or mere noise, continue to intimidate.[96] Their contrived dissonance betrays the possibility, in Deleuze and Guattari's conception, of a sober consistency.[97] If it were the case that these narrow understandings of nature-sounds (*Naturlauten*) remained the only response to modern disenchantment, or if these new difficulties were not "reflected within themselves," incorporated as the artwork's ownmost antagonism and, eventually, worked through (*Aufarbeitung*) or "composed out" in order to ward off an impending decay into regressive or stunted consciousness, music might, indeed, be justifiably accused of "forgetting [. . .] what has been achieved."

---

[94] Eshun, *More Brilliant than the Sun*, 164–5, 188; Chris Cutler, "Plunderphonia," in *Audio Culture*, ed. Christoph Cox and Daniel Warner (New York: Continuum, 2010).

[95] T. W. Adorno, "Perennial Fashion—Jazz," in *Prisms*, trans. Samuel Weber and Shierry Weber Nicholsen (Cambridge, MA: MIT Press, 1984) 128; "Zeitlose Mode – Zum Jazz," in GS10.1, 61. This thesis on bodily alienation holds true, even if Adorno failed to hear the moment of resistance to it in jazz, which is achieved by, in part, setting in motion the mimetic tension between the suffocating tone of cityscape traffic and the horn ensemble. This thesis also holds true, despite the fact that Adorno could not anticipate another form of resistance in the Black expressive tradition, namely the emergence of funk or breakbeat, which could only be fully realized after urbanization and electronification, but are already implicitly present in, for instance, the Presto to Beethoven's late C-sharp Minor Quartet.

[96] Deleuze and Guattari, *A Thousand Plateaus*, 346.

[97] Ibid., 344.

It might, that is to say, be accused of "vindicat[ing] insanity as health,"[98] of sanctioning *literal* schizophrenia: an amnesia that only feigns its revolutionary, deterritorializing force, but in fact—paralleling the flakiness and enveloping power of drug use—lacks the necessary synthetic moment to change art, let alone the world.[99] Following Adorno's criticism of Stravinsky in the *Philosophy of New Music*, this shortcoming would, moreover, suggest that the transition from a technique that emphasizes, for instance, narrative unity, polyphony, harmony (*Stimmigkeit*), and the steady or syncopated pulse to a technique that, instead, stresses overtones, timbre, discord, minimalism, and that floating play of simultaneously articulated tone colors, might be unwittingly following a more general, regressive social tendency. "[A]nxiety in the face of dehumanization is," as Adorno expresses it, "[potentially] transformed into the joy of its unveiling, and ultimately into the pleasure of the death instinct."[100] Rather than anticipating revolutionary transformation, such flouting of the past would, in short, signal the point where music becomes "*proud* to negate the concept of the human in collusion with the system of dehumanization,"[101] instead of preserving its memory by inaugurating the long awaited, but repeatedly suppressed, all-sided development of the faculties.[102]

Humanism *Résumé*

Everything turns on how one responds to the inadequacy of bourgeois humanism and the degree to which one begins resisting the compartmentalization that, through the division of labor, has no doubt made technical advances abstract, one-sided and, therefore, tethered to this reified, borderline narcotic obliteration of memory.[103] Should one, following the Nietzschean adage, kick the humanism of the past over the edge when it is on its last leg or, even worse, celebrate and

---

[98] Adorno, *Philosophy of New Music*, 127; *Philosophie der neuen Musik*, 158.
[99] Deleuze and Guattari, *What Is Philosophy?*, 165.
[100] Adorno, *Philosophy of New Music*, 127; *GS12*, 156–7.
[101] Ibid., 127 (my emphasis; translation modified)/*GS12*, 157.
[102] See, also, T. W. Adorno, "*Kranichsteiner Vorlesungen*," in *Nachgelassene Schriften, Abteilung IV*, vol. 17, ed. Klaus Reichert and Michael Schwarz (Berlin: Suhrkamp 2014), 447–540. In the 1966 Darmstadt lecture from this collection, "Funktion der Farbe in der Musik," the dialectic of humanization and dehumanization expresses itself in the difference between a musical color that is organized immanently and a musical color that is isolated from its immanent structure. The suggestion is that insofar as the latter has lost its relationship to the past or the preceding moments of musical articulation, it is symptomatic of the destruction of experience.
[103] Cf. Katherine McKittrick and Sylvia Wynter, *Sylvia Wynter: On Being Human as Praxis* (Durham, NC: Duke University Press, 2015).

encourage, along the lines of Nick Land's accelerationism, the ritualistic process of destruction?[104] Perhaps one should, on the contrary, attempt to fulfill it, to realize that the human element was only ever gestured to on an ideological level, as a promise, and never materialized in reality, never capable, *ceteris paribus*, of rising to a material circumstance in which the full development of each becomes synonymous with the full development of all? In contrast to virtually the whole of French philosophy proceeding in the wake of Althusser's anti-humanism,[105] Adorno avoids what might be described as the inclination to blame the conceptualization itself as the source, not the expression, of the problem. As if one could undialectically think away the exclusionary, racist impulse of all hitherto existing humanism, without so much as even touching the one-sided, alienated production process that has, objectively speaking, needed to annihilate the historical memory of advancements in (musical) technique. "If the tendency toward the spatialization of music," writes Adorno, "defends itself, with good reason, against the dictum that insists on the *invariant anthropological nature of the senses*—as established by nature the eye is always an eye, the ear an ear—at the same time it must not refuse, in the rage for identity, to recognize its other."[106] The anthropological limit is not, as is now glaringly obvious, *the* limit. In reality, however, becoming-human was never, especially in classical German philosophy, a matter of cohering to an essentialism grasped either in advance, prior to historical *praxis*, or somehow existing in the pristine, undistorted past.[107] This is another way of saying that, following both Marx's and Cage's imperative, the potential for a new ear was always equal to the potential for a new type of production—one that has finally overcome precisely this objective alienation by preserving, in Benjamin's words, both the hatred and the nourishing "spirit of sacrifice" (*Opferwillen*) at work in the history of the oppressed, that is, the history of technically organized resistance to the ongoing process of domination, where the theological drive for rest, not "progress," guides the struggle, lest the sinew

---

[104] For a critique of Land's neo-reactionary philosophy, see Benjamin Noys, *Malign Velocities: Accelerationism and Capitalism* (Winchester: Zero Books, 2014).

[105] Louis Althusser, *The Humanist Controversy and Other Texts*, trans. G. M. Goshgarian (New York: Verso, 2003). Cf. Rosi Braidotti, *The Posthuman* (Malden, MA: Polity Press, 2013).

[106] Adorno, "On some Relationships between Music and Painting," 69.

[107] The need to grasp the significance of the moment of social praxis as the still deferred unity or realization of philosophy is of course already at work in Marx's early reading of Feuerbach. Missing this moment, which I am here associating with a still unrealized humanism, is likely the basis of Althusser's misreading of the 1844 manuscripts, in which he accuses the young Marx of backsliding into a religious conception of transparent knowledge. Louis Althusser, *Reading Capital*, trans. Ben Brewster (New York: Verso, 2009), 16. For what, in my view, is a far better reading of the dialectical character of the young Marx, see Bloch, "Changing the World or Marx's Eleven Theses on Feuerbach," in *The Principle of Hope*, ed. Ernst Bloch (Cambridge, MA: MIT Press, 1995), 249–86.

(*Sehne*) of its greatest strength atrophy.[108] Instead of forsaking the truth-content (*Wahrheitsgehalt*) of humanism, the point, then, is to live up to it by following the immanent dialectic of nature-history, which moves, then and now, by way of extremes.[109]

Semblance, Praxis, and the Non-pulsed End of Dialectics

Expressed musically, the rippleless, liquid-still, body without organs, the non-pulsed, floating (*schwebend*) attempt at opening (the ear and body as whole) onto a new, cosmological world, recoils back (*umschlagen*) into its other, namely absolute polyphony, the idea of a constellational totality, of a kaleidoscopic or rhizomatic entwinement between those simultaneously moving blocks of tone color: so-called micropolyphony. Melody is withheld so that it can, perhaps, one day return. The lullaby warmth of wood instruments is retained by denying them expression, by playing out the steel resonance of electronification. Yet, this idea of an all-sided development, which would alone preserve both extremes, alone maintain the innovations of the past while nonetheless trying to go beyond them, guarantees success as little as the celebratory,[110] affirmative return of song, of melody, can be foreseen. Sensing the negativity or nonidentity between a desperately needed political *praxis* and the semblance-character (*Scheincharakter*) that infects all art, Adorno goes so far as to say that "it has been [. . .] impossible to bring authentic music into being."[111] The best attempts are superior precisely because they at least admit the sorrow (*Trauer*) of this immanent failure: their political deadlock. For art is not immediately political,

---

[108] Benjamin, "On the Concept of History," 394/*GS*1.2, 700.

[109] Adorno writes in *Minima Moralia*, 89/*GS*4, 98, that "[i]n the innermost recesses of humanism, as its very soul, there rages a frantic prisoner who, as a Fascist, turns the world into a prison." But, as he elsewhere notes, knowing full well that to posit the inhuman is to preserve the human dialectically, something of humanism "survives" when the artist refuses to "yield to any pressure of the ever more overwhelming social organizations of our time," and instead, "express[es], in full command of meaning and potentialities of today's processes of rationalization, that human existence led under its command is not a human one." When the artist is, in other words, "ready to challenge, by its very appearance and its determined irreconcilability, the dictate of the present man-made but merciless world," a negative glimpse of a humanity that is *not yet* shines through. T. W. Adorno, "What National Socialism Has Done to the Arts," in *Essays on Music*, ed. Richard Leppert (Los Angeles: University of California Press, 2002), 387; "What National Socialism Has Done to the Arts," in *GS*20.2, 429. Fred Moten's conception of the "not-in-between," which he derives from C.L.R. James, implies this same extremism, this same deferred longing for the human that cannot be achieved by way of the middle road. Moten, *Black and Blur*, 1–12.

[110] For more on the ambivalence of the celebratory moment, that is, on the with-and-against oscillation of the primal scream that needs diffusion, needs and strives after universalization or a "public," see Moten, *Black and Blur*, vii–xiii.

[111] Adorno, "Vers une musique informelle," 322/*GS*16, 540.

even if it is a corrective to knowledge or even if it is a refracted, contradictory attempt to make politics political for the first time. Whoever forgets this insight becomes a victim of the spell of *praxis* itself, the urgency of which plagues, and ultimately defeats, every living organism. Advanced music is, similarly, confronted with what might be called an historical impasse that, unlike the easy, reformist middle road, can no longer tolerate faking its *pathos*,[112] or feigning reconciliation with nature while it, conveniently enough, discards these technical advances in another round of ritual self-destruction. In its guiltless yes-saying, its joyous affirmation, it perpetuates the history of the exploitation of nature or "becomes a song of triumph" by asserting that what was inflicted on nature was ultimately worth it.[113] It thereby squanders, in Benjamin's words, the "creations whose possibility slumbers in [nature's] womb,"[114] or fails to reflect, in Adorno's terms, art's "inextricable conflict with the idea of the redemption of suppressed nature."[115] The semblance (*Schein*) of art must, in this respect, go under (*untergehen*), and yet it can't, despite its ownmost desire to become *praxis* or become the actual reconciliation that it can only, as yet, present (*darstellen*) in neutralized form. Such a predicament, doubtless afflicted with negativity, with a suffering *lack*, a bad infinity, which itself propels further developments in the curse of natural-history, is perhaps best summed up by Adorno's refrain against Benjamin's thesis on technology. In an urge to "step outside of themselves," all critical artworks seek to open up the, so to speak, window and take an auratic breath of fresh air.[116] The hastiness of practice, of natural-historical self-preservation, negates this hope, despite and because of its necessity. Art, allegedly a misnomer because of its immediate identity with the creativity of all becoming,[117] with the song of all animals, is, in truth, not life but rather an expression of the unresolved lineage of domination, the *Schuldzusammenhang* of the living. It should therefore come to an end, as Hegel predicted.[118] This is what Adorno means when, against Deleuze's false humility, he says that "the song of birds is found beautiful by everyone," "[y]et something frightening lurks in the song of birds, because it is not song that it obeys, but rather the spell [of nature] in which it is enmeshed."[119] Song is not yet.

---

[112] Adorno, *Philosophy of New Music*, 35/*GS*12, 44.
[113] Adorno, *Aesthetic Theory*, 160/*GS*7, 240.
[114] Benjamin, "On the Concept of History," 394 (translation modified)/*GS*1.2: 699.
[115] Adorno, *Aesthetic Theory*, 160/*GS*7, 240.
[116] Ibid., 63/*GS*7, 100.
[117] Deleuze and Guattari, *A Thousand Plateaus*, 300.
[118] The contrast between this view and Deleuze and Guattari's conception of the cosmos itself [becoming] art should be obvious. Deleuze and Guattari, *A Thousand Plateaus*, 346.
[119] Adorno, *Aesthetic Theory*, 66 (translation modified)/*GS*7, 105.

The Nonidentity of Nature and History

Without exaggeration one could say that searching for the so-called cosmological element in music—so frequently cited with reference to Stockhausen, Cage's famous description of *Imaginary Landscape No. 1*, Afro-futurism, and, before any of these attempts, George's poem from Schoenberg's *Entrückung* finale—became the overarching need of critical music in the post-tonal era. At the same time, this need remains, at present, blocked, incapable of being realized in the world, just as it was during the initial experimental phase. The "I feel the air from another planet" moment,[120] the space-travel ambiance and the laser-beam bite, which have marked so much electroacoustic music since Adorno's death, always border on forgetting that, like the automatically guided astronaut and the automatically guided drone bomb, technology has heretofore been nothing other than a heteronomous force, that is, a depersonalized, streamlined process that, in Horkheimer's ominous words, has "dropped the driver [and] is racing blindly into space."[121] "It should be enough," Adorno maintains, along these lines, "to remember that there is no atmosphere in the cosmos [*Weltraum*] and thus no air from the other planets."[122] Does the program laid out by Deleuze and Guattari, guided by the thesis that nature = history,[123] confront this objective current, this objective antagonism at play in the relation between art and *praxis*, technology and nature? Or does it, like Nietzsche's criticism of the allegedly pure drive for truth, make art practical simply by wishing it were so? In this way, remaining faithful to the Frankfurt School position, which, on the contrary, demands that we follow the extreme similarity between nature and history, until the smallest difference between them, the minutest chance or nonidentity, reveals itself might still be the more apt approach.

The Desecration of Silence

However this dilemma is decided, it is virtually impossible to deny the fact that the cold, lifeless asphalt on which the character Hamm from Beckett's *Endgame* wheels his mutilated body is history's answer, expressed in art, to this need

---

[120] Adorno, "Vers une musique informelle," 318/*GS*16, 536–7.
[121] Max Horkheimer, *Eclipse of Reason* (New York: Continuum Press, 2004), 87.
[122] Adorno, "Vers une musique informelle," 318/*GS*16, 536–7.
[123] Deleuze and Guattari, *Anti-Oedipus*, 25.

for air, for a cosmological "opening onto a world."[124] It is not for nothing that the promised reconciliation of the echo is allegorically presented as woman trapped in the narcissism of man.[125] The heliotropic flowers of a new day, of history "rising in the sky," cannot, as they do in the grass from Ovid's tale or the dirt from Hirschbiegel's *Untergang*, grow in desiccated asphalt. In music, this same process of absolute suffocation is expressed in the piercing barbs of Penderecki's *Threnody*, when the fingertips of the victims of Auschwitz and the Atomic Bomb dig, in absolute desperation, into the concrete walls of the camp. Punishment is the only natural law (*Naturgesetz*) that ever was. There is only air to breathe in the outer ring of hell. Beyond the choice between Adorno's and Deleuze's philosophical musicology, the more pressing question might, therefore, be: does *any* music confront this impasse, this Beckettian imperative to avoid the desecration of silence,[126] to avoid the spell of nature that continues to forswear those who, in Jean Améry's unforgettable image of peace, want to stop the healing process of biological and social time by, paradoxically, undoing the past?[127] Refusing to turn away from the infinite wound, or refusing to resolve it, as if its reverberation were not, to this day, constituting every moment of natural and social history, Adorno returns once more to Beethoven and the choral moment internal to the movement song:

> Order [*Ordnung*] that shuts itself up in its own meaning will also shut itself away from the possibility above order. Vis-à-vis theology, metaphysics is not just a historically later stage, as it is according to positivistic doctrine. It is not only theology secularized into a concept. It preserves theology in its critique, by uncovering the possibility of what theology may force upon men and thus desecrate. The cosmos of the spirit [*Kosmos des Geistes*] was exploded by the forces it had bound; rightful justice befell it [*ihm widerfuhr sein Recht*]. The autonomous Beethoven is more metaphysical, and therefore more true, than Bach's *ordo*. Subjectively liberated experience and metaphysical experience converge in humanity [*Humanität*]. Even in an age when they fall silent, great works of art express hope more powerfully than the traditional theological texts, and any such expression is configurative with that of the human [*konfiguriert mit dem des Menschlichen*]—nowhere as unequivocally as in moments of Beethoven. Signs that not everything is futile come from sympathy with

---

[124] Deleuze and Guattari, *A Thousand Plateaus*, 337; Samuel Beckett, *Endgame & Act Without Words* (New York: Grove Press, 1958).
[125] Cf. Luce Irigaray, "Women on the Market," in *This Sex Which Is Not One*, trans. Catherine Porter (New York: Cornell University Press, 1985).
[126] Adorno, *Aesthetic Theory*, 134/GS7, 203.
[127] Jean Améry, "Resentments," in *At the Mind's Limits*, trans. Sidney Rosenfeld and Stella P. Rosenfeld (Bloomington: Indiana University Press, 1980), 72.

the human [*Sympathie mit dem Menschlichen*], from the self-reflection of nature in the subject [*Selbstbesinnung der Natur in den Subjekten*]; it is only in experiencing its own naturalness [*Naturhaftigkeit*] that the genius of nature rises above [*entragen*].[128]

Even if composing like Beethoven is no longer possible after the idealist cosmos has been justifiably exploded,[129] the subjectivity that he wrenched from history continues to speak, since it remains a testament to something more than what is simply the case, more than genius feigning superiority over nature once again. This suggests that in composing *with and against* convention, that which convention rigidly divides (*was die Mode streng geteilt*) can be reunited or, in Deleuze and Guattari's language, reassembled into a new block, into a new, unanticipated transversal. It also suggests that the production of subjectivity, as a moment in the process of reconciliation with objectivity, remains essential to the task of grasping that ceaselessly sought-after, "mind-independent" or nonintentional nature. Hence, in this context, nature is not the flow of "natural" phenomena, not the image of green shrubbery, wild beasts, and mountainous landscapes undisturbed by humankind. If anything, the latter comprise the real, much-maligned anthropomorphisms.[130] Nor is it the hypostatization of the "facts," the picture-thinking in which present-day, positivist science, that is, the Hegelian understanding,[131] regresses to myth by collecting empirical or neurological data, yet, in the next breath, forgetting the speculative moment that would set this data in its proper place, that is, within a dynamic, ever-fluctuating natural-historical constellation. "[O]nly that which has no history is definable," remarked Nietzsche.[132] This silent, non-subsumed naturalness (*Naturhaftigkeit*), this surplus (*Mehr*), accordingly recedes before those reifications that remain shut in (*verschließen*) on themselves. Especially insofar as the trembling or tender moment immanent to consciousness remains blocked from self-reflection, the parasitic outgrowth (*Schmarotzerauswuchs*)

---

[128] Adorno, *Negative Dialectics*, 397 (translation modified)/*GS6*, 389–90.

[129] Adorno, *Beethoven*, 160/*NS1*, 231.

[130] As if mimetic similarity, or the formal and material likeness between animals and humans and, more generally, between subject and object, were not the source of solidarity. As if denying this fact were not the source of the ancient taboo on *eros*.

[131] See, for example, G. W. F. Hegel, *Hegel's Phenomenology of Spirit*, trans. A. V. Miller (New York: Oxford University Press, 1977), 37. See, also, Adorno's analysis of how the strength of Hegel's philosophical experience leads him far beyond the limits of positivism well before the latter was fully formed, in T. W. Adorno, *Hegel: Three Studies*, trans. Shierry Weber Nicholsen (Cambridge, MA: MIT Press, 1993), 55; *Drei Studien zu Hegel*, in *Gesammelte Schriften*, vol. 5, ed. Rolf Tiedemann (Frankfurt a.m.: Suhrkamp Verlag, 1972), 296.

[132] Friedrich Nietzsche, *On the Genealogy of Morals*, trans. Walter Kaufman (New York: Vintage: 1989), 80.

of thought continues to mirror the state, continues to fancy itself something fundamentally different from the traumatic origin from which it springs. Nature cannot, in this way, abide the exchange principle that, as abstraction, as the loss of memory, refuses to lean into or identify *with* the immanent difference of identity, refuses to reflect that which has yet to unfold, yet to reveal itself to our woefully detemporalized epistemology.[133] To play on a Benjaminian theme, nature, in this critical sense, is better understood as the *not yet recognizable* or the *not yet heard*.[134] It is the opaque, the inaccessible to thought, the longing that wants to break with the false immediacy of the present system of rank and class, with the *ordo* whose music still follows the petrified, rhythmic modes of historical time. It is, moreover, the mute sorrow (*Trauer*) that wants to sing, that wants to find a voice and a *people*, wants to become, as Kracauer once put it, folk song, but can't under the current, inhuman (*unmenschlich*) configuration of domination.[135] To remember the nature in the subject, then, signifies nothing other than staying true to that emancipatory drive that is immanent to all natural-historical desire.

Critique of Pseudo-Praxis

The notion that apes "seem objectively," in Adorno's dialectical construction, "to mourn [*trauert*] that they are not human" is not simply an exaggeration designed to highlight the inadequacy of thought in relation to its object.[136] It is just as much a statement about the socially necessary form of appearance under the present conditions of domination, about the impossibility of nature appearing

---

[133] Adorno, *Negative Dialectics*, 331–4/*GS*6, 324–8.
[134] Benjamin, "On the Concept of History," 390; *GS*1.2, 695.
[135] Siegfried Kracauer, "The Mass Ornament," trans. Barbara Correll and Jack Zipes, *New German Critique* 5 (Spring 1975): 67–76, 76. For further consideration of the social suppression of this possibility of folk music, see Max Paddison, *Adorno's Aesthetics of Music* (New York: Cambridge University Press, 1993), 118. While helpful in showing the crisis conditions to which critical music responds, Paddison, in my view, misunderstands the "subject" of advanced compositional technique when he claims that this subject is, on Adorno's account, necessarily the bourgeois subject. This claim is both tautological and an hypostatization. Adorno insists, on the contrary, that the measure of successful critical music cannot be reduced to the "standpoint" epistemology that is so prominent in identitarian discourse. In mirroring a Sainte-Beuvean form of analysis, categories such as expression, technique, truth-content, form, and subject matter all border on being eclipsed. For a look at how the force of subjectivity can be subsumed neither under any standpoint nor any abstract technique (e.g., the tone row), see Alastair Williamson, "New Music, Late Style: Adorno's 'Form in the New Music,'" *Music Analysis* 27, no. 2/3 (July–October 2008): 193–9.
[136] Adorno, *Aesthetic Theory*, 113, *GS*7, 172. For an analysis that aims, in part, to grasp the subjective moment in objectivity as well as the objective moment in subjectivity, see Richard A. Lee Jr., *The Thought of Matter: Materialism, Conceptuality, and the Transcendence of Immanence* (New York: Roman and Littlefield, 2016).

to critical consciousness as anything other than a missed chance. For, like all natural-historical organisms, apes also shudder before an ever-threatening, defuse system of predation and hunger and, in conformity with the nirvana principle, yearn to annihilate it. Like our longing to give voice to sorrow, their voiceless gestures signal a *dialectical* humanism that, *to critical consciousness*, is neither bourgeois, nor essentialist, neither affirmative, nor leaping ahead of itself in heroic feats of practice. In contrast to all pseudo-becomings and pseudo-praxis (*Scheinpraxis*), where the preservation of the past in the present moment is disavowed, so that the past, in fact, inadvertently dominates it, a "fully developed humanism," itself a "fully developed naturalism,"[137] knows that only the echo, that is, the *deterritorialized* refrain, can reconcile. It knows that this suffering, which originates in prehistorical cataclysm, lives on, haunting or, more accurately, forming "society" and all of its socio-biological reproductions, so long as we refuse to turn around and answer it or so long as we refuse to admit that no animal, including so-called man, has in actuality deterritorialized the cosmic and elemental refrain of the ancient spell: the toil of insecurity, of unfulfilled labor. No epistemological category can escape this objective limit to the appearances, this as-structure in which political semblance continues to veil social domination, in which natural selection persists because patrician and plebian, feudal lord and vassal, continue to appear as characters wholly distinct from bourgeois and proletarian. "If the lion had a consciousness, his rage at the antelope he wants to eat would be ideology."[138] His rage, like ideology, would subside, however, if food, of both the spiritual and material kind, were finally made plentiful to every living organism, if second nature finally left behind the radical insecurity of first nature.

The Mute Song of Justice

Will there one day be a people with ears to hear this echo of nature in history? Will they thus join together (*einstimmen*) in the secularized chorus that is alone a match for the gathering, fascist momentum? Will *die Klage* become *die Klänge* of reconciliation, of justice? Will anyone ever succeed, as Homer promised, in singing an epic song of peace, so that its silence finally drowns out the noise?[139]

---

[137] Karl Marx, "Private Property and Communism," in *Collected Works*, vol. 3, ed. James S. Allen et al. (New York: International Publishers, 1975), 296.
[138] Adorno, *Negative Dialectics*, 349/GS6, 342.
[139] T. W. Adorno, "Parataxis: On Hölderlin's Late Poetry," in *Notes to Literature*, vol. 2, trans. Shierry Weber Nicholsen (New York: Columbia University Press, 1992), 148; "Parataxis: Zur späten Lyrik

Will the machining of the voice rescue the sorrow of all imprisoned creatures, after the Alte Oper, the allegory of civilization, has been reduced to rubble? There is no denying that all signs point to one more sorrowful answer in a series of catastrophic answers. And yet, as Deleuze and Guattari never forgot, the totality is moving fast, beyond our comprehension. It has, in reality, passed us by well before we have heard its ramifications. There is no telling, then, whether the "sound molecules of pop music are at this very moment implanting here and there a people of a new type, singularly indifferent to the orders of the radio, to computer safeguards, to the threat of the atomic bomb."[140] There is just as little certainty regarding whether the radio dome, that is, the ionosphere or skywave off of which these molecules are now refracted, is currently forming a new echo that could one day be laid hold of. In Adorno's terms, the overpowering order of things produces an impenetrable spell, but it is, in the end, only a spell.[141] The futility of all oppression is manifest precisely when that oppression becomes total. Hence, "[e]ven if the dynamic was always the same, its end today is not the end."[142] Music is the voice that speaks for the end of natural-history.

Hölderlins," in *Gesammelte Schriften*, vol. 11, ed. Rolf Tiedemann (Frankfurt a.m.: Suhrkamp Verlag, 1972), 490.

[140] Deleuze and Guattari, *A Thousand Plateaus*, 346.

[141] T. W. Adorno, "Late Capitalism or Industrial Society?" in *Can One Live after Auschwitz?*, ed. Rolf Tiedemann (Stanford, CA: Stanford University Press, 2003), 125; "Spätkapitalismus oder Industriegesellschaft?" in *GS8*, 370.

[142] T. W. Adorno, "Reflections on Class Theory," in *Can One Live after Auschwitz?*, ed. Rolf Tiedemann (Stanford, CA: Stanford University Press, 2003) 110 (translation modified); "Reflexion zur Klassentheorie," in *GS8*, 391.

Excursus II

The Sorrow Song of Nature

Even those of harsh and unyielding nature will endure gentle treatment: no creature is fierce and frightening if it is stroked.

—Seneca, *On Anger*

There is no help except from music.

—Adorno, *Introduction to the Sociology of Music*

Wreckage Universalized

In his historico-philosophical analysis of *Trauerspiel*, Benjamin claimed that sorrow (*Trauer*) is more than a feeling that accompanies a particular genre of German dramatic performance. As "play *for* the sorrowful," he contended, on the contrary, that sorrow play is, at bottom, a type of musicality that emerges from a conflict between the communicative barriers of "human" language and the object of expression.[1] The "interplay [between sound and meaning] must find its resolution," writes Benjamin, in this vein, "and that redemptive mystery is music."[2] The play *on and of* sorrow is thus produced for and by a particular type of person confronted with a particular set of natural-historical relations. It is compensation for the alienated, modern subject, who suddenly finds herself thrust before a debased, fractured world. The fall (*Untergang*) of nature into the creaturely, itself now infected with death and damnation, into a universal diaspora that, consorting with the devil, has lost the security of a teleological and hierarchized metaphysics, is a decisive turning point.[3] So too is the moment when the faith in dialogue, the alleged transparency of language, which was so

---

[1] Benjamin, *Origin of German Tragic Drama*, 119 (translation modified)/*GS*1, 298.
[2] Benjamin, "The Role of Language," 59–61, 61/*GS*2.1, 137–40, 139.
[3] Compare this falling, secularizing movement to what Angela Davis has called the "nonteleological character of blues consciousness." Davis, *Blues Legacies and Black Feminism: Gertrude "Ma" Rainey, Bessie Smith, and Billie Holiday* (New York: Vintage, 1998), 77.

crucial to Greek tragedy, dissolves. In this "musicked speech,"[4] this historically grounded sensitivity for the phonetic side of the word, it is as though the husk of meaning and signification were burnt up in the atmospheric descent, leaving only the cold, lifeless interior—a ruin—of the ancient *ordo*.[5] Nature mourns because she is mute, because, as Benjamin puts it, she is betrayed (*verraten*) by language along the salvific arc of translation, of name-giving.[6] This suggests that the element of *Trauer*, which, as Adorno rightly insisted, is constitutive of *all* art, can be distilled from a wide range of musical and literary genres.[7] In particular, the perceptive listener will notice the degree to which the "sorrow songs" of the African diaspora stand out as, so to speak, allegorical ciphers that at once protest against and submit to this fatalistic condition. If, in other words, German baroque drama resembles, as Benjamin argued, early twentieth-century Expressionism,[8] there is reason to believe that a similar play of forces unite baroque *Trauer* to the "sorrow" upon which the so-called blues of the Black radical tradition are played.[9] For the other to the European revelry, forced to *steal away* (*sich fortstehlen*) before Schiller's triumphal procession, is undoubtedly the colonized, raced subject, the wretched of the earth. The vagabond's folk song is the moan of the dispossessed on its way to music. Theorists have, of course, long maintained that the "blues" is not merely one genre among others but rather a kind of *ethos*, or a way of comporting oneself in relation to this imprisoned condition. This is why there are "bluesmen" and "blueswomen," and one must *have* the blues in order to be capable of *playing* them. Just as play (*Spiel*) is, in Benjamin's conception, *for* the sorrowful, *for* the homeless, the blues is *for* those who are guilty without having, in truth, committed a crime. In fact, the ambivalent lament that cries out against this fateful guilt-nexus (*Schuldzusammenhang*),[10] the oscillation between, on the one hand, a *resignation* that acquiesces to the prognosticated sentence and, on the other, the *onward* that endures or, despite the unbearable odds, holds out hope for the promised land, for an escape along the Jordan River, is essential

---

[4] This is Amiri Baraka's description of the blues, which is here being connected to the phonetic sensitivity of *Trauerspiel*. See D. H. Melhem, "Revolution: The Constancy of Change," in *Conversations with Amiri Baraka*, ed. Charlie Reilly (Jackson: University Press of Mississippi, 1994), 214.
[5] Compare this burning of the husk during the descent to Benjamin's conception of the burning ascension into the realm of the ideas in Benjamin, *Origin of German Tragic Drama*, 31/*GS*1, 211.
[6] Benjamin, "The Role of Language," 60/*GS*2.1, 138.
[7] Adorno, *Aesthetic Theory*, 52/*GS*7, 84.
[8] Benjamin, *Origin of German Tragic Drama*, 53–6; *Ursprung des deutschen Trauerspiels*, 234–6.
[9] Following Moten, *Black and Blur*, I am concerned with the conceptualization of Black radicalism as fundamentally tied to the theoretical, practical, and lyrical prefiguration of a postcolonial future. See, also, Cedric Robinson, *Black Marxism: The Making of the Black Radical Tradition* (Chapel Hill: University of North Carolina Press, 2000).
[10] Benjamin, "Fate and Character," 201–6, 204/*GS*2.1, 171–9, 175.

to this song that would come to guide, in Amiri Baraka's view, every authentic iteration of jazz, to say nothing of electroacoustic experimentation.[11]

Totality

W.E.B. Du Bois's classical conception of the sorrow song brings this metaphysics of the wearied and worn, this hopeless clinging to hope, into sharp relief. Paralleling Benjamin's conception, for Du Bois too it is always a question of how and under what conditions "language can express sorrow,"[12] how, that is to say, music can give voice to the "unvoiced,"[13] after the security of the old regime, the old *episteme*, has been devastated by colonization, slavery, and their perpetuation by other means.[14] In the same way as Shakespeare, by virtue of his affinity and difference to German baroque drama, must be understood, on Benjamin's account, as the outermost star lighting up the constellation of *Trauerspiel*, or in the same way as the Bachian fugue—polyphonic song as such—must be understood, on Adorno's account, in relation to outermost developments of Beethoven's late style,[15] so the countless stars, both proximate and remote, which orbit and ultimately constitute the image of the African American spiritual, must be critically placed by theory, if one is to adequately grasp the possibilities that are still slumbering in nature, still waiting to burst forth. From the first, unamplified murmurs of blues-based jazz to the Caribbean and European, Middle Eastern, and African hybridizations, critique aims to illuminate this constellational totality in its ongoing movement. When read off of the present, ever-fluctuating whole, unrecognizable connections, that is, previously hidden links, and undeveloped, long-gestating themes, begin to sound their grievance anew, begin to emerge in the full light of their recognizability. The incipient

---

[11] Leroi Jones (Amiri Baraka), *Blues People: The Negro Experience in White America and the Music that Developed from It* (New York: Morrow Quill, 1963), 17. For further discussion of what I am calling the "onward" element of the blues, see Davis's analysis of the determination to "keep walking" or "keep moving" in Davis, *Blues Legacies*, 75–9. For better understanding of the concept of resignation, see T. W. Adorno, "Resignation," in *Critical Models: Interventions and Catchwords*, trans. Henry W. Pickford (New York: Columbia University Press, 2005), 289–93; "Resignation," in *Gesammelte Schriften*, vol. 10.2, ed. Rolf Tiedemann (Frankfurt a.m.: Suhrkamp Verlag, 1972), 794–9.
[12] Benjamin, "The Role of Language," 59–61, 59/*GS*2.1, 137–40, 138.
[13] W. E. B. Du Bois, *The Souls of Black Folk* (New York: Oxford University Press, 2017), 169.
[14] For more on the perpetuation of slavery by other means, see Angela Davis, "From the Prison of Slavery to the Slavery of Prison: Frederick Douglass and the Convict Leasing System," in *The Angela Y. Davis Reader* (Malden, MA: Blackwell Publishers, 1998), 74–95.
[15] T. W. Adorno, "The Function of Counterpoint in New Music," in *Sound Figures*, trans. Rodney Livingstone (Stanford, CA: Stanford University Press, 1999), 123–44.

meaning of the totality is still, in short, waiting to be understood, even if that totality is also, in its current form, the false.[16]

Plugging the Sorrow Song into the *Trauergesang*

Consider, for example, Du Bois's claim that the red bricks of Jubilee Hall bear the allegorical imprint of "the blood and dust of toil."[17] Implied in this reading of the *allos*, the cypher of a *different* world in which the "Veil" will be rended and "the prisoned [...] go free"[18] is a song whose melody is, first and foremost, based on the voice of the past, the exiled, or the "fugitive and the weary wanderer."[19] Hence, it could be said that, like Adorno's Alte Oper, the music of the famous Nashville concert hall recuperates the unanswered sigh of the first slaves, the "we" who, in truth, preceded the colonial settlement and may well, for that reason, echo the lament of the forgotten indigenous population too.[20] A remembrance of prehistory in which song returns to something wholly understood and yet cloaked, devoid of out-and-out determination, is noticeably at play in this conceptualization.[21] Bringing him unmistakably close to Benjamin, Du Bois emphasizes what might be called a preconscious understanding, where the conceptless concept, or judgmentless (*urteilslos*) judgment of music,[22] is closer to language as such (*überhaupt*), precisely because it, paradoxically, rubs the meaningful-nexus (*Sinnzusammenhang*) of the coercive word against the grain. The mute or silent (*stumm*) element of nature, which is best approximated by music, not, to state it differently, by the nature-dominating abstraction of the word,[23] can only truly be heard with the help of an ear that, as Du Bois puts it, senses that "the music [of the imprisoned] is far more ancient than the words." As he also expresses it, describing both the "cradle song" that, in an earlier period, still carried a remnant of the African language and cadence and, for the later generation, had undergone the "method of blurring" between Black-and-white

---

[16] Adorno, *Minima Moralia*, 50/GS4, 55. Adorno's famous claim that the "whole is the false [*Unwahre*]" does not imply that one could or should renounce the task of thinking the movement of the totality. To do so would mean forfeiting the power of critique.
[17] Du Bois, *The Souls of Black Folk*, 167.
[18] Ibid., 176.
[19] Ibid., 173.
[20] Ibid., 175.
[21] Cf. Deleuze, *Logic of Sense*.
[22] Adorno, *Beethoven*, 11/NS1, 32.
[23] This is not to say that the abstract word somehow falls outside of the totality in a crude dualism. It too follows the movement of the dialectic. It too is recuperated and transformed in relation to the phonetic or sonic moment. These must, in other words, be understood as interpenetrating moments.

traditions: "[its] message is naturally veiled and half articulate. Words and music have lost each other and new and cant phrases of a dimly understood theology have displaced the older sentiment."[24] At a particular stage in production, word and sound become divided, even at odds or antagonistic to one another. The enclosure without generates the alienation of the sensorium within. This fallen, meaningless state, which has destroyed memory, or the "warp and woof" of storytelling on which the wisdom of an older way of life was based,[25] ultimately infects every aspect of nature. The split between the two is, in fact, the material basis of the modern music of grief and mourning. One gropes when one has no other recourse. The cant externality foisted upon the phonetic substance reminds one, moreover, of the trite, clumsy features of *Trauerspiel*. Words are inadequate, but their human, all-too-human attempt at expressing this plight is not the heart of these sorrowful works of art. The fact that the theology is now Christian, that the language and concepts belong to the fosterland, points to an antinomy. Amiri Baraka's claim that early blues artists took up entertainment for the first time is certainly true, but emphasizing this misses the truth-content, the sorrow song, immanent to the blues. As Angela Davis has noted, the banal and cant words, the "love ballads," are more than love ballads about private life.[26] The "man" outside the door of Elmore James's famous song is also the "man" of the police state, the capitalist axiomatic, in Deleuze's terms, which incessantly suppresses the nomadic war machine, not just the jilted or unfaithful lover.[27] Thus, the words are based on the fragments, the detritus picked up and reassembled, inherited from the master, and constrained, as the Fisk Singers were once constrained, by the "limitations of allowable thought."[28] But they also gesture to a beyond, that is, to a radical deterritorialization of what has hitherto been the case. The limits entailed in the double or triple line verse and, later, the imposition of the twelve-bar progression are the secret strength of this deceptively narrow music.[29]

[24] Du Bois, *The Souls of Black Folk*, 171.
[25] Ibid., 175–6. Du Bois uses the same weaving metaphor that Benjamin uses to describe storytelling in Benjamin, "The Storyteller," 149/*GS2*, 447.
[26] Davis, *Blues Legacies*, 81.
[27] Deleuze and Guattari, *A Thousand Plateaus*, 351–423.
[28] Du Bois, *The Souls of Black Folk*, 174.
[29] For further consideration of how the analysis of form in the traditional European sense cannot be easily grafted onto the *a priori* self-reflexivity of the blues and Black expression, see Fumi Okiji, *Jazz as Critique: Adorno and Black Expression Revisited* (Stanford, CA: Stanford University Press, 2018), 28–9. This excursus follows Okiji's lead in that the limited attention that Adorno pays to the lived contradiction of Black experience in his criticism of jazz often effaces the subtle play on the antinomies that constitute this form of expression. As Theodore Gracyk has shown in Gracyk, "Adorno, Jazz, and the Aesthetics of Popular Music," *Musical Quarterly* 76, no. 4 (1992): 526–42, even on a technical level Adorno at times lapses into a reductionism or generalization that misses the particular. The constellating of both the experiential and technical developments that form the aphorisms of this excursus are intended, then, as lines of flight that, if followed, might begin

Immanent to it is something uncompromising, something that Richard Iton has suggested is a minstrelsy protesting against minstrelsy.[30] Admittedly, the sorrow song on its way to the advanced blues "blends" with the ruling order and therefore seems reformist, heteronomous, even whitewashing in the way that Paul Whiteman's arrangements would eventually integrate "unruly," Black jazz for white consumers. But it also bends in another direction, since its expression remains unpolished, broken, inarticulate.[31] It will at times play the coded game of salability,[32] passively adapting to Tin Pan Alley's top-down demand for freshly minted "race records," yet the sadness of those who, in the end, refuse to accept anything other than "a truer world," justice, and the "God of Right"[33] also breaks through in the refracted, quivering voice and, later, in the crackling distortion of the amplified guitar. Without directly stating it, or perhaps even directly knowing it, the longing for an escape from the Mississippi Delta is encompassed in Du Bois's delineation of these early, post-bellum spirituals.

Anticipatory Echo

One need only recall the classical figure Charlie Patton, one of the first blues artists to be recorded by monopoly capital. In his work, the entire arc can be detected in cell form. Before the electronification of the instrument, at the stage of the mere phonographic recording, the non-diatonic features of the blues, that is, its sliding and blurring technique, are already present. Toward what is the famous "blues note," the quarter tone, bending, when it begins as the *glissando* of the voice? What memory trace is being revealed? Is it a different scale, a West African inheritance bursting through the limits of European convention, as Baraka and others, once claimed?[34] Perhaps. One thing is inescapable, as far as the origin (*Ursprung*), that is, as far as the emergence of the new, in contrast to the "first," is concerned: when the artist musters enough strength to make the words

---

revealing how, on Adorno's own terms, the critical potency of Black music has not been fully considered. Compare, also, this approach of reading with and against Adorno to Robert W. Witkin, *Adorno on Music* (New York: Routledge, 1998), 160–80.

[30] Richard Iton, *In Search of the Black Fantastic: Politics and Popular Culture in the Post-Civil Right Era* (New York: Oxford University Press), 210–18.

[31] It is not accidental that Adorno uses very similar language to describe the aesthetic potential of so-called Kiddy's Cinema in order to contrast it with the slick and polished form of the socially sanctioned kind. T. W. Adorno, "Transparencies on Film," in *The Continental Philosophy of Film Reader*, ed. Joseph Westfall (New York: Bloomsbury, 2018), 274; "Filmtransparente," in GS10.1, 353.

[32] Adorno, *Introduction to the Sociology of Music*, 32.

[33] Du Bois, *The Souls of Black Folk*, 169, 175.

[34] Jones (Baraka), *Blues People*, 25.

audible, they are undeniably frail (*schwach*). Without perceiving just how much they have neglected to grasp the critical, non-biographical truth-content of this music, some authors speculate that Patton had a speech impediment.[35] Far more important here is the sense that, in works such as *Pea Vine Blues*, the failure to clearly enunciate the lyrics is compensated for with a moaning, Gould-esque, hum.[36] And Patton is certainly not the only bluesman or blueswoman to embody this scat-like tendency, this progressive regression to nonsense, immanent to the song of grief.[37] Along with Texas Alexander, his moan anticipates Son Houses's *Pearline* and Howlin' Wolf's *Moanin' at Midnight*. The orality of the colonized speaks, as Édouard Glissant highlighted, against the immobilizing force of the written word.[38] In *Pea Vine Blues* specifically, the horizontal line of the linguistic phrase not only prematurely cuts off, only to be concluded by the guitar's melody, reminding us that the voice is no longer satisfactory, that it must be "machined" if it is to succeed at expressing the expressionless. The words themselves also start to blend, monophonically, with the notes of the acoustic guitar. Hence, this voice of sorrow is in a process of *becoming-instrument*. It is being "trained," as Houston A. Baker Jr. has underscored in his attempt to determine the onomatopoetic or mimetic character of the Black expressive tradition.[39] As the words themselves *swing low*—"I think I heard the Pea Vine when *she blowed*"—the "blow" of the "train" is sung in the same, lower register that rumbles from Patton's Stella Grand.[40] The chariot of the old world becomes the locomotive of the new, industrialized one, which ineluctably points to the "backdoor," Mississippi Central route to Chicago. Du Bois was already on the trail of this longing for the north-bound exodus from Jim Crow essential to the lullaby when he showed that the Bible phrase "Weep, O captive daughter of Zion" was transformed by the freed slave into the "weep-a-low" of the "Africanized," Christian hymn. A similar becoming-train is operative when a "mystic dreaming" turns Ezekiel's lament into the verse: "There's a little wheel a-turnin' in-a-my heart."[41] These are mimetic

---

[35] See, for example, Robert Palmer, *Deep Blues: A Musical and Cultural History of the Mississippi Delta* (New York: Penguin Books, 1982), 65–6.
[36] See the earlier fragment entitled "Gould, the Benjaminian."
[37] For more on the progressive character of regression, see Herbert Marcuse, *Eros and Civilization: A Philosophical Inquiry into Freud* (Boston, MA: Beacon Press, 1966), 19.
[38] Édouard Glissant, *Caribbean Discourse: Selected Essays*, trans. J. Michael Dash (Charlottesville: University Press of Virginia, 1989), 123.
[39] Houston A. Baker, Jr., *Blues, Ideology, and Afro-American Literature: A Vernacular Theory* (Chicago: University of Chicago Press), 8.
[40] In another striking example of the similarities between Du Bois and Benjamin, Du Bois describes how the rumbling thunder of the American South seemed like it was "mournful" to the colonized. Du Bois, *The Souls of Black Folk*, 172.
[41] Ibid., 174.

improvisations syncopated against the minstrel band's debasement, which almost always follow the sinking, downward trajectory all the way to the low-down, gutbucket, bottom: to death.[42] On the one hand, Patton's "you done me wrong" performs the sado-masochistic fluctuation between the accuser and the accused so essential to the guilt-nexus of the blues. Mama, Papa, and Me are all blamed, depending on the situation, and always in the mornin', when one awakens, after what was, by no means, Brahms's *gute Nacht*. Folk songs such as *Must Have Did Somebody Wrong* and *Stormy Monday* come to mind in this context. They have been taken up and reinterpreted by countless artists. The most intense moments almost always come back to the feeling that only death will release one from the curse of intermundane existence. On the other hand, a critical ear cannot miss the prophetic significance of the unamplified, instrumental riff in-between Patton's singing verse. The piercing silence that it momentarily conjures up signals a desire to explode, to break out of the confines of unamplified music. With each hard attack, each percussive emphasis, a negativity built into the ever-sameness of this guilt structure flits past. The repetition of the guitar makes it possible. And yet, this expressive potential could not realize itself until that same interval, that play between the silent and the signified, was amplified and accompanied by a larger ensemble, until the harmonica, snare, and Hammond organ were layered on top of its driving momentum in, for instance, the work of Muddy Waters and, subsequently, the "metaphysics of youth" of the early Allman Brothers Band.[43] This is the moment when the dialectic between augmentation and diminution is laid bare.[44] Both sides need the electroacoustic flow, if the natural-historical process is to be set back in motion, against the bewitching circle of territorialization. Their potential—stored up labor—is based on a potential stored up or "jammed" (*gestaut*) in the advances of industrial production in general. Seizing control of it, rechanneling it, is the precondition of this rhythm, this gathering intensity, one day transcending Patton's limit. Then, and only

---

[42] For further consideration of this *scatological* tendency, see Gilroy, *The Black Atlantic*, 198.

[43] Walter Benjamin, "The Metaphysics of Youth," in *Selected Writings*, vol. 1, ed. Michael W. Jennings (Cambridge, MA: Harvard University Press, 2003), 6–17; "Metaphysik der Jugend," in *Gesammelte Schriften*, vol. 2, ed. Rolf Tiedemann and Hermann Scheppenhäuser (Frankfurt a.m.: Suhrkamp Verlag, 1974), 91–104. For an analysis of the developments that followed from the incorporation of the church organ and the Hammond B-3 in the Black expressive tradition, see Mark Anthony Neal, *What the Music Said: Black Popular Music and Black Public Culture* (New York: Routledge, 1999), 26–34.

[44] This dialectic of augmentation and diminution should be thought as a supplement to Fred Moten's conception of an augmentation that is too frequently, in my view, disconnected from its other. In other words, the implications of Moten's appeal to the transformative potential of augmentation cannot be fully grasped unless one points to the manner in which technical reproduction has simultaneously opened up a note shortening capacity that reaches to the molecular or infinitesimally small level. See, for example, Moten, *Black and Blur*, 118–33.

then, are the outermost consequences, the razor-sharp caesura of, for instance, a wah-wah that juts through the silent abyss of this brief interval, realizable. Then, and only then, does the decolonization of song become dangerous in the way that Saidiya Hartman has described Sukie's resistance to the white master's enjoyment.[45] An even more emphatic *onward* than Patton's initial gesture is, in other words, anticipated in his simple ostinato, his double-time rhythmic *feel* that, like a crackling wick, is about to ignite, but cannot as yet do so, since it remains bound, with Verdi and Wagner on another plane of consistency, to the solo song. Patton is still, in a word, alone with his minor instrument.[46] Who will come to his rescue? Who will amplify this weak potency and make it part of a collective ensemble. Who, or what, will enlarge the echo[47] or connect "the most diverse longitudes and latitudes, the most varied speeds and slownesses,"[48] so that Glissant's ideal of genuine transformation, of consenting not to be a single being (*un seul*), is finally made possible?[49]

Stomping Out the Dialectic

Even if Albert Murray correctly maintained that the music of the blues should not be straightaway conflated with the melancholy of the spiritual or gospel,[50] one cannot avoid observing the manner in which sorrow remains preponderant (*vorrangig*) for the former. The frivolity or swinging good-ol'-time of the Saturday night honky-tonk or jazz club is hardly evidence to the contrary, especially in light of the coerced merriment, the "stepping it up lively," of plantation life to which this festivity arguably remains fastened.[51] Whereas gospel is allegedly reserved for "praying" the blues, seeking redemption, or submitting to the ponderous weight, blues music is said to be characterized by the task of ridding oneself of the blues as such, "playing" them, stomping them out, so that the devils finally flee the scene.[52] Mapping

---

[45] Saidiya Hartman, *Scenes of Subjection: Terror, Slavery, and Self-Making in Nineteenth-Century America* (New York: Oxford University Press), 41.
[46] Compare this sense of a "minor" instrument with Deleuze's conception of a "minor" literature and becoming-minoritarian in Gilles Deleuze and Félix Guattari, *Kafka: Toward a Minor Literature*, trans. Dana Polan (Minneapolis: University of Minnesota Press, 1986).
[47] Gilles Deleuze, "Boulez, Proust, and Time: 'Occupying without Counting,'" *Angelaki* 3, no. 2 (1998): 69–74.
[48] Deleuze and Guattari, *A Thousand Plateaus*, 309.
[49] Moten, *Black and Blur*, XV.
[50] Albert Murray, *Stomping the Blues* (Boston, MA: Da Capo Press, 1989), 51.
[51] Hartman, *Scenes of Subjection*, 36.
[52] Murray, *Stomping the Blues*, 17.

the broader, natural-historical metamorphosis pinpoints the degree to which this distinction is, however, conceived on the basis of an undialectical, abstract opposition. This is to say that playing the blues is certainly grounded, in part, on the secularization process, on the ever-growing rationalization and disenchantment (*Entzauberung*) of life. Its inner dialectic cannot, therefore, be grasped without the element of mockery, the lightheartedness (*Heiterkeit*) that,[53] through play, generates distance from the dire *praxis* of the racist political situation or makes music, as Jacques Rancière has demonstrated, part of the disinterested "aesthetic regime of art."[54] But this newly emergent, modern emphasis on the play element (*Spielmoment*) conceals the movement of the whole or the underlying unity between these apparent opposites. Play neither extinguishes semblance (*Schein*),[55] nor succeeds in exorcizing the demons whose persistence is, in truth, the precondition of the socially necessary need for semblance (*Schein*). The charmer who was to replace Socrates and charm away (*epádein*) the fear of death with a lullaby has yet to arrive.[56] As if that which the negation negates were not preserved in the negation. As if the haunting moment, the grunts and groans of the worksongs, did not persist in, for example, Howlin' Wolf's or Willie Brown's recordings, especially when, without ceremony, the coda to these songs flippantly ends in classical fashion with a strumming dim-da-da-do. In retrospect, the melancholy or sorrow of the gospel-blues appears all the more to be constitutive of blues music in general, even if the rhyming cheerfulness is an essential means through which it first surfaces and is temporarily quelled. The complete separation of the two terms is, in actuality, more characteristic of contemporary light music (*Leichtmusik*) than anything else: the fulfilled slackening of the tension (*Spannungsverlust*) in which music regresses to the taming discipline of sport.[57]

---

[53] T. W. Adorno, "Is Art Lighthearted?" in *Notes to Literature*, vol. 2, ed. Rolf Tiedemann, trans. Shierry Weber Nicholsen (New York: Columbia University Press, 1992), 247–53; "Ist die Kunst heiter?" in GS11, ed. Rolf Tiedemann (Frankfurt a.m.: Suhrkamp Verlag, 1972), 599–608.

[54] Jacques Rancière, "The Aesthetic Revolution and Its Outcomes," in *Dissensus*, trans. Steven Corcoran (New York: Continuum, 2010).

[55] This dialectical formulation of the relation between semblance and play should be contrasted with Benjamin's claim in the "Technology" essay that, in film, play completely extinguishes semblance. My view is that, following Adorno's criticism, Benjamin eventually reconsidered this conception. See Benjamin, "The Work of Art in the Age of Its Technological Reproducibility: Second Version," 127/GS7.1: 368–9. This approach should also be contrasted to Murray's undialectical conception of the relationship between the profane and the holy in, for example, Murray, *Stomping the Blues*, 31.

[56] Plato, *Phaedo*, in *Five Dialogues*, trans. G. M. A. Grube (Indianapolis, IN: Hackett, 2002), 116.

[57] T. W. Adorno, "The Aging of the New Music," in *Essays on Music*, ed. Richard Leppert (Los Angeles: University of California Press, 2002), 181–202, 188; "Das Altern der Neuen Musik," in GS14, 143–67, 152.

Blind Myth

Be that as it may, situating the mythical return of the figure of Teiresias, that is, the blind, prophetic, blues musician—for instance, Blind Willie Johnson and Blind Lemon Jefferson—is all but impossible without this dialectical perspective, this critical understanding of the movement of natural-history. The static element, that is, the still unresolved, mute sorrow, continues to make a claim (*Anspruch*) on us,[58] especially in an era that seems to have renounced the blues altogether but nonetheless remains chained to its basic, formal structure. These blind figures of the gospel-blues are not anomalies, then, as Murray implies when he calls them "sobering sideshows" to the main event.[59] Their underemphasis constitutes their higher rank. They are the "split-off elements of truth [*abgespalten Elemente der Wahrheit*] that reality has handed over to the growing domination of nature."[60] Moreover, "[t]he splinter in your eye," the wound that comes with this banishment, is not a hindrance but rather "the best magnifying glass."[61] Blind Willie Johnson, in particular, demands critical understanding, since his music embodies the full development of the slide guitar in embryonic form: a soothsayer's vision of the future not altogether different from Patton's. The slide is, of course, renown for its mimetic resemblance to bird song, and Teiresias did, after all, receive his prophecy, on Callimachus's account, from the song of birds. With a glass bottle from the apothecary taking over the technique honed on the diddley bow, it is as though equipment—the machine— were better suited to sound the mimetic truth that only the pharmakon, which magically wounds and heals simultaneously, can successfully deliver us from the disease.[62] In the case of Johnson's music, there is something indescribably out-of-step, something fundamentally untimely (*unzeitgemäß*), at play in his calming, slow, dirge-like tempo. An ancient wound speaks in this humming song, this attempted unification between the voice and the instrument. Like the melancholy of Shostakovich's late quartets or the motionless sorrow of variation XX from Beethoven's *Diabelli Variations*, this music appears to have lost the

---

[58] Walter Benjamin, "On the Concept of History"/GS 1.2, 691–706, 694.
[59] Murray, *Stomping the Blues*, 54.
[60] Adorno, "The Aging of the New Music," 192/GS14, 157. Murray is, of course, well aware of this appropriation by domination when he speaks, for instance, of the "gospel-fad pop hits" in Murray, *Stomping the Blues*, 30. Bringing him especially close to Benjamin, he is likewise eminently sensitive to the mute nature of the so-called blue demons that haunt the blues as such in his striking introduction on the allegorical character of the blues.
[61] Adorno, *Minima Moralia*, 50/GS4, 55.
[62] For further consideration of what is implied here, namely that mimetic "magic" brings us closer to the object than abstract science, see Adorno and Horkheimer, *Dialectic of Enlightenment*, 7/GS3, 26–7.

strength to kick up a fuss, to do anything but *resign* itself before inevitable defeat. This could account for why the lullaby, Adorno's return to the *Lied*, and Deleuze's becoming-child of music are so pronounced in, for example, *Dark Was the Night*. A mature anguish, as though it had transmigrated from ancient Egypt to ancient China and the Middle Passage, comes to the fore in Johnson's incomparable call and response, his "restatement and echo,"[63] or antiphonal play between the voice and technology. This music knows how protracted and unbearable every iteration of slavery, direct and indirect, has been, and this is why it heralds, in homage to Platonic anamnesis, a condition that has broken the yoke of slavery. James Baldwin's short story about the blues captures its physiognomy like no other. Hoping "that the hand which strokes [the audience's] head will never stop,"[64] the musician of the redemptive blues "seemed to soothe a poison out of [the listeners]; and time seemed, nearly, to fall away from the sullen, belligerent, battered faces, as though they were fleeing back to their first condition, while dreaming of their last."[65] Thus the *lulling* character of Johnson's music, as well as its theological dimension. In contrast to mere resignation, however, this music has, in truth, ascended to a level of wisdom, beyond the alleged insight of the philosopher and the fool, for whom history is still the terrain on which justice is realized.[66] In Glissant's terms, the art of the colonized embodies a "despair which is not resignation," a despair which, pessimistic though it may be, stubbornly insists upon fighting on its own terrain, on giving voice to *comment c'est*.[67] Adorno tersely describes this phenomenon when he similarly contends that "ever since Plato's doctrine of anamnesis the not-yet-existing has been dreamed of in remembrance, which alone concretizes utopia without betraying it to existence."[68] It is hard to imagine a more accurate depiction of Johnson's portamento confrontation with existence, with the indeterminate composition of *how it is*, than this adherence to the ban on graven images. The *dux* and

---

[63] Adorno, "The Natural History of the Theatre," 77/*GS*16, 320.
[64] James Baldwin, "Sonny's Blues," in *Going to Meet the Man* (New York: Vintage Books, 1993), 115.
[65] Ibid., 129.
[66] William Faulkner, *The Sound and the Fury* (New York: Vintage International, 1990), 76.
[67] Glissant, *Caribbean Discourse*, 104. Adorno references this title to Samuel Beckett's novel three times in *Aesthetic Theory*. This "novel" contains no punctuation and thus, on the one hand, keeps open the accents and lacuna for comedic, horrifying, or mundane emphasis. On the other hand, this work presents the fragmented memory of objective spirit, of the torture involved in no longer being able to synthesize experience amid the "mud" from which the narrator speaks. Hence, the play on the French "how it is" (*comment c'est*) and "to begin" (*commencer*) attempts to give voice to the negativity of experience. As Glissant implies, it is only in a mimetic immersion with how it is that the allegory of the new begins to shine forth. See Samuel Beckett, *How It Is*, trans. Samuel Beckett (New York: Grove Press, 1964).
[68] Adorno, *Aesthetic Theory*, 132/*GS*7, 200. Compare this conception of utopia to Deleuze and Guattari's brief discussion of the "negative dialectics" of the nonpropositional concept in Deleuze and Guattari, *What Is Philosophy?*, 99–100.

comes of this song, long traced by anthropologist to the African continent, but not altogether dissimilar from the soaring call and response of Brahms's *Double Concerto in A minor*, is a remembrance that, against the emptiness of homogenous time, points to what will one day be only by tarrying with what has passed away. Together, they echo across continents. Together, both voices, dead- and living-labor, give us an aural hint of how things will one day sound in the messianic light: full of "rifts and crevices," "indigent and distorted," which is to say, reconciled, because they too will have passed away in the *fulfilled* space of the future.[69] The sliding pitches, already hinted at in Patton's languishing hum and echoed in "Ma" Rainey's whining, trumpet voice, are the plaint of the colonized subject, which must accordingly be thought together with moments, that is, "stars" in the constellation, as seemingly distant as the tremolo cry of old-time music, the Appalachian doom that knows no escape from poverty save the momentary respite of an accompanying, polyvalent banjo. Zoom out and you'll see it. Enlarge the echo and you'll hear it. The song of decolonization, of postcolonial futurity,[70] stubbornly includes the white, dispossessed wage-slave as well and must, therefore, be located beyond the borders of the southern United States, even if it is inflected in a singular and always changing way there. How else could one account for the wavering-pitch that constitutes, for example, so much of Indian classical music? The wax applied to the colonizer's instrument, the violin, bends the borders, disobeys the semblance of natural law, that is, the fixed segments of the fret, in this instance too. The difference between the master's and the slave's music might be summed up, then, by the fact that, in the great works of the latter, the secret despair of Socrates's victorious declaration about the constancy of the soul—the basis of private property—is exposed. Neither the swan nor any of the creatures of natural-history sing in celebration of impending death.[71] They long to be other than what they have been. They posit immortality because possibilities were stolen from them, because "no reform has sufficed to do justice to the dead," and because the "injustice [*Unrecht*] of death," that is, the injustice of having not lived well, is unthinkable to both reason and the natural-historical impulse from which it emerges.[72] The celebration, if there is one, is ambivalent through and through, just as Frederick Douglas's remembrance of the screeching agony of his raped aunt was both necessary and impossible.[73]

---

[69] Adorno, *Minima Moralia*, 247/GS4, 281.
[70] Moten, *Black and Blur*, 21–6. For further consideration of Deleuze's complicated relationship to postcolonial theory and practice, see the essays gathered in Simone Bignall and Paul Patton, *Deleuze and the Postcolonial* (Edinburgh: Edinburgh University Press, 2010).
[71] Plato, *Phaedo*, 123.
[72] Adorno, *Negative Dialectics*, 385/GS5, 378.
[73] Moten, *Black and Blur*, X.

It would take the mimesis of rage in Max Roach and Abbey Lincoln's *Triptych* to pay it adequate respect in music, to avoid selling the past too cheaply in an imperative of short-term memory or worse, anti-memory.[74] The central question is thus, as both Adorno and Fred Moten have framed it: How can one give voice to this suffering without betraying its dignity,[75] how can one diffuse it without diluting it, especially in an era when the concept and material reality of a "public" is either fraught or altogether blocked?[76]

Silent Torture

The always expected helping hand, the precondition, in Jean Améry's account of the healing, biological time-sense of humanity, never did come to relieve the anguish of millions upon millions of victims.[77] For them, both inside and outside the borders of Europe, torture lasted the thousand years that the Third Reich prognosticated.[78] The incommunicable trauma that echoes in the music of the colonized and ghettoized is thus *lulled* by Johnson and, over time, by his inheritors, namely Elmore James, Earl Hooker, and Duane Allman, because it *has to be* lulled if the persecuted are to survive, if they are to endure the unendurable.[79] The similarity between the dream of this slide-guitar lineage and the soothing measure taken by several decolonizing musicians is unmistakable to the perspicuous ear. Moments as diverse as the initial, Beethovian rustling from Kayhan Kalhor's *Silent City*, the *onward*, uncompromising bass-drop from Geoffrey Oryema's *Exile*, as well as the gentle, trembling departure of the bass-voice in Paul Robeson's tribute to *Joe Hill* all challenge the status quo by *stilling* the frenzied delirium of the modern cityscape. They have no choice but to do so. For the twentieth- and twenty-first-century city, to which the dispossessed

---

[74] Deleuze and Guattari, *Thousand Plateaus*, 21, 294, 297. One is tempted to say that there is a violation of the dignity of the dead in this anti-memory imperative. It is noteworthy that acute suggestions such as Adorno's concerning the similarity between the archaic element in Bach's c-sharp minor Fugue in volume one of the *Well-Tempered Clavier* and Beethoven's *String Quartet No. 14 in C-sharp Minor* are virtually absent from an analysis that follows this prescription. Adorno, *Beethoven*, 56/*NS*1, 91–2.

[75] T. W. Adorno, *Aesthetics*, trans. Wieland Hoban (Medford, MA: Polity Press, 2018), 71; *Ästhetik*, in *Nachgelassene Schriften, Abteilung IV*, vol. 3, ed. Rolf Tiedemann (Frankfurt a.m.: Verlag, 1994), 116.

[76] Moten, *Black and Blur*, X. Cf. Adorno, "The Aging of the New Music," 199/*GS*14, 165–6: "The primitive fact of the matter cannot be kept silent, that today the alienation between music and the public has so rebounded against music that the material existence of serious musicians is seriously threatened."

[77] Améry, "Torture," 28.

[78] Améry, "Resentments," 78.

[79] Glissant, *Caribbean Discourse*, 132–4.

migrate for scraps of livelihood, obeys one principle and one principle alone: that of work discipline. Knowing that the rate of exploitation will not, under any circumstance, slow, that this social form cannot, therefore, do anything but provoke more anxiety, more "noise making," and more "killing time" designed to drown out unconscious desperation or vent a pent-up aggression that has no other outlet, is the first step in cultivating a genuine endurance.[80] The escape to the North was, in short, hardly an escape. Small wonder that the "carry-me-backs," in which a return to the South persisted as part of the ambivalent song of the Great Migration, emerged in tension with Billie Holiday's more defiant, *Strange Fruit*.[81] Successfully calming the discontents of civilization is not, then, reducible to simple pacification, even if pacification—a necessary moment in the process of mimetic doubling—comprises the bad conscience of all art. Rather, this feature of decolonizing song suggests that the task of adequately rescuing the suffering of the past remains incomplete. It will, in actuality, require taking up this ambivalent song of protest again and again, transposing it, re-situating it in the totality, by means of the most advanced technology, in and through lines of connection, transversals or diagonals, lattice weaves or fractal variations, that were previously buried or hidden. Any other attempt at remembrance would determine the limit of capital from outside of capital, instead of searching for it in the crevices, the "pockets of silence,"[82] or the minimal, molecular loci of untrammeled, tender nature, which still, despite appearances, constitute the present, wholly mediated reality.[83]

Was die Mode streng geteilt

Perhaps, in keeping with this logic of continually returning to an originary trauma for the sake of one day overcoming it,[84] the alternative spatiotemporal

---

[80] Adorno, *Introduction to the Sociology of Music*, 16/GS14, 194; T. W. Adorno, "On the Fetish-Character in Music and the Regression of Listening," in *Essays on Music*, ed. Richard Leppert (Los Angeles: University of California Press, 2002), 310; "Über den Fetischcharakter in der Musik und die Regression des Hörens," in *GS14*, 44.

[81] Hartman, *Scenes of Subjection*, 30.

[82] Adorno, "On the Fetish-Character in Music," 289/GS14, 15.

[83] Cf. James Baldwin, "Of the Sorrow Songs: The Cross of Redemption," in *The Cross of Redemption: Uncollected Writings*, ed. Randall Kenan (New York: Vintage Books, 2010), 148: "Aretha dared to 'steal' the song from Otis because not many men, of any color, are able to make the enormous confession, the tremendous recognition, contained in 'try a little tenderness.'"

[84] Kodwo Eshun, "Further Considerations on Afrofuturism," in *The New Centennial Review* 3, no. 2 (Summer, 2003): 287–302. In contrast to *More Brilliant than the Sun*, in this reconsideration Eshun seems to part ways with his earlier, Deleuzian stance on anti-memory in favor of the "countermemory" of the colonized.

formation rehearsed in the production of the work of art can be best understood when guided by Adorno's dialectical conception of fashion or convention (*Mode*). For Adorno, "fashion [*Mode*] is not, as the prejudice implies, abrupt change, but rather the infinitesimally lulled [*gemildert*] vibration of historic unfolding in the midst of coagulation." "Fashion [*Mode*] is the infinitely slow," he continues, "represented [*vorgestellt*] as sudden change."[85] The music that follows in Johnson's wake calls out the actual sluggishness of the social order by becoming what the latter hides in representation (*Vorstellung*). It militates against the notion that the latest thing has moved on to anything other than the same old hat, that it has, in other words, actually deterritorialized the false security of commodification, the provisional hiding place (*Unterschlupf*),[86] or overcome the abjecting logic of the first lullaby. This is why, although derived from a different set of forces or unfolding on a different plane of consistency, one can trace cross-cultural links between this blues legacy and, for instance, the melancholy of Ingram Marshall's electroacoustic elegy, *Entrada: At the River*, or the monotonous, softened wonderings of Laurie Spiegal's *East River Dawn*. The increasing speed of the market's turnover, powered today by the infinite debt of the state,[87] the cacophony of anarchic, uncoordinated social relations, is exposed by the steady lament, by the "calming and stabilizing, calm and stable, center in the heart of chaos."[88] It says: go on with your clamor; go on with your restlessness. You too shall pass, for you are not, in reality, genuine repetition, but rather a generalization based on the unchanging relations of production.[89] The fact that this song refuses to keep up with the speed of circulation, that it insists on the *onward* that was once singularly proclaimed in the transitional oboe to the death march of the *Eroica Symphony*, evokes an essential truth of the dialectic of natural-history: although it is definitively needed, the merriment of the swinging, boogie-woogie groove is a socially necessary palliative.[90] As Alban Berg's *Wozzeck* made palpable, after the sado-masochistic repetition compulsion is unveiled as the law of natural-history itself, after the horror of the hunt, of the escape-and-capture dialectic of civilization, has come into the glaring light, it is virtually impossible to dance the *Ländler* without either becoming farcical or an outright insult to the dead.

---

[85] Adorno, *Sociology of Music*, 203/GS14, 404.
[86] Adorno, "On the Fetish-Character in Music," 311/GS14, 45.
[87] Deleuze and Guattari, *Anti-Oedipus*, 216–17.
[88] Deleuze and Guattari, *A Thousand Plateaus*, 311.
[89] Deleuze, *Difference and Repetition*, 1–27.
[90] This critique of the so-called groove, which insists upon thinking the dialectic between measured and unmeasured time, or between movement and the standstill (*Stillstellung*), should be contrasted to Mark Abel's *Groove: An Aesthetic of Measured Time* (Boston, MA: Brill, 2014).

Dreambird

At the same conjuncture when film was beginning in Deleuze's natural-historical account to link the cinematographic image to sensory-motor activity, when an arborescent narration of the relationship between past and present signaled in, for instance, the flashback plucking of the harp aimed to preserve the conventions of the novel, the "smearing" slide guitar was, alternatively, pointing to a dreamscape, a becoming-bird, whose visual analogue is the dissolve technique of the camera gaze.[91] The soft plucking and strumming of the lute are not the modern guitar's only bequest. As the slide blurs the notes, Henry Dumas's "Christian" hymn about the allegedly unbroken circle, the preservation of the multigenerational struggle in memory, comes to mind.[92] Is it a conservative, dead-weight, an immobilizing force that stifles creative intensity, like the "down filling" of the novel on which the "sleepyhead" bourgeois of the twentieth century rest?[93] Or perhaps it is the moment when this very immobilization, this burden or debt to one's forebears, to the foundational "masters" of music and literature,[94] generates an understanding of the virtual that, in reality, precedes the practical narrowness of sensory-motor activity, the means-ends logic that invisibilizes the so-called Bergsonian pure recollection?[95] If it is either of these, then one must assume that modern sorrow drives song to within an earshot of the human limit, gesturing in this same musical blur to what in film became the "pure optical and sound situations" of the avant-garde.[96] This is the case not only because of the rupture in the ordinary course of time that music such as Johnson's or Son House's performs but also because the "not-in-between" of this music,[97] its intransigent negation of the empirical realm, is a concrete embodiment, an imageless image, of utopia. A dance devoid of this dialectical tension between semblance and reality, between, as Deleuze puts it, an occupying that, on the one hand, counts and, on the other hand, resists counting altogether,[98] would betray the goal of the

---

[91] Deleuze, *Cinema 2*, 13.
[92] Henry Dumas, "Will the Circle Be Unbroken?" in *Echo Tree: The Collected Short Fiction of Henry Dumas* (Minneapolis: Coffee House Press, 2003). See, also, Moten's discussion of this work in Moten, *Black and Blur*, 90–1.
[93] Benjamin, "Theories of German Fascism," 315/GS3, 242.
[94] For a closer look at the pragmatic and, indeed, Deleuzian choice to avoid origin stories and aggrandizing the "masters" of music such as Robert Johnson, Tupac, or Karlheinz Stockhausen, see Eshun, *More Brilliant than the Sun*, 001-[004].
[95] Deleuze, *Cinema 2*, 54.
[96] Ibid., 9–18.
[97] Moten, *Black and Blur*, 2–12.
[98] Deleuze, "Boulez, Proust, and Time," 69–74.

autonomous work of art before it begins: envisioning a world beyond the spell of *praxis*.

Forced Quantity

Shifts in tempo, like those of volume, ready-to-hand today with either the real-time turn-of-the-knob or the painstakingly slow process of cutting and slicing the oscilloscope patterns of the digital-audio-workstation, become the dialectical motor to music.[99] In truth, the unstable, molecular vibrations of the graphic inscription, the mnemonics seared into either the body itself or the written page, were always the motor. "Material-force" or "matter-flow" hardens into the "unreal reality" of a form that cannot, at the same time, contain it.[100] This is why speed produced amid slowness or slowness produced amid speed, the work of art—semblance (*Schein*)—in determinate opposition to the spatiotemporal organization of the status quo, subtly tweaks the contents, the color, or the material elements of embodied sound. A minor, but all-important axial turn

---

[99] The implications of this development in mechanical reproduction, in which the written score loses precedence over the digital inscription, should be compared to Adorno's conception of musical reproduction in T. W. Adorno, *Towards a Theory of Musical Reproduction: Notes, A Draft, and Two Schemata*, trans. Wieland Hoban (Malden, MA: Polity, 2006); *Zu einer Theorie der musikalischen Reproduktion: Aufzeichnungen, ein Entwurf und zwei Schemata*, in *Nachgelassene Schriften*, Abteilung I, vol. 2, ed. Henri Lonitz (Frankfurt a.m.: Verlag, 2005). While Adorno is primarily concerned with problems of performance and interpretation, or of following the dialectic between the "subcutaneous" elements of a composition and their reification via notation and culture industry habituation, there are more than a few suggestive moments in this text that are applicable to recent technological developments. For example, his discussion of how a plethora of radio performances might enhance the discovery of the "right" interpretation, instead of detracting from it (142/184), points to how the endless editing capacity of the digital audio workstation (DAW) could be deployed in the attempt to unearth tensions that are sedimented in the musical material. In this sense, the "second nature" of both the bad and good interpretations of recorded performances becomes a "third nature," a third immediacy that is congealed in the automatically transposed digital patterns and itself waiting for further modification. Composition and the studio start, in this way, to take precedence over performance, but this precedence itself then recoils back upon performance, so that improvisation, instead of a technique bogged down by fidelity to a score, becomes a qualitatively different mode of musical production. This state of affairs, of course, goes well beyond the indeterminate compositions and non-traditional forms of notation of the previous century.

[100] For further consideration of how Deleuze and Guattari attempt to resist what Adorno calls the alleged "higher level essentiality" of form on which the history of idealism rests, see Deleuze and Guattari, *A Thousand Plateaus*, 410–12; Gilles Deleuze, "Making Inaudible Forces Audible," in *Two Regimes of Madness: Texts and Interviews 1975-1995* (Cambridge, MA: MIT Semiotext(e), 2006), 156–60, 160. Adorno, *Metaphysics: Concept and Problems*, 4/NS14, 14. An essential aspect of this resistance to what would amount to an undialectical conception of form consists in the fact that, whether as a pre-capitalist or capitalist regime, an oral or written tradition, or a nomadic or state machine, no ontological prioritization of one side over the other can be justified if form is itself a material variation in a material continuum. For further consideration of Adorno's dialectical understanding of the first and second nature of the "material" of music, see Paddison, *Adorno's Aesthetics of Music*, 149–83.

eventually takes place.¹⁰¹ Which *ritornelli* are sped up or slowed down, which are stretched out, molecularized, combined, or contrapuntally differentiated, naturally makes all the difference. As Schelling detected before anyone, maintaining such a tightrope balance comprises the aesthetic truth-content of the dialectic between quantity and quality from Hegel's *Science of Logic*.¹⁰² Long before he would come to theorize the world-historical significance of technical reproduction, Benjamin understood something of this gambling logic too. The compulsion to increase or decrease tempo, in fact, constitutes the predicament of the modern, European artist, as much as it inflects the colonized subject's task of creolizing the master's language. In Glissant's formulation, echoing Deleuze's Bergsonian appeal to the virtual over the practical, an "accelerated nonsense created by scrambled sounds" becomes an increasingly salient feature of colonized language.¹⁰³ As a "nonfunctional" poetics that cannot be decoded by the colonizer, its whispering shouts and shouting whispers are, moreover, punctuated by the drum-like, respiratory rhythm of the voice. Whenever such desperate movements, such "forced poetics" or "defensive reflexes," develop against the ruling conventions (*Mode*), pathways connecting ostensibly disparate cultures and historical periods can be detected.¹⁰⁴

Scatting across Cultures

For Benjamin, Werfel's 1915 work, *Die Troerinnen*, drew comparison to Opitz's baroque drama. This was because, "in both works," Benjamin argued, "the poet was concerned with the mouthpiece [*Sprachrohr*] of lamentation and its resonance. In both cases what was therefore required was not ambitious artificial developments, but a verse-form modelled on dramatic recitative."¹⁰⁵ *Sprechgesang* or recitative, the intermediate between speech and actual song, becomes a more pressing need precisely when the means or, more accurately, one's command of them, deteriorates. The speaking pipe, megaphone, or tubed instrument (*Rohr*) is supposed to be the counterforce, the technical means of preserving the echo of lamentation, but midway along the path of rerouting, the artist finds herself incapable of telling the old tale, of capturing the reverberation of the scream.

---

[101] Adorno, *Negative Dialectics*, xx/GS6, 10.
[102] G. W. F. Hegel, *Hegel's Science of Logic*, trans. A. V. Miller (Atlantic Highlands, NJ: Humanities Press International, 1969), 314–26.
[103] Glissant, *Caribbean Discourse*, 124.
[104] Ibid., 121–9.
[105] Benjamin, *Origin of German Tragic Drama*, 54 (translation modified)/GS1.1, 235.

Should she sing or should she have recourse to the epic form of storytelling that constituted all art before the devastation of modernity and colonization? Does she have any choice in the matter? In the case of Werfel and Opitz, the solution was a fragmented combination of the two options, where language tries to break out of the strictures of a now-inadequate or now-suppressed speech by speaking the song of lamentation. In the blues, something similar happens, however, the instrumentation of the voice becomes stronger, eventually wins in the "wrestling match,"[106] instead of the, as it were, speech-ification of the instrument. This is the material basis of the entrance of the scat technique onto the historical stage. A need for epic narrative remains, but it fails to find an outlet and must, therefore, regress if it remains static or falls behind the latest technically mediated possibilities. This struggle—the process of hybridization as such[107]—inexorably propels a new tempo and a new orality in the breathy song of speech, the breathy speech of song, and even the breathy or auratic echo of the instrument's "machined," coagulated voice. The emergence of contemporary mumble rap, in which the lyrics become less significant than the rhyme, is a notable expression of this ongoing problematic. So too is the *blurring* of words themselves, for example, hollerin' haulin', see and sea made easy, or bails tolled and bells toned.[108] Such a problematic in the dynamic of song, which deploys zeugma and syllepsis as well, may even constitute the progressive regressions at play in the childlike and, for that reason, *more* resilient "yeas," "ayes," and "uhs," which punctuate the "break" between so many hip-hop verses. The strife of the voice on its way to instrumentation and back, whether in the mouthed, stabilizing, "beatboxing" beat or in the towering, instrumentalized plaint that softens the contours of speech, begins to account for why, as Benjamin continues his comparison, he asserts that "[t]he analogy between the endeavors of the baroque and those of the present and the recent past is most apparent in the use of language."[109] Language longs to become the language of things. The eruptive thingliness immanent to its articulation can no longer be repressed.[110] Human language fails to do it justice. Even more strikingly, this "musicked" language functions by way of an "acceleration" (*Forcierung*) in Benjamin's understanding.[111] And this acceleration, which is characteristic of both artists, Werfel and Opitz, even appears to be

---

[106] Deleuze, "Boulez, Proust, and Time," 73; Deleuze and Guattari, *A Thousand Plateaus*, 309.
[107] See Homi K. Bhabha, *The Location of Culture* (New York: Routledge, 1994).
[108] For further consideration of this Afrodiasporic tendency to progressively regress into nonsensical phonemes, see Michael Veal, "Starship Africa," in *The Sound Studies Reader*, ed. Jonathan Sterne (New York: Routledge, 2012), 454–67, 462.
[109] Benjamin, *Origin of German Tragic Drama*, 54/GS1.1: 235.
[110] Moten, *Black and Blur*, 99.
[111] Benjamin, *Origin of German Tragic Drama*, 54/GS1.1: 235.

the means whereby the resonance of nature-sound becomes eloquent, that is, becomes a remembrance of sorrow worthy of the nonhuman, opaque essence.[112] While John Osborne's translation renders this term "exaggeration" (*Forcierung*) and thus succeeds in apprehending something of the incommunicability of this modern aesthetic procedure, it misses the mark substantially in another respect. In fact, the German term is frequently used in the economic context of expediting circulation, as well as with reference to the quickening of the heartbeat. If increasing the speed of the turnover-time (*Umschlagszeit*) of production is the condition of selling below the socially necessary average,[113] then doubling this beggar-thy-neighbor logic in presentation, modifying its pacing mimetically or *forcing* a new rate in the auratic breath as it undergoes instrumentation, seems to be the first condition of combating the semblance of capitalist inevitability. Bearing in mind the degree to which this changed tempo cannot be actualized in an abstract or one-sided relation to its contents, the second condition appears to be a sense of "communal existence,"[114] that is, the emergence of a public that could respond to this "fallen" state by beginning to co-enact (*mitvollziehen*), consummate, or carry forth the music of the "we," the shared composition of the Afrodiasporic resistance, which dissolves the artist-spectator dichotomy, the specialist-layperson, stage-audience, binary, or fails.[115] Hence, baroque *Trauer* approaches the sorrow of the Black expressive tradition insofar as it is the lack of a "public" that plagues both traditions.[116] As with post-bebop jazz, Deleuze and Guattari's contention that rhizomatics equals pop analysis is not forfeited by its unorthodox methodology or its vertiginous form of presentation; it is,

---

[112] Glissant, *Caribbean Discourse*, 133. Much work still remains to be done on how one should think Glissant's decolonizing attempt to create opaque structures in relationship to the frequent attempts in the Frankfurt School to grasp the opaqueness of the object itself. For consideration of a possible approach, see Tom Huhn, "Kant, Adorno, and the Social Opacity of the Aesthetic," in *The Semblance of Subjectivity: Essays in Adorno's Aesthetic Theory*, ed. Tom Huhn and Lambert Zuidervaart (Cambridge, MA: MIT Press, 1997), 237–58.

[113] Karl Marx, "Results of the Immediate Process of Production," in *Capital: A Critique of Political Economy*, vol. 1, trans. Ben Fowkes (New York: Vintage Books, 1977), 1019.

[114] Benjamin, *Origin of German Tragic Drama*, 54/GS1.1, 235.

[115] Cf. Attali, *Noise*, 135. As will become evident below, this emphasis on failure should be contrasted with Réda Bensmaïa's reading of Deleuze and Guattari's Kafka, where abundance, success, and vitality are undialectically conceived as the proper way to understand Kafka's oeuvre. Lines of flight are inextricably bound, on the contrary, to lines of torpor. Even if Kafka finds a temporary "escape route" from the spell of the family in, for example, the becoming-animal tales, this does not mean that he avoids, in Benjamin's conception, the guilt-nexus of the living. Bensmaïa, "The Kafka Effect," in *Kafka: Toward a Minor Literature*, trans. Terry Cochran (Minneapolis: University of Minnesota Press, 1986), ix–xxi.

[116] For an excellent analysis of how this absent people or absent public ignites the practical effort of the work of art in Deleuze's theory, see Daniel W. Smith "'A Life of Pure Immanence': Deleuze's 'Critique et Clinique' Project," in Gilles Deleuze, *Essays Critical and Clinical*, trans. Daniel W. Smith and Michael A. Greco (Minneapolis, MA: University of Minnesota Press, 1997), xli–xlv.

rather, strengthened, since these elusive (*flüchtig*) elements guard against the reactionary notion that the public already exists, that it is already self-conscious, equipped with an adequate form of communication,[117] or that, having ascended to the level of autonomous, cooperative self-production, it has already achieved the much-maligned, Lukácsian subject-object synthesis.[118]

State of Nature

The violence of the auction block, of separating families for the sake of accumulation, is only the beginning of the objective constraint to the coproduction of anti-bourgeois, common space: the prerequisite of real emancipation. Eventually, the same separation, now in the form of the population control of the carceral state, would regenerate a similar "scene" or staging of false reconciliation, of false joviality and entertainment produced for and by the white imaginary, since the commodity form through which all of this emerges—neutralized—would also remain essentially unchanged. So long as the static, organizing mechanism of social reproduction goes unchallenged—the few commanding the (racialized) labor of the many—the formal clumsiness of the resulting disparate aesthetic traditions is all but guaranteed. For, in the last analysis, the music of the solo song falls flat when confronted with *collective* sorrow. An historical context characterized by decline appears, in this way, to bind each of these aesthetic comportments. In other words, the old adage holds: the emancipation of the workers and colonized must be the task of the workers and colonized themselves, not the task of a group of insurrectionists, (music) specialists, or colonized intellectuals.[119] Thus the *a priori* guilt of the work of art, the objective character of which escapes Deleuze and Guattari's analysis.[120] The consequence of living in this condition is that, as Benjamin puts it, "like expressionism, the baroque"—

---

[117] Deleuze and Guattari, *A Thousand Plateaus*, 24. This position should, of course, be distinguished from the prevailing, liberal conception of communication articulated in Jürgen Habermas, *The Theory of Communicative Action: Reason and the Rationalization of Society*, vol. 1, trans. Thomas McCarthy (Boston: Beacon Press, 1984).

[118] Georg Lukács, *History and Class Consciousness: Studies in Marxist Dialectics*, trans. Rodney Livingstone (Cambridge, MA: MIT Press, 1971).

[119] See Frantz Fanon, *The Wretched of the Earth*, trans. Richard Philcox (New York: Grove Press, 2004), 9–13.

[120] Adorno, *Aesthetic Theory*, 39/GS7, 64; Deleuze and Guattari, *Kafka*, 32. By Deleuze and Guattari's own admission, the alleged superficiality or "surface movement" of guilt in Kafka's stories, which is allegedly overcome via a comedic exaggeration, is necessarily plugged into the bureaucratic hell of the novels. This in part grounds the claim that Kafka finds an escape path instead of outright liberation. The latter anarcho-liberal consolation is hardly the type of intensity that could assuage the *objective* character of the guilt-nexus.

and one could add, post-bellum, Afrodiasporic art as well—"is not so much an age of genuine artistic achievement as an age possessed of unremitting artistic will."[121] This is not to say that the art of the Black radical tradition is without its profound accomplishments. Indeed, this culture constitutes virtually every aspect of important American art and in ways that, to state it once more, are not coded for or understood by the signifying norms of the *Herrenvolk*.[122] The difficulty uniting these different manifestations of *Trauer* rests, on the contrary, on what happens when the "unremitting" (*unablenkbar*) will is faced with not being in control of its own body, the affective variations of which extend, let there be no mistake, beyond the physical barriers of "individuated," bourgeois atoms. If, as Saidiya Hartman has elucidated it, the pleasure of the master class is predicated on feigning outrage, but ultimately, in liberal fashion, disavowing the suffering condition of the racialized other, it is doubtless true that the volition of the colonized and propertyless will require an outlet, an object, and it will, moreover, *need* a collective, political organizing mechanism, a technology, to succeed at giving voice to the "multiple-cry." Yet it simply will not find one. The absent politics, which is to say, the absent technique that could resist the domination of nature that reduces this multiplicity, in Deleuze's terms, to the image of thought, to a commodity, was and is missing.[123] The flow is jammed (*gestaut*).[124] The condition under which each variety of *Trauergesang* surfaces is akin, then, to being caught in a nightmare, shaking oneself endlessly in desperation, attempting to wake up, only to discover that you were never asleep, that you are still in the camp, still in the iron cage, unacknowledged by your brothers and sisters, and alienated from the technical means, the quantitative intensity or the mobilizing force, that would be capable of turning the tide,[125] shifting the flow, or breaking through the congestion. As Leo Löwenthal once expressed it, describing the physical and spiritual imprisonment of living under National Socialism, imagination cannot help but atrophy in this *state* of terror, this *state* of nature.[126] The problematic of modern music, that is, the politics of technique that would genuinely serve as a primer to the reorganization of each and everyone's relation to the body (politic), can thus be summed up as a confrontation in which the forces separating the unremitting will from its object

[121] Benjamin, *Origin of German Tragic Drama*, 54/*GS*1.1: 235.
[122] For a striking example of the preservation of a non-normative and even hostile code, see C. L. R. James, *Black Jacobins: Toussaint L'Ouverture and the San Domingo Revolution* (New York: Vintage Books), 18.
[123] Deleuze, *Difference and Repetition*, 129–68.
[124] Deleuze and Guattari, *Anti-Oedipus*, 33; Adorno, *Aesthetics*, 128/*NS*, 204.
[125] Améry, "Resentments," 75.
[126] Leo Löwenthal, "Terror's Atomization of Man," *Commentary: A Jewish Review* 1 (1945/1946): 1–8.

reach a feverish pitch. The resulting music will be called "noise" by interested parties.[127] The compulsion of the object itself drives the next development, despite and because of the lack of technical mastery, despite and because of the lack of public or *people*. Measuring the matter against itself, against what it claims to be and against what it has unwittingly assumed, illuminates just how much it was irresistibly driven out of itself (*weitertreiben*). The matter breaks through, in other words, when it can no longer be restrained, when the immanent negativity, the pre-cognitive suffering, has accumulated enough intensity to explode the blockage between the in-itself and the for-itself, between the potency that one contains within oneself—nature, the more (*das Mehr*)—and the repressive form that it is currently taking.[128]

Fateful Improvisation

Several vectors emerge from this natural-historical dialectic of the blues. They form what could be called the musical embodiment of "double consciousness," which so frequently centers on the becoming-train of music.[129] In the first place, the inadequacy of the oral, linguistic, and conceptual form of narration in both ante- and post-bellum song generates a new type of epic narration, a new type of material confrontation with the unremitting will. To be sure, the ambivalent "carry-me-backs" that both Hartman and Davis have highlighted will continue for some time, up to the present. The critical point, however, is that, in the superior works, the long, Odyssean or Jewish journey of old is being rearticulated, *retrained*, precisely because of the inadequacy of the unamplified, acoustic, and disinherited conceptual means. Wagner's placement of the horn off of the stage is not the only mode of broadening the horizon and echo of the escape-train longing. After Patton's first gesture at the instrumental continuation of the vocal melody, Bill Broonzy—among others—takes the, so to speak, next step. In him, the raw quiver of the "natural" voice drops away from the construction. Unlike

---

[127] Cf. Tricia Rose, *Black Noise: Rap Music and Black Culture in Contemporary America* (Hanover, NH: Wesleyan University Press, 1994); Attali, *Noise*, 7.

[128] T. W. Adorno, *An Introduction to Dialectics*, trans. Nicholas Walker (Malden, MA: Polity Press, 2017), 32–33.

[129] Compare this Du Boisian "double consciousness" to Eshun's attempt to illustrate the Deleuzean concept of multiplicity by appeal to a "triple consciousness" and "quadruple consciousness" in Eshun, "Further Considerations on Afrofuturism," 298. My view is that this attempt to overcome the purportedly bad dualism of dialectics is too quick to forget the material basis of the real illusion, namely the condition of propertied and propertyless subjects and the concomitant division of mental and physical labor. See, also, Okiji, *Jazz as Critique*, 31–48.

the soft nylon of their "classical" counterparts, the colonized steal away on the steel metal resonance of nomadic metallurgy.[130] For instance, in Broonzy's famous *Shuffle Rag*, a strummed chord progression, jolly like the iterant life of Luzana Cholly from Murray's tribute to the onomatopoeia of Black expression, follows from an introductory, Paganini-esque cadenza.[131] In epic works like these, the so-called chops of the virtuoso are the harbinger of the journey to come. Grounded rhythmically and harmonically in this initial flirtation, the main theme, exposition, and development then unfold. They parallel the solution to baroque immobility that was discovered in nineteenth-century Europe but already latent in Bach's preludes. They are structured by an affinity, to be more specific, with the journey-bound yearning of the great, non-vocal, instrumental symphonies and concerti of the earlier, European epoch. Badan Powell's astonishing, Brazilian transposition of Bach's *Prelude in C minor* into his *Prelúdio* for guitar is one of the outermost stars in this non-vocal constellation. Cotton pickin' suppleness overcomes the rift in the continents, revealing with every circular arpeggio the Latin core to the German winter. Before this, Broonzy was similarly embodying the Kantian concept of genius without, of course, knowing it.[132] Assured that reason's anchoring critique of metaphysics would not lead him astray,[133] his solo guitar mimics the sublimity of the heroic individual's sea-bound, *c-c* riding quest. Like so many others of its kind, his instrumental works are far from being mere serenades on a theme of unfaithful love. Will his claim to individuality win the day, will he prove the metaphysical basis of his agency? Has life really been transformed into *easy living*, or does the Delta Flood of '27, nature as allegory of the wreckage of civilization, continue to devour all possibilities? Everything suggests that the *onward* merriment on which Broonzy's joyful instrumentalization of song is based, that is, the *gestus* of having finally found an escape route, having finally won the Faustian gamble, is secretly a memento mori. The moment when the chord progression temporarily falls away is critical. The same holds for the increased intensity of the young Duane Allman's subsequent, amplified music, when the instrumental accompaniment to his "band" or "troupe" of *jongleurs* likewise comes to an outright halt in, for example, the cadenza to *You Don't Love Me*. In the stop-time—*secessio plebis*—of these moments, the soloist is lonelier than any document of existentialism could proclaim. The more the semblance

---

[130] Deleuze and Guattari, *A Thousand Plateaus*, 411.
[131] Albert Murray, *Train Whistle Guitar* (New York: Vintage Books, 1974).
[132] Kant, *Critique of the Power of Judgment*, trans. Paul Guyer and Eric Matthews (New York: Cambridge University Press, 2000), 186–97.
[133] Kant, *Critique of Pure Reason*, trans. Paul Guyer and Allen W. Wood (New York: Cambridge University Press, 1988), 354.

of happiness illuminates the solitary *Charakter* on the stage, the more the silence threatens to envelope.[134] Agile, the sinister hand glides up and down the neck of the guitar in search of the place to stop, in search of the right note. A melancholy as red and black as Joachim's cadenza to Brahms's *Violin Concerto* glimmers. That so much could be *riding* on this infinitesimally small, improvisational moment, that such pressure could weigh on the "choice" of when to stop the movement of the nimble hand and place the fingers, of how to inflect or accent the next note, is evidence, despite appearances, of the persistence of empirical unfreedom, of the unresolved, prehistorical ritual of "reading" the text of nature.[135] In Benjamin's conception, the "moment of danger," not the boasted spontaneity indicative of an already achieved liberation, is at the root of this reading, as it were, of the entrails, this deciphering of the riddle of the future written in the stars.[136] The spell of performativity lives on, then, in these aleatory moments, since, upon closer examination, they betray just how much the blood-soaked rites of the origin are still casting their shadow. Outside of the closed circle of the theater, missing the mark could, indeed, mean death, could, indeed, mean punishments from the gods or, today, punishment from the sacrosanct market. Thus the disability to the show of ability, the secret unhappiness to happiness, or the poverty to a "wealth" that remains bound up with myth and remains, for that reason, tied to the rules of astrological prediction, to the priests—administrative, managerial functionaries—who, in ever-new form, legitimate the master's stockjobbing swindle. The fate of fortune (*Glück*), of receiving charity from what befalls (*fällt*) the victor, not in glory but by chance (*Zufall*), continues to rain down on the victim, regardless of her merit, her efforts, and, most importantly, regardless of her need.[137]

Weathering the Storm

In the face of this betrayal, it might be said that the onward-resignation dialectic of the blues expresses itself in the oscillation between Chuck Berry's *Johnny Be*

---

[134] Benjamin, "Fate and Character," 201–6/*GS*2.1, 171–9.
[135] For an examination of how this improvisational moment is constituted by asubjective and nonrepresentational elements and thus in need of the Deleuzean concept of the assemblage, see Nick Nesbitt, "Critique and Clinique: From Sounding Bodies to the Musical Event," in *Sounding the Virtual: Gilles Deleuze and the Theory and Philosophy of Music*, ed. Brian Hulse and Nick Nesbitt (Burlington, VT: Ashgate, 2010), 159–80.
[136] Benjamin, "On the Mimetic Faculty," 722/*GS*2.1, 213.
[137] Benjamin, "On the Concept of History," 390/*GS*1.2, 694.

Good vitality and the guilt-nexus of Skip James's and T-Bone Walker's "I go down to pray." Before this, however, the movement between these prototypical blues works, which parallels the movement between abundance and poverty,[138] can be traced to the affective oscillation between two earlier works from the same repertoire, namely *Summertime* and *Sometimes I Feel Like a Motherless Child*. In the former, the living is easy, the gamble is won, and the escape from both the coercion of sharecropping and racist, KKK violence seems to be secured. In the latter, slavery lives on in the convict leasing and Jim Crow system and, in no time, the terror of familial separation at the auction block will become an even colder form of rationalized, administrative logic, namely the form of domination in the era of carceral Keynesianism.[139] It is not for nothing that, despite their contrasting tenor, these sorrow songs follow, as Samuel A. Floyd Jr. has noted, a similar harmonic scheme.[140] The logic of major and minor modulation, of inverted and augmented pathos, guides the transformation of the rising, sweet chariot into the descending Number Nine, both of which promise evacuation but ultimately return, in failure, to an Old Testament punishment of the innocent. This constitutes their fatalistic *Charakter*. The trope of being buried *deep down*, of letting the flood engulf you when the levee breaks, of repenting for the wrong you've done and, in the end, reading the writing on the wall,[141] brings the blues closer and closer to the *Trauer* of the baroque, to say nothing of the *Trauer* of "life" after Auschwitz. What is more, the "sometimes" theme, which consists of that moment when *weathering* the false sovereignty of the blues no longer feels possible, is always on the verge of supplanting the short-lived optimism. The wizened codger, who has lived through the worst—direct slavery—levies his "told ya so" against the youth who disobeys the Manichean cosmos.[142] The asceticism of a church credo that, eternalizing the misery of a socially produced condition, is confident that those who indulge in the forbidden fruit, the devil's music, "have it comin'," forms the horizon of this epic *anagnorisis*. Both outcomes of the game (*Spiel*) of fate are, after all, dictated by the benevolent master himself, the personification of capital. Can anything other than devastation be expected if the active agent is to go on setting the terms of the game from above, that is, with an uncontested monopoly on violence backing it and an equally stupefying

---

[138] Baker, Jr., *Blues, Ideology, and Afro-American Literature*, 8. See, also, Susan McClary, *Conventional Wisdom: The Content of Musical Form* (Berkeley: University of California Press, 2000), 38.
[139] Mike Davis, *Ecology of Fear: Los Angeles and the Imagination of Disaster* (New York: Metropolitan Books, 1998), 416.
[140] Samuel A. Floyd, Jr., *The Power of Black Music: Interpreting its History from Africa to the United States* (New York: Oxford University Press, 1995), 218.
[141] Adorno, *Negative Dialectics*, 360/GS4, 353.
[142] Murray, *Train Whistle Guitar*, 108–9.

veneer of legitimacy that attends the juridical form of bourgeois right? Absorbing fresh batches of newly freed up, strikebreaking wage-labor was largely, in reality, the top-down goal of the Great Migration.[143] In retrospect, it is obvious that it could do nothing to abolish the racialized division of labor, which stood at the origin of this era of accumulation, and is now reproduced via the command and control, automated targeting system of the racist divide and conquer police state.

Bury Me Deep

Before this well-greased form of the control society,[144] honed inside and outside of direct warzones, would put an end to virtually every authentic protest; before domination would, as it often seems today, become so totalizing that merely suggesting, let alone acting, for sake of a world devoid of prisons and the police would produce, with pushbutton precision, a second-nature chorus of raging denunciations concerning the impracticality of the proposal—before all this, there was Elizabeth Cotton's music.[145] Only in the downfall of the beautiful semblance (*schöner Schein*) is the theological impulse strong enough to withstand the coming onslaught: the antiquatedness of man.[146] In Cotton's work Paul Gilroy's call to think the African and Jewish diaspora alongside one another rings out against the rising "organic composition of man."[147] An old, grainy, red-tinted black-and-white video recording retains the *hic et nunc* of her *Freight Train*.[148] It is difficult to imagine a more haunting recuperation of the aura than Cotton's song. Her voice, which sings out of key, performs the frail

---

[143] Warren C. Whately, "African American Strike-Breaking from the Civil War to the New Deal," *Social Science History* 17, no. 4 (Winter, 1993): 525–58.

[144] Deleuze, "Postscript on the Societies," 3–7.

[145] Cf. Angela Davis, *Are Prisons Obsolete?* (New York: Seven Stories Press, 2003), 9–21. Cotton's nomadic desire for the escape train should be held in tension with Trixie Smith's famous "Freight Train Blues," which points to just how much the onward-resignation dialectic is fundamentally gendered. For a discussion of this phenomenon in relationship to black feminist literature, see Samantha Pinto, *Difficult Diasporas: The Transnational Feminist Aesthetic of the Black Atlantic* (New York: New York University Press, 2013).

[146] Anders, *Die Antiquiertheit des Menschen Bd. I: Über die Seele im Zeitalter der zweiten industriellen Revolution* (München: C.H. Beck Verlag, 2002).

[147] Adorno, *Minima Moralia*, 229/GS4: 259–60.

[148] The lyrics to *Freight Train* are as follows: "Freight train, freight train, run so fast / Freight train, freight train, run so fast / Please don't tell what train I'm on / They won't know what route I'm going / When I'm dead and in my grave / No more good times here I crave / Place the stones at my head and feet / And tell them all I've gone to sleep / When I die, oh bury me deep / Down at the end of old Chestnut Street / So I can hear old Number Nine / As she comes rolling by / When I die, oh bury me deep / Down at the end of old Chestnut Street / Place the stones at my head and feet / And tell them all I've gone to sleep / Freight train, freight train, run so fast / Freight train, freight train, run so fast / Please don't tell what train 'm on / They won't know what route I'm going."

uncertainty that comes with renouncing the desire for recognition. Integration and assimilation are not the language of this incomparably delicate, broken cry. If she wants the train to pick up speed, if she desires that it should "run so fast," this is because it might yet depart in peace, like the *Abgesang* of the first cradle song, like the dreamscape dissolve of a shimmering cymbal. Cotton knows that not even the dead are safe so long as the victor continues to win.[149] She wishes to be buried near the tracks, so that the echo of those who longed to flee the guilt-nexus of the living will not be forgotten. The echo reconciles because it carries the sorrow beyond the confines of her present imprisonment. Like the message in the bottle, a promise that the word will be answered by another people, in a faraway land, is announced in this folk music. Insofar as it fleetingly, gently, departs, even though, as in the Book of Lamentations, it was initially a shriek, an outburst of mere *Naturlaut*, the echo attests to the idea that human toil will one day come to an end. For even the screams of torture sink back into the abyss from which they came. In this sense, the becoming-train of music embodies what Adorno calls "the transmutation of metaphysics into history."[150] Cotton has not sought escape via the nether regions of religion, nor by way of what amounts to the same thing in updated form, namely the curse of Oedipal imitation. Her technique parallels Benjamin's conception of *Versenkung*, of an immersion that, in the presentation of *Trauerspiel*, sinks down to confront the pain face to face.[151] The alternating bass style of her cotton pickin' fingering gives her the needed dexterity to become similar to the rhythm of the train. She has found the cure in the poison of labor. She both resists and submits to the cursed superstition that the gambler needs to lay the bet with her own hand. Resembling Broonzy, the decisive moment comes when the epic instrumentation takes over from the initial flirtation, in this case, the first, lyrical statement, which is addressed to and pleading for mercy from the "freight train, freight train" itself, not one of nature's so-called organisms. After four verses, the rhythm of the train spoken of in the lyrics is echoed in the *onward* of the guitar progression itself and the melodic line that repeats the now-perfected, vocal refrain. The instrument has the last word. The lyrics trail off into the distance before the industrial rejoinder of the guitar does the same. As much as this music critiques the fatalistic *resignation* of the old, mist-enveloped regions, there still appears to be but one mode of atonement for those who, in Benjamin's understanding, have been subjected to the ideology that natural life is synonymous with guilty life: *ars*

---

[149] Benjamin, "On the Concept of History," 391/GS1.2, 695.
[150] Adorno, *Negative Dialectics*, 360/GS6, 353.
[151] Benjamin, *Origin of German Tragic Drama*, 232/GS1.1, 406.

moriendi supplanting *ars vivendi*.[152] The truth-content of this false projection concerning the possibilities that are dormant in nature consists of the fact that it at least refuses the affirmative character of the culture industry, which always reduces happiness to mere life (*bloßes Leben*), to what is tautologically already the case anyway.[153] Heretofore, "only death," writes Adorno, in a similar context "[has been] an image [*Gleichnis*] of undistorted [*nicht entstellten*] life."[154] Nothing but the very bottom, absolute nothingness, avoids the false *cravings* of false society. And, as both James Baldwin and Primo Levi have illustrated, one has to know this *scatological* bottom intimately to be in a position to preserve the utopian mountaintop from which it is differentiated.[155] The extremes touch. The antinomy of the sorrow song appears. It might as well be copied verbatim from Jean Améry's ethics: to communicate torture adequately one would have to torture the listeners themselves.[156] This obviously cannot be justified, even if it were directed at the persecutors.[157] Yet, renouncing the attempt to communicate the ineffable betrays a complicity with the lifeless mechanism of the administrative world, which, now as ever, places a taboo on the shudder that first stirred genius to rise above the natural-historical spell of myth. The taboo on mimesis, on becoming anything other than what is, prevails.

Transpositional Metaphysics

One might think that, in the face of the *Trauer* of this communicative congestion (*Stauung*), a reprise examining Deford Bailey's significance for the blues would be in order. Instead, one mostly finds passing lip service and historicism when it comes to the great harmonica player. Bailey is thought to be a quaint anomaly, worth remembering for being a Black patron to the white Ole Opry, but not a significant musician whose inclinations bear on contemporary practices,

---

[152] Ibid., 131/GS1.1, 310.
[153] Benjamin, "Critique of Violence," 251; GS2.1, 201. See, also, Giorgio Agamben, *Homo Sacer: Sovereign Power and Bare Life*, trans. Daniel Heller-Roazen (Stanford, CA: Stanford University Press, 1998); Jacque Derrida, "Force of Law: The 'Mystical Foundation of Authority,'" in *Acts of Religion*, trans. Mary Quaintance (New York: Routlege, 2002), 228–98.
[154] Adorno, *Minima Moralia*, 78/GS4, 86.
[155] Primo Levi, *Survival in Auschwitz*, trans. Stuart Woolf (New York: Simon & Schuster, 1986), 22–37; James Baldwin, *Go Tell It on the Mountain* (New York: Vintage Books, 1980), 228–30.
[156] Améry, "Resentments," 77.
[157] For a further look at this problematic concerning the degree to which both the work of art and philosophy are compelled to cause pain in the reader, see Kestin Sutherland, "The Poetics of *Capital*," in *Capitalism: Concept, Idea, Image*, ed. Peter Osborne, Éric Alliez, and Eric-John Russell (London: CRMEP Books, 2019), 203–18.

especially insofar as the outermost logic of this sorrowful movement points ineluctably to the *becoming music of noise*. Even Floyd, Jr., who is otherwise a definitive authority on the role of the train in Black expressive music, relegates Bailey to a passive observer of the train, unlike Duke Ellington, who is allegedly more conversant with its polysemic meanings.[158] To counter this misinterpretation, the reader should recall Benjamin's conception of the "nonsensuous similarity" at play in mimetic activity.[159] Half a decade after Arthur Honegger's *Pacific 231*, which he almost certainty never heard, and nearly two full decades before Pierre Schaeffer's *Étude aux chemins de fer*, Bailey was already so absorbed in the task of emulating the wheel-churning rhythm and steam dispensing whistle of the train that he abandoned the melodic line, a residue from the unamplified era of "human" song, altogether. One misses an all-important trajectory in the development of music when one fails to note the precociousness of this peculiar mimesis, this particular form of machining the voice. It is not only impossible to fully access these sounds, which are, of course, sensuously different but *nonsensuously* similar to the train sounds themselves, without first having the amplification of the microphone, on which the harmonica rests, at one's disposal. The exhaling intervals of the voice or the up-and-down, expanding-and-contracting thrust of the diaphragm also have to catch steam, as it were, before this non-Oedipal imitation could become possible. Startlingly, the stop-time of the solo guitar or solo trumpet is also at play in Bailey's oral interlude. This transforms the conventional story about the blues and jazz virtuoso. Well before the greatest expressions of the amplified blues would *play out* this stop-and-go *play on* silence, the becoming music of Bailey's hissing whistle "sang" in mechanized protest to the traditional instrument. Why should he, as Cage asked, look for expression in the instruments from the age of manufacture? And why stop at the *external* combustion engine, instead of, in keeping with Hegel's objective spirit, pressing on to the next synthesis, the *internal* combustion engine and beyond? Similar to Coltrane's *Drum Thing*, which brings this stop-time *feel* to an outright standstill (*Stillstellung*), to the dark mystery of rumbling timpani and bass thunder echoing from the smoke-filled distance, Bailey had earlier gestured to an enlargement (*Erweiterung*) of the territory of music.[160] In

---

[158] Floyd, Jr., *The Power of Black Music*, 222.
[159] Benjamin, "On the Mimetic Faculty," 721/GS2.1, 211.
[160] This is Kant's term for synthetic *a priori*, that is, metaphysical, experience. It is precisely this technical modification that "adds to" or, as it is often translated, "amplifies," experience, granting it, albeit negatively, its metaphysical content. Immanuel Kant, *Prolegomena zu einer jeden künftigen Metaphysik*, in *Sammtliche Werke*, Band 3, ed. J. H. Kirchmann (Leipzig: L Heimann's Verlag, 1876), 75.

him, *embouchure* becomes the means of deterritorialization. The instant he and Little Walter plug in, the echo of the harp reverberates across instruments, its temporal core preserved.[161] Once again, Deleuze and Guattari's fictional, post-human runner comes to mind.[162] As the saliva accumulates, overflowing his lips, regression to the good breast is now,[163] after millennia of repression, recuperated in the spiritualization of music. The unrelenting tempo is so exhausting that the musician *on the run* spits through his teeth trying to catch it, trying to breathe it, trying to become a music that echoes in his ribs and dances up and down his spine. The teeth-gnashing physiognomy of the electroacoustic era finds its other in the downbeat of the runner's foot drop. A low-down bass reverberates from his heel back up to his inner ear, as if the harp had itself become a brain or grown an ear canal in the soundhole of the twanging, amplified guitar.[164] The long-distance, mythical hunt for prey is relived on a new plane. A new ensemble, with a new arrangement of the sensorium, is latent. Soon, with the rise of whammy and delay pedals, the guitar will become a steel drum, the steal drum a voice. Pitch shifters and tube screamers will likewise transpose this sliding harmonica resonance into a guitar that heads downward like the retracting hangar bays of an aircraft carrier. Keeping up with the pace and machinic echo of these inhuman, fossil-fuel powered forces requires transformation, in contrast to representational fidelity.[165] Nietzsche's dictum that sedentary life (*Sitzfleisch*) is a sin against the spirit, so that philosophical thinking requires walking, is antiquated.[166] Philosophy requires a speed that is fast enough to break the sound barrier. As a transitional instrument in the era of electronics and the effects rig, the breadth of the harmonica's resonance, the titanium strife that echoes from it, is exemplary at teaching this *transpositional* insight. Bailey's version of the becoming-train of music does not, then, so much anticipate the "fuzzy aggregates" of Coltrane's *Om* or Merzbow's *Pulse Demon*, as it encodes an oral need in the *noise* of free jazz. The howlin,' terrifyingly lonely, becoming-animal scream that, up to the present, calls from beyond the mountainous horizon on moonlit evenings could not reach the heavens, could not protest god's criminal absence, without the steam trumpet chime of the locomotive.

---

[161] Adorno, *Negative Dialectics*, 371/*GS6*, 364.
[162] Deleuze and Guattari, *A Thousand Plateaus*, 305.
[163] Cf. Julia Kristeva, *Melanie Klein*, trans. Ross Guberman (New York: Columbia University Press, 2001), 61–2, 81–8.
[164] Cf. Elizabeth Grosz, "Deleuze, Ruyer and Becoming-Brain: The Music of Life's Temporality," *Parrhesia* 15 (2012): 1–13.
[165] Deleuze, *Difference and Repetition*, 262–77.
[166] Friedrich Nietzsche, *Twilight of the Idols*, in *The Anti-Christ, Ecce Homo, and Other Writings*, trans. Judith Norman (New York: Cambridge University Press, 2005), 160.

Advanced Decay

A little-known, live trio jam by George Lewis, Mark Dresser, and Anthony Braxton from the 1985 Jazz Middelheim Festival in Antwerp exemplifies this voice-based, "post-metaphysical" variation.[167] A steady stream of *ritornelli* are gathered and contrasted in the trio's sonic mimesis of the industrial cityscape. Yet the machine is broken. It spews out scraps of nature: humans. It sputters. It spits. Lewis squawks out sounds with his mouth that sound like an engine. The trombone forsakes its identification with itself, that is, with the clearly delimited, harmonious ensemble of standardized *organon*. In the concluding moments, Braxton's saxophone can only offer false starts and rasping desperation. Is this play or is it the convulsions of the abused? The laser beam cuts of Dresser's bowed, upright bass, which, until Paul Chambers, was merely a plucking instrument for jazz, anticipate Kaija Saariaho's scratching, shaking textures, the, so to speak, ripping tissues of which drift away, like the electric clacking of cicadas that approximate the passing airplane from above. The refrain guides these improvisations. There is, despite the untrained ear's riposte, consistency here. This noise is, in other words, on its way to music, even if our ears are not predisposed to hear it. Only now, striking the right *noise*—not the right "note"—between Lewis's and Braxton's call and response is the precondition of uncovering the hidden eloquence of dead-labor. Now there are *choral* voices steaming through the circuits of the entire apparatus (*dispositif*). When, in the digital era, they start to overflow—the so-called clipping or redlining moment—the mature artist will capture these voices of the dead, hold the dissonance, play one ringing, broken note off of the strident overtone of the others, all the while teasing, negatively, that consonance might, at some point, return. That the first murmurs of this would emerge before complete amplification and digitification suggests that the naïve pleasantness of Bailey's earlier sideshow imitation—is it not produced, in part, for the white, exoticizing imaginary?—is not its dominant feature. His music just as much points, by way of Braxton's trio and others, to what would become the preponderant need of critical music in the coming century: the task of seizing control of the electroacoustic flow, making music dangerous, like Sukie's *vagina dentata*,[168] lest the neutralizing spell

---

[167] For a further look at how Braxton's music might be linked to Deleuzean rhizomatics and the practice of improvisation, see Jeremy Gilbert, "Becoming-Music: The Rhizomatic Moment of Improvisation," in *Deleuze and Music*, ed. Ian Buchanan and Marcel Swiboda (Edinburgh: Edinburgh University Press, 2004).

[168] Hartman, *Scenes of Subjection*, 41, 47.

of the capitalist axiomatic absorb the breakout attempt yet again. As soon as the melody and the traditional instrument have become problematic, Sun Ra, Giulia Loli, Pimmon, and Kim Cascone are already on the horizon, the "tool" and the "effect" are already becoming the active instrument.[169] Reverse-delay pedals play the musician, not vice versa. The echo is the vanguard.

Fugitive Life

A cross-cultural, transnational need for noise, for seizing control of the dissonant overtone immanent to consonance, unites these iterations of the sorrow song. It persists, as static and as obstinate as the bass-drone of Thomas Pynchon's sun, which everyone and no one can hear.[170] It remains, as pesteringly proximate as it always was, pulsing within and across territories, even if—excluding, for instance, Braxton's work, Terry Riley's compositions, or Julius Eastman's queer circuit-jamming—musicians have seldom gleaned the underlying unity. This neglect might be attributable, first and foremost, to what Adorno calls the elusiveness (*Flüchtigkeit*) of natural beauty. In contrast to Hegel's aesthetics, which in Adorno's assessment sides too easily with the prevailing conditions, this force that is "not-quite-graspable" (*nicht ganz zu Greifenden*), that, by virtue of its transience (*Vergänglichkeit*) or ephemerality, evades the capture (*einfangen*) of domination, is in fact nothing other than the vital element (*Lebenselement*) of the work of art itself.[171] Fred Moten calls it the "constant escape" of the Black aesthetic.[172] Nonidentity is, to express this essential phenomenon differently, the truth of identity. The former is the constitutive outside of the latter, or it is, as James Baldwin once put it, the Black conscience to the white autarky.[173] Adorno, who is to this day accused of racism when it comes to his critical analysis of jazz, is thus exceptionally close to Moten, as well as Deleuze and Guattari, for whom this elusiveness is associated with the nomadic war machine, that is, the minoritarian drive to sidestep the state's sedentary and appropriative logic.[174]

---

[169] Kim Cascone, "The Aesthetics of Failure: 'Post-Digital' Tendencies in Contemporary Computer Music," in *Audio Culture*, ed. Christoph Cox and Daniel Warner (New York: Continuum, 2010), 392–8.
[170] Thomas Pynchon, *Gravity's Rainbow* (New York: Penguin Books, 1973), 695.
[171] Adorno, *Aesthetics*, 24/NS3, 43.
[172] Moten, *Black and Blur*, 84–5.
[173] James Baldwin, "The White Man's Guilt," in *Collected Essays*, ed. Toni Morrison (New York: Library of America, 1998), 723. For an analysis of constitutive exclusion as it applies to political agency, see Sina Kramer, *Excluded Within: The (Un)Intelligibility of Radical Political Actors* (New York: Oxford University Press, 2017).
[174] For an analysis that, in addition to situating Adorno's critique of light music, also dispels this alleged racism and collates a slew of similar, counter narratives, see Richard Leppert, "'Commentary' to

Wieland Hoben's recent translation of Adorno's *Aesthetic Lectures* is, of course, correct to render *Flüchtigkeit* as "elusiveness," but the perceptive listener will hear an additional connotation. Given Adorno's emphasis that, on the one hand, this vital-element eludes the determinations (*Bestimmungen*) of world spirit and, on the other hand, is characterized by an "impossibility-of-being-pinned-down" (*Nicht-sich-dingfest-machen-Lassen*), *Flüchtigkeit* also connotes something of the "fugitive," of refusing to be arrested.[175] It will not, in short, be taken into custody. Just as Adorno had earlier, in collaboration with Horkheimer, linked the mimetic faculty to the criminal element that militates against all reification and all lawfulness,[176] now, in 1958, as he began his first foray into the subject matter that would become *Aesthetic Theory*, natural beauty was itself the, as it were, fugitive or volatile moment that constitutes the internal "law of motion" (*Bewegungsgesetz*), the unfolding dialectic, between art beauty and natural beauty.[177]

Technical Ecology

Think again of the *need* for amplification and technical reproduction. Think also of the critical-dialectical compulsion (*Zwang*) that would turn the solo song into the multiple-cry and, in so doing, extend the sorrow song to the sorrow song *of nature*, to multispecies solidarity. Is it not the case that mastering these technical advances is the precondition of unleashing the hidden, fluid, and ephemeral peregrinations of nature? Music is not the haphazard agglomeration of technical progress. Technical advances, on the contrary, recoil back upon and necessitate transformations in the relations of production. These transformations eventually turn the proto-bourgeois, that is, ear-plugging individualism, powered on the enslavement of others, into the shared odyssey of a dynamically contrasted, polyphonic composition. It is only at a late hour that we glimpse the truth of

---

'Music and Mass Culture,'" in *Essays on Music*, ed. Richard Leppert (Los Angeles: University of California Press, 2002), 327–72.

[175] Adorno, *Aesthetics*, 24/NS3, 43. This dialectic of fugitivity and captivity is also thematized in T. W. Adorno, "Short Commentaries on Proust," in *Notes to Literature*, vol. 2, ed. Rolf Tiedemann, trans. Shierry Weber Nicholsen (New York: Columbia University Press, 1992), 182; "Kleine Proust-Kommentare," in *Gesammelte Schriften*, vol. 11, ed. Rolf Tiedemann (Frankfurt a.m.: Suhrkamp Verlag, 1972), 212. For a look at the role of the fugitive in Deleuze's thought, in particular as it relates to empiricism as a "fugitive" and African American science, see Britt Rusert, *Fugitive Science: Empiricism and Freedom in Early African American Culture* (New York: New York University Press, 2017), 17–20.

[176] Adorno and Horkheimer, *Dialectic of Enlightenment*, 189/GS3, 260.

[177] Adorno, *Aesthetic Theory*, 77–8/GS7, 120–1.

the whole, namely the history of capitalism as the history of either extinction or emancipation, species-annihilation or species-recognition. Weather systems predicting the breadth and flow of the so-called nuclear winter were among the first indicators of this global, "world ecological" perspective.[178] When consciousness eventually rises, then, to the level of conceptualizing "ecologies of sensation,"[179] that is, dynamic, affective, and conceptual, geopolitical assemblages that resist the stultifying epistemology of the Euclidean "point," this is only because the narrowness of the old, trumped up, *causa sui* metaphysics became self-evident in the face of the crisis of technical reproduction. In music, from Steve Reich to John Adams, and the Bang on a Can Ensemble, the American school of minimalism teaches that the steady pulse of the electroacoustic flow lets you *play* the pulse, ride the wave of the looping, piano echo, instead of the individuated notes or differentiated "points" of sound. The contours have faded.[180] But an entire fossil-fuel infrastructure had to first be in place for this qualitative transformation to be recognized. The war had to disenchant and immobilize. Eros had to become sick, as Deleuze says.[181] Now one can, to be sure, turn the dial of the one continuum, switch on and slide up and down the one, infinitely modulating variation of the cosmological mixing board.[182] Now Broonzy and Cotton's epic impulse can spread out, so to speak, with the "wettening" effect of signal processing and filtering. Yet with each advance, the pressure mounts. Recognition almost always takes place, as Jasbir Puar has emphasized, either as a "epistemological corrective,"[183] that is, without practical consequences, or via the pacified and circumscribed space of the elitist artworld. Another way to describe these developments of the electronic age is to say that, after amplification and technical reproduction, and after what could also be described as the *blur* between the environment and the "self" that once seemed to stand over and against it, it *seems* virtually impossible to stop the deterritorializing momentum. The dangerous flow *seems* to be on the verge of absolute discharge. Hence, the half-missed note of the guitar solo, the "choppy" misfire of improvisation and, similarly, the "muted" rhythm chords, now reverberate an inward groan, a

---

[178] Justin McBrien, "Accumulating Extinction: Planetary Catastrophism in the Necrocene," in *Anthropocene or Capitalocene*, ed. Jason W. Moore (Oakland, CA: PM Press, 2016), 116–37, 126.
[179] Jasbir K. Puar, *The Right to Maim: Debility, Capacity, Disability* (Durham, NC: Duke University Press, 2017), 4.
[180] Deleuze, *Cinema 1*, 11.
[181] Deleuze, *Cinema 2*, 24.
[182] Deleuze locates this emergence of the infinite variation machine of modernity, in contrast to the more static and hypostatized, "stamped form" of the old metaphysics, in the figure of Leibniz. See Gilles Deleuze, *The Fold: Leibniz and the Baroque*, trans. Tom Conley (Minneapolis: University of Minnesota Press, 1993), 19.
[183] Puar, *The Right to Maim*, 18–36.

broken sob, which music could not previously capture. Fingers mourn as if they had throats. Thomas Hood's rhyme stings like never before.[184] The stillness of the break between the echoing, dissonant note that flits past, escaping the totality, and the notes or chords that explicitly follow it often evokes that brief, perilous moment before dynamite is about to ignite. The engine revs before taking off. The shockwave of a revolver ricochets off city streets and high-rises. One hears an ambulance, a siren call, the state of emergency, in this elusive noise. All it takes is a grazing of the fingerboard. These intolerably loud caesuras to the meaningful-nexus (*Sinnzusammenhang*), which the apparatus of capture, the policed ears of the state, aim to silence, should be harder and harder to contain, harder and harder to deny today, so obviously are they instances of, so to speak, "overflow," of potency pulsing at and, eventually, over, the edge.[185] When such volatility has, moreover, been tubed, flipped, and rippled, and when the improvisational moment has, similarly, been driven *onward* by the steady tap of the ride cymbal, by the fixed beat of a mimetically modulated railroad crossing bell, a semblance of the stifled possibilities of the species cannot help but come to fore with even greater intensity. The contrast between extremes is essential. Chaos juxtaposed to stabilizing uniformity reassures. The shelter of the latter incites the desire to join the former, or slowly but surely test the limit.

Decontextualization

The concept of negativity is not on the side of idealism. The earth-shattering sublimity of a Beethoven timpani resounds all the more when, by virtue of technical reproduction, it is ripped from its original context, transposed to a mountainous landscape, and syncopated against an actual crash of lighting.[186] The silence between the thunderous crash and the antiphonal, "late" beat of the drum echoes inwardly. Because she mourns, nature is mute. It is as though the eroding sediment from these same mountains were grieving, as the rocks from Hegel's *Phenomenology* do, over missed opportunities. On the other, affirmative

---

[184] For a discussion of Thomas Hood's "Song of the Shirt," see William Morris, *News from Nowhere and Other Writings* (New York: Penguin Books, 2004), 100.

[185] Deleuze and Guattari, *A Thousand Plateaus*, 452–3.

[186] For further consideration of how decontextualization like this might, in the era of hi-fidelity reproduction, either preserve the old, socially determined hierarchy of the senses or perhaps even foment an alternative form of technically mediated, "general intellect" memory, see John Mowitt, "The Sound of Music in the Era of Its Electronic Reproducibility," in *The Sound Studies Reader*, ed. Jonathan Sterne (New York: Routledge, 2012), 213–24.

side, the beat that does in fact hit the mark, that confirms what was anticipated in protention,[187] can give courage, just as soul music and the Afrofuturist vector that emerges from it would eventually ward off the *funk* of the blues by *becoming the funk*. Bootsy Collins compressed into a narrow circuit, pulsed with AC voltage to the nth power, becomes Victor Wooten, Mike Gordon, and Oteil Burbridge. The latter have honed a multigenerational, uniaxial force and can now command this explosive flow beyond the irresistible drop of the "one" that once boomed on the stage of James Brown's incessant, church-choir repetition.[188] The bass becomes a canoe: steady, rowing, guiding you through the forest river of your dreams. It becomes the *basso continuo* of old, only now it is electrified and it is silver.

Moon Satellite

Benjamin's surrealist, x-ray vision approaches the edge of the ego.[189] The dose of stupidity needed to loosen up the reification, however, is not, as Kodwo Eshun claimed, so much hashish as the combination of psychedelics and technically reproduced music.[190] Blasted out of its original context and supplemented by music, the coldest winter evening reverses into the greatest warmth, for the moon, previously blocked, peeks through the clouds and, like the process of production itself, temporarily illuminates the truth from behind our backs. Time swells.[191] The optical and sonorous unconscious converge. The glow of the moon is like the afterimage of an atomic bomb. The blinding white light reflected off of the snow-covered landscape reveals the black capillaries, in negative, of your eyes. As the line between dreaming and waking-life begins to dissolve, as the inside and outside, nature and history, push and pull on one another, the rhizomatic blood vessels become one with the rhizomatic tree branches and the countless, marble shadows that they cast on the snow-white floor of the forest. Leibniz called these lines the marble veins of the infinite cosmos.[192] Benjamin called them the wooded entrails of the unconscious.[193] You are nothing but one

---

[187] Edmund Husserl, *The Phenomenology of Internal Time-Consciousness*, trans. James S. Churchill (Bloomington: Indiana University Press, 1964).
[188] Gilroy, *The Black Atlantic*, 202.
[189] Benjamin, "Surrealism," 212/GS2, 302.
[190] Eshun, *More Brilliant than the Sun*, 53.
[191] Cf. Walter Benjamin, *The Storyteller: Short Stories*, ed. Sam Dolbear et al. (New York: Verso, 2016), 55.
[192] Deleuze, *The Fold*, 4.
[193] Walter Benjamin, "Dream Kitsch: Gloss on Surrealism," in *Selected Writings*, vol. 2.1, ed. Michael W. Jennings (Cambridge, MA: Harvard University Press, 2003), 3–5, 4; "Traumkitsch," *Gesammelte Schriften*, vol. 2, ed. Rolf Tiedemann and Hermann Scheppenhäuser (Frankfurt a.m.: Suhrkamp Verlag, 1974), 620–2, 621.

variation in the infinite variations of the great machine that never began and will never end.

Neutralization

What might be termed, following Moten's analysis, the lyrical moment, the howlin', inarticulate sigh, which carries the expressionless moan of the oldest worksongs well into the twenty-first century, seems to be suppressed at virtually every turn by the culture industry. Deterritorialization reterritorializes with woefully deceptive consequences. The problem of genuine improvisation in contrast to the reified schema of mass production remains unresolved, since it is not clear that the stored up, accumulated breakout attempts have, from indeterminate composition to free jazz, succeeded at achieving anything but a reinscription of the same trap that has always haunted music. In fact, the "phonetic substance" of all music, the "smooth space" or non-communicative texture from which intelligible, meaning-bearing signification issues forth, cannot find a voice but through this confrontation with the state, with, that is to say, the "popular" culture of the commodified circuits or the compressing limits of striated space.[194] After the sorrow song has been transformed and preserved by the machined, amplified voice or, understood on a macrological plane, after the state appears to have wholly appropriated the iterant, fugitive element—think of the notorious dilutions of white rock-and-roll—the natural-historical dynamic is, to be sure, altered forever. Laurie Anderson's tin-can voice expresses the frailty of resistance to this dynamic like few others. Wendy Carlos proved Donna Haraway's thesis, that we were always cyborgs—especially Bach and Beethoven—fifty years ago.[195] What was previously inaudible does, indeed, become audible. But this means that what was previously elusive is also on its way to being neutralized by the process of rationalization. The murderous, *hollerin'* revenge of Josh White's mule, who, tired and beaten from the endless *haulin*,' is not a mule but a creaturely worker, is thinned out and pacified over time. Everyone disowns Paul Robeson in the end.[196] Stagolee is captured, packaged, filtered, and dolled out in meager portions to the spiritually starved. The masochistic lonely crowd,

---

[194] Deleuze and Guattari, *A Thousand Plateaus*, 474–5.
[195] Donna Haraway, "A Cyborg Manifesto: Science, Technology, and Socialist-Feminism in the Late Twentieth Century," in *Simians, Cyborgs and Women: The Reinvention of Nature* (New York: Routledge, 1991), 149–81.
[196] Iton, *In Search of the Black Fantastic*, 34–9. See, also, Gerald Horne, *Paul Robeson: The Artist as Revolutionary* (London: Pluto Press, 2016).

in truth, prefers noise making to drown out the unbearable screams instead of free-time,[197] which would only drive home the fact that our autonomy has been stolen from us, that we would not know what to do with ourselves if we were not, at every moment, collecting data, that is, really subsumed, abstract value, for the owners of property and blood. The *horror vacui* is too much to bear. The abyss of the soul from which revolutionary *praxis* must spring is never confronted. The positivist spirit has transformed space into an anechoic chamber.

Co-enactment

Who is in a position, given this context, to push *onward* to what Adorno and Edward Said understood by the concept of late style, to the radical deterritorialization of musical form, which anticipates the radical deterritorialization of the internal and external division of labor?[198] Doing so would, minimally, require "surrendering" (*Überlassen*) or "following" (*suivant*) the matter itself, giving oneself over to the dissonance, in homage to Hegel, wherever it might take you.[199] Adorno illuminates this conflict with utmost precision. One understands virtually nothing of his critique of jazz unless one grasps the degree to which everything, for him, turns on the tensions between what he calls the minstrel (*Musikant*) element of music and the potential for its co-enactment (*Mitvollzug*).[200] "Torn halves of an integral freedom" that do not add up when pieced back together, the tension between them mirrors the tension between the nomad and the state that Deleuze describes.[201] Their difference must, accordingly, be understood, for both thinkers, as dynamic and interpenetrating, capable of reversals, condensations, and inversions. Instead of an abstract opposition, in which the former would somehow be on the side of critique, and the latter on the side of ideology, the troupe or band, that is, the iterant or elusive element, which is

---

[197] For further consideration of this all-important concept of the masochistic lonely crowd in Adorno's thought, see T. W. Adorno, "Democratic Leadership and Mass Manipulation," in *Gesammelte Schriften*, vol. 20, ed. Rolf Tiedemann (Frankfurt a.m.: Suhrkamp Verlag, 1972), 267–86. For more on the compulsion of noisemaking or making a racket (*Radau*), see Adorno, *Introduction to the Sociology of Music*, 46/GS14, 226, as well as Deleuze and Guattari, *Anti-Oedipus*, 55.

[198] Edward Said, *On Late Style: Music and Literature Against the Grain* (New York: Vintage Books, 2007).

[199] Adorno, *Aesthetics*, 84/NS, 136; Deleuze and Guattari, *A Thousand Plateaus*, 409: "matter-flow can only be *followed*"; "To follow the flow of matter is to itinerate, to ambulate."

[200] T. W. Adorno, "Kritik des Musikanten," in *Gesammelte Schriften*, vol. 14, ed. Rolf Tiedemann (Frankfurt a.m.: Suhrkamp Verlag, 1972), 67–107.

[201] T. W. Adorno and Walter Benjamin, *The Complete Correspondences* (Cambridge, MA: Harvard University Press, 2001), 130.

forced to "keep moving" against the capitalist axiomatic, cannot avoid eventually becoming congested or jammed (*gestaut*), in Adorno's framing, "interrupted, blocked, or plugged up," in Deleuze's.[202] Expression runs into convention, dies out by virtue of it, or becomes reified in the process of performing the service of entertainment. Adorno insists, in other words, that this congestion process (*Stauungsvorgang*),[203] which he says might on occasion propel genuine thinking and thereby differentiate itself, in anticipation of Deleuze, from stupidity,[204] is thrust upon all acts of musical production, even if, in the case of mere minstrelsy or mere entertainment, the possibility of self-reflection, of breaking out of the jam in and through the jam, is ultimately forfeited. The logic of sense is not yet thinking: percept and affect need the concept, just as the concept needs percept and affect.[205] Confronting this congestion (*Stauung*) that might, following this logic, be understood as the widening gyre of subsumption under the commodity form, and that Adorno also associates with the stuffiness (*Muff*) of the "classical" music and operetta of his parents' generation,[206] is the condition for the possibility of entering into the work in an unanticipated way. *Ministralis*, like gleemen, have official duties to perform for the empire, but there is always something more at play for those who simultaneously stand inside and outside of society, at once exoticized and abjected, pariah and parvenu.[207] Uncertainty might, that is to say, generate the fantasy of becoming the fifth instrument in the quartet, co-enacting the unfolding of its composition, surrendering to its inner tensions and resolutions, to its train (*Zug*) of development. Succeeding at this becoming-music means both clearing the musty air and, above all else, reinvigorating the dynamic movement of the mimetic faculty, which is always blocked just before turning back upon itself and recommencing the movement of becoming-other once again. Hence, coproduction or co-consummation (*Mitvollzug*) implies a regulative idea in which both musician and listener approximate full immersion with the music itself: "structural listening."[208]

---

[202] Gilles Deleuze, "Life and Literature," in *Essays Critical and Clinical*, trans. Daniel W. Smith and Michael A. Greco (Minneapolis: University of Minnesota Press, 1997), 3.

[203] Adorno, *Aesthetics*, 128/NS3, 204.

[204] Deleuze, *Difference and Repetition*, 150.

[205] Deleuze and Guattari, *What Is Philosophy?*, 183.

[206] Adorno, *Introduction to the Sociology of Music*, 33/GS14, 212.

[207] For an analysis that attempts to identify the anachronism of applying Marx's conception of the proletariat's power to the present circumstance, see Adorno, "Reflections on Class Theory"/GS8, 373–91. Adorno's point is that if the proletariat has been wholly subsumed under bourgeois relations, it no longer exists both inside and outside of society simultaneously and, for that reason, arguably loses its revolutionary strength.

[208] For a criticism of this conception of "structural listening," see Rose Subotnik, "Toward a Deconstruction of Structural Listening: A Critique of Schoenberg, Adorno, and Stravinsky," in *Deconstructive Variations: Music and Reason in Western Society* (Minneapolis: University of

Stuffy Troubadour

One can understand, in this respect, why Adorno would associate the minstrel moment that stops at mere minstrelsy with the bourgeois customer who consumes the exchange-value of the music instead of perceiving its objective features, who asks of it that it "give" him something for his precious dollar, instead of considering what the work might demand of him. The minstrel-like moment, as a constitutive moment of all art, especially the experimental avant-garde, which in Adorno's lifetime was already starting to embody the "comic quality of [an] aged youth,"[209] is the moment when the work either pushes beyond itself, measuring itself against itself, or betrays its inner necessity: the need of the "we" that can only be answered in and through technical modification. Putting on the mask, histrionics, or the play (*Spiel*) of the circus troupe of vagabonds, are all, of course, unavoidable for an art that needs critical distance from the suffocating positivism of the false world. Yet, as Alexander Kluge has incisively shown, this, so to speak, rolling with the punches, or this adaptation to the culture industry, is lethal when it fails to reflect the degree

---

Minnesota Press, 1996). Unfortunately, there are a series of misreadings of Adorno's materialist conception of music criticism in this influential piece. For instance, Adorno's appeal to the preponderance of the object is far from being, as Subotnik claims, an adherence to Kant's and Eduard Hanslick's unwitting projection of the Western scientific "neutral" gaze onto the musical material. His method does not by any means imply, as she also claims, that the onlooker arrives at a transparent understanding of the material. Such abstract universalism is, in fact, the exact opposite of Adorno's dialectical claim. It is telling, in this regard, that Subotnik makes no mention of atomistic listening, the dialectical other to structural listening. Far from embodying the very historicism that Benjamin identified in the figure of Fustel de Coulanges, Adorno's ideal of objectivity does not consist of searching, as Subotnik says, for the work's "original sense," for how it really was or is in and of itself without subjective mediation as a necessary moment in cognition. On the contrary, Adorno's concept of structural listening implies resisting the dehistoricizing destruction of experience and, instead, searching for each work's truth-content, for its unreconciled relationship to the present domination, which can only ever come to the fore in a tension-filled and opaque constellation, and can only ever offer a fleeting glimpse of redemption. Adorno's alleged incapacity to countenance "moral indeterminacy" is actually closer to Subotnik's incapacity to countenance a world beyond the relativizing violence of commodity relations. Adorno says that, on principle, interpretation is infinite (*Aesthetic Theory*, 186/GS7, 277), that is, dynamically mediated and becoming recognizable in the midst of the latest developments, the latest repetitions of the old danger. Giving oneself over to the structure, as Hegel insisted, as well as searching for the necessity that would drive forward the next development or overcome the previously incompatible demands are not marks of cultural elitism, as Subotnik implies, they are evidence of fidelity to the possibility of something other than the status quo. In political terms, there is no possibility of emancipation without a vanguard that has sublated the previous shortcomings of the previous struggles. Anything less than this critical turn amounts to claiming that Marx, for example, is a cultural construct and therefore as false and as true as the next theorist. For a further examination of how this charge of Adorno's subjectivism or "individual preference" is actually the object revenging itself on the one who makes the accusation, see Adorno's aphorism, "Unfair Intimidation," in Adorno, *Minima Moralia*, 69–70/GS4, 76–7. For a look at how this stance, namely that there is something for everyone so that everyone can be accused of arbitrariness, is nothing other than the ideology that preserves the rigidity of the class system, see Adorno, *Minima Moralia*, 194/GS4, 219.

[209] Adorno, *Aesthetic Theory*, 24–5/GS7, 44.

to which the balance of forces have irreversibly changed. What once spoke becomes mute, regresses to kitsch. Neither autonomous music nor so-called popular music are immune to this. The tired workers, in need of entertainment as a "shot in the arm,"[210] are too exhausted to leave the false security of the bourgeois home for the art of the public square, which doesn't exist anyway. It should come as no surprise, then, that they are equally ill-equipped to hear the refrain that echoes from the *Zirkuskuppel*: "I'd like to see the man, who after Auschwitz, tries to stop us from saying something that has to be said."[211] After the social death of slavery, the same necessity of the new categorical imperative doubtless migrates into Afrodiasporic art. This begins to show why, especially in the face of the racism of minstrelsy in the US context, Adorno maintains, in a rarely cited passage, that "jazz has its unquestioned merits." Its "presence of mind, [. . .] concentration," and sense of "tonal and rhythmic differentiation"[212] potentially set it apart from the conventionality of so-called high art, not least when the latter maintains its art-religious pretensions or, similarly, disavows just how much the "immediacy" of the sensuous is actually mediated to its core and thus in need of an immanent-critical, philosophical moment to glean what still remains possible for music and politics after (*nach*) catastrophe. "The social function of jazz," writes Adorno, "coincides with its history, the history of a heresy that has been received into mass culture."[213] Today, this heresy has been identified as the Afro-pessimist trap.[214] There appears to be but one way out after the economy of desire of the culture industry is revealed to be structurally racist, or after redemption has, in Frank Wilderson Jr.'s conception, been systemically eliminated as a possibility for Black subjects.[215] "Certainly jazz has the potential for a breakout from this culture," continues Adorno, attempting to hone in on the antinomy of art in the modern and, by implication, post-bellum era. But this, he notes, is probably only possible insofar as the breakout is performed by "those who were either refused admittance to [mass culture] or [are] exasperated by its mendacity."[216] When jazz is received, or more accurately, appropriated by,

---

[210] Adorno, "Is Art Lighthearted," 248/GS11, 599–600.
[211] Alexander Kluge, *Artist Under the Big Top: Perplexed* (West Germany: Kairos-Film, 1968).
[212] Adorno, *Introduction to the Sociology of Music*, 33/GS14, 212.
[213] Ibid., 33–4/GS14, 212–13.
[214] See Orlando Patterson, *Slavery and Social Death: A Comparative Study* (Cambridge, MA: Harvard University Press, 1985).
[215] Frank Wilderson III, "Afro-Pessimism and the End of Redemption," *Humanities Futures*: https://humanitiesfutures.org/papers/afro-pessimism-end-redemption/ (accessed July 5, 2019). For a criticism that claims that Wilderson is too fatalistic, on the one hand, and tends to invisibilize, on the other, the real struggle against anti-Black racism, see Greg Thomas, "Afro-Blue Notes: The Death of Afro-pessimism (2.0)?" *Theory & Event* 21, no. 1 (January 2018): 282–317.
[216] Adorno, *Introduction to the Sociology of Music*, 33–4 (translation modified)/GS14, 212–13.

the demands of commodity production, this is tantamount to what Adorno describes in "On Jazz" as jazz unwittingly veiling its commodity character,[217] or refusing to admit the social mediation—the reproduction of the State—from which it tries to distinguish itself. Hans Zimmer and Arvo Pärt, to say nothing of the earlier barbarism of Sibelius's nationalism, do the same. No wonder they, in contrast to Schoenberg, Penderecki, and Ornette Coleman, are consumed with such unreflective glee, while the latter are disclaimed, the second the fixed chord structure drops away, under the pretense of "incomprehensibility." Even if, following the innovations of be-bop, advanced jazz musicians parted ways with the exchange-value of the swinging, big band dance number, such veiling persists, both within and without jazz, insofar as the critical link between mimesis and rationality—their ongoing dialectic—is severed. Consumed with the same aloofness and disinterest that makes a mockery of the white bourgeois, "classical" music connoisseur, the Black bourgeois, jazz connoisseur borders on forgetting the degree to which the racist political spell must, musically speaking, be "reflected within itself," "composed out," or incorporated as an internal problematic.[218] Anything short of this *Aufarbeitung* would fall behind the immanent, technically mediated, potential for freedom.[219] Anything else would miss the expressive openings that are not the same today as they were yesterday and will be tomorrow. In thus swearing off art as the refuge for mimetic activity,[220] irreparable damage is done to the *praxis* in whose name political commitment allegedly acts.

Planned Spontaneity

Certain variations in the history of jazz, which Adorno likely never heard,[221] or perhaps overlooked, no doubt succeed at rising to this level of autonomy,

---

[217] T. W. Adorno, "On Jazz," in *Essays on Music*, ed. Richard Leppert (Los Angeles: University of California Press, 2002), 473; "Über Jazz," in *Gesammelte Schriften*, vol. 17, ed. Rolf Tiedemann (Frankfurt a.m.: Suhrkamp Verlag, 1972), 78.
[218] Adorno, "On some Relationships between Music and Painting," 68/GS16, 630–1.
[219] Fanon, *Wretched of the Earth*, 145–80, makes a similar point on the prospect of decolonial freedom via a flexible or historically mediated understanding of national culture.
[220] Adorno, *Aesthetic Theory*, 53/GS7, 86.
[221] Jeffrey Nealon, *Post-Postmodernism: or, The Cultural Logic of Just-in-Time Capitalism* (Stanford, CA: Stanford University Press, 2012), 107–8. Though brief on the jazz question, Nealon is decisive for showing how much Adorno's critique mirrors Amiri Baraka's denunciation of the whitewashing commodification of swing. He also notes that Adorno likely never heard many of the experimental iterations of jazz that could be said to be on the side of autonomous music.

to what, in *Aesthetic Theory*, he came to call the recoiling modification of the drives, the process, that is to say, of mimetic *Vollzug*.[222] But, if the secret schema uniting the concept and intuition, mimesis and rationality, is revealed to be the schema of production;[223] if, in Deleuze's terms, all "individuated" desire is linked to a larger, machinic apparatus of *desiring production*, it follows that the logic of sense will assume a different "form" during virtually every cyclical revolution in the technical forces of production. "New" works and "new" riffs in the spontaneous blues or jazz solo will frequently move, despite some temporary success, in lockstep with the demands of expanded reproduction, which, of course, needs new markets and must, therefore, find new consumers, especially when the production of sheet music and the support of large-scale ensembles are no longer cost-effective.[224] Frederic Rzewski touched upon something essential concerning this attempt to either resist or adapt to domination, this trial (*Revisionsprozeß*), in Adorno's words, of life against life.[225] In the former's conception, the graceful recovery of the initial, unconscious, "wrong" note, in which a second "wrong" note justifies the initial fumble, constitutes the spirit of authentic improvisation.[226] Benjamin too sensed the inescapability of this dynamic when he maintained that the "presence of mind" of revolutionary practice has to retroactively hear the secret of the missed chance that would have averted the catastrophe, that would have jammed the circuitry of so-called progress if only one had been more alert. "Were you really unaware of this? Didn't the dead person's name, the last time you uttered it, sound differently in your mouth? Don't you see in the flames a sign from yesterday evening, in a language you only now understand? And if an object dear to you has been lost, wasn't there—hours, days before—an aura of mockery or mourning about it that gave the secret away."[227] The mimetic refuge of art prepares the way, as it were, for "second reflection,"[228] even if it arrives on the scene too late. When it avoids adaptation to death, that is, when it avoids mere representational imitation, it extracts the truth from the error. It hears the nonidentity that was already implicit in the moment, the mockery or sorrow that would unfold the next day.

---

[222] Adorno, *Aesthetic Theory*, 112/GS7, 171.
[223] Adorno and Horkheimer, *Dialectic of Enlightenment*, 98/GS3, 146.
[224] Neal, *What the Music Said*, 26–32.
[225] Adorno, "Short Commentaries," 176/GS11, 205.
[226] Frederic Rzewski, "Little Bangs: A Nihilist Theory of Improvisation," in *Audio Culture*, ed. Christoph Cox and Daniel Warner (New York: Continuum, 2010), 267.
[227] Walter Benjamin, *One-Way Street*, in *Selected Writings*, vol. 1 ed. Michael W. Jennings (Cambridge, MA: Harvard University Press, 2003), 482–3; *Einbahnstraße*, in GS4, ed. Rolf Tiedemann and Hermann Scheppenhäuser (Frankfurt a.m.: Suhrkamp Verlag, 1974), 141–2.
[228] Adorno, *Negative Dialectics*, 44/GS6, 54.

Precognitively, and yet mediated by the history of cognition, it senses with bodily dexterity the countless "omens, presentiments, [and] signals [that] pass day and night through our organism like wave impulses," and it sets them in motion, as if with a divining rod.[229] This preserves the involuntary, aesthetic moment in cognition without tossing out cognition—itself congealed technology—in a reactionary appeal to mystical immediacy. The difficulty, then, consists in the fact that the "wrong" note has been revealed as a wrong note in determinate relation to the totality. The error is the world-historical error, the Middle Passage and Auschwitz, which respectively open and close this era of accumulation. How can any of these "notes" be made right, asks Adorno? How can a correction be demanded from those who never wanted to take part in the victorious procession? And how can one avoid betraying this impulse to overcome calamity, to heal the sickness in the next phrase, with a music that would, in so doing, effectively proclaim that chattel slavery was an "operational mishap," that the camps were an anomaly along the path to economic prosperity?[230] Answers to this tonic-dominant, conflict-resolution logic are not forthcoming, since it is the matter itself—*fundamentum in re*—that withholds them. The point is to ignite upon the antinomy. Adorno's criticism of jazz pivots, in this way, on the fact that jazz production—doubtless similar to the state-subsidized *auteurs* and "art-music" composers of Europe—threatens to flee the impossible guilt of playing the next note. Art is, indeed, as Beckett said, a desecration of silence.[231] Finding meaning in the totality before the light of the hidden *terminus ad quem* has arrived violates the *Bildverbot*.[232] The "measure of convalescence,"[233] that is, the capacity or incapacity of the proletariat to heal and thus exercise power, is forfeited by leaping ahead of itself, forgetting that for every line of flight, there is also a line of torpor, resignation, and acquiescence. There is greater strength in admitting, as opposed to acting out against, one's weakness. As Horkheimer once said, punishment lurks behind the inability to love the good that is impotent. Hating the sight of the weak, it seeks revenge over the fact that this good has been, from time immemorial, powerless.[234] Instead of being a corrective to *praxis*, that is, instead of giving us a negative glimpse of a world beyond *praxis*, beyond the

---

[229] Benjamin, *One-Way Street*, 483/GS4, 141.
[230] Améry, "Resentments," 67.
[231] Adorno, *Aesthetic Theory*, 134/GS7, 203. Although it is not frequently noted, the false immediacy of the allegedly pure and unmediated "soul" is a criticism that extends, in Adorno's philosophy of music, to Wagner as well. See Witkin, *Adorno on Music*, 166–7.
[232] Adorno, "Essay as Form," 13/GS11, 21
[233] Benjamin, *One-Way Street*, 487/GS4, 148.
[234] Max Horkheimer, *Dawn and Decline*, trans. Michael Shaw (New York: The Seabury Press, 1978), 146.

realm of "price,"²³⁵ almost every act of improvisation mirrors what might be described, in political terms, as the undialectical conception of the dichotomy between spontaneism and economism of the Comintern, as well as the failed attempt to forge an alliance between the internationalist *Négritude* movement and the US civil rights struggle.²³⁶ In both cases, the Archimedean point is missed:²³⁷ on the one hand, the delicate balance between a particular, aleatory moment that, as Hegel showed, is itself a crystallization of the universal; and, on the other, a universal that, preserving difference in the midst of similarity, cultivates the trust needed for genuine, transnational solidarity.

Cruel Pragmatism

Torture, which, far from simply "de-worlding" an already artificial tradition, in reality, accelerates the adaptation of people to blind collectives, is also what generates the separation of the mind from the body in the first place.²³⁸ Unworthy of its name, consciousness has heretofore been nothing but a reaction formation that preserves that separation in masochistic repetition. Adorno's conception of mimetic co-enactment might, accordingly, be characterized as the process by which music attempts to bridge the gap, by which it seeks to reactivate the synesthetic entwinement of the collective and individual, conscious and unconscious, sensorium. Unfortunately, however, the cool hanging cigarette of the front man does more fetishistic work than is initially believed.²³⁹ The false authority of a stylized, scopophilic ego-ideal stands, in the figure of the creative "artist" or "genius," above the fray, removed from the body politic and thus implicitly disparaging the possibility of co-production. The eye supplants the ear.²⁴⁰ The conductor's baton exposes him as a farcical archetype with a

---

²³⁵ Immanuel Kant, *Grounding for the Metaphysics of Morals*, trans. James W. Ellington (Indianapolis, IN: Hackett Publishing, 1993), 40.
²³⁶ Iton, *In Search of the Black Fantastic*, 49–53. This failure to follow the dialectic of the individual and the whole, to hear the we in the I, as Coltrane described it, parallels Fumi Okiji's claim that too much jazz criticism has fluctuated undialectically between the primitivist thesis and the ideology of bourgeois-liberal individualism. Okiji, *Jazz as Critique*, 16–17, 28–29.
²³⁷ Adorno, "Marginalia to Theory and Praxis," 274/*GS*10.2, 777.
²³⁸ Elaine Scarry, *Body in Pain: The Making and Unmaking of the World* (New York: Oxford University Press, 1985); T. W. Adorno, "Education after Auschwitz," in *Can One Live after Auschwitz?*, ed. Rolf Tiedemann (Stanford, CA: Stanford University Press, 2003), 27; "Erziehung nach Auschwitz," in *Gesammelte Schriften*, vol. 10.2, ed. Rolf Tiedemann (Frankfurt a.m.: Suhrkamp Verlag, 1972), 684.
²³⁹ Adorno, "On the Fetish-Character in Music," 310/*GS*14, 44.
²⁴⁰ For an excellent historical account of the manner in which this domination of the eye over the ear or this "hierarchy of the senses" is related to both Italian Futurism and French Surrealism, see Douglas Kahn, *Noise, Water, Meat: A History of Sound in the Arts* (Cambridge, MA: MIT Press, 1999), 45–68.

blunted sword. Benjamin did not miss the implication here either. Gambling, he says, addresses itself to *all* the senses.[241] Some forms of improvisation truly take a chance. Some have nothing to lose. Fetishistic listening and the cult of personality that comes with it, on the contrary, place a taboo on this entwined reactivation, this, as it were, rhizomatic rerouting of the nose and the ear, the tongue and the eye, in favor of a market-sanctioned clairvoyance. Nowhere is such a taboo more poignantly presented than in Roberto Rossellini's *Rome, Open City*, when the door swings between a jazz radio jingle and the deafeningly silent attempt to circumvent torture. Only reified consciousness could go on producing unambiguously affirmative music in the face of fascism. A puffed-up radicality prevails, since the formal freedom of bourgeois right and, today, the increasing gender and racial parity of participation in commodity production are not seen for what they are: modifications in the composition of the profit system that, in truth, preserve the colonialist order in updated form.[242] During international tours designed to combat the "Soviet threat," Dizzy Gillespie and Louis Armstrong were explicitly doing the bidding of the US State Department.[243] The only difference is that today the State Department does not need to intervene. Domination, and the American exceptionalism through which it circulates, is automatic. The empire's music blares from the slums of the global south to the industrial service centers. It should not be forgotten that every café in Weimar Germany similarly declared its revolutionary intension with Dixieland "hot jazz" playing *in the background*.[244] This was and is pseudo-practice (*Scheinpraxis*), in the final analysis, despite the musical innovations and despite the fact that the German and US contexts are, of course, qualitatively different. Disagreeing with this assessment cannot, then, be chalked up, in opposition to both Ralph Ellison's and Adorno's disdain for political *engagement*,[245] as the mere aversion

---

[241] Walter Benjamin, "Short Shadows (II)," in *Selected Writings*, vol. 2.2. ed. Michael W. Jennings (Cambridge, MA: Harvard University Press, 2003), 699–702, 700; "Kurze Schatten (II)," in *GS4*, ed. Rolf Tiedemann and Hermann Scheppenhäuser (Frankfurt a.m.: Suhrkamp Verlag, 1974), 425–8, 426.

[242] For further consideration of this deterritorializing and reterritorializing movement, or this play on inclusiveness through which the racist order of the state is perpetuated in the "post-racial" era, see Jason Michael Adams, "The King's Two Faces: Michael Jackson, the Postracial Presidency and the 'Curious Concept of Non-white,'" in *Deleuze and Race* (Edinburgh: Edinburgh University Press, 2013), 168–89. The other essays in this collection also go a long way toward illuminating Deleuze's dynamic understanding of race and racism, especially insofar as this understanding requires grasping just how much desire, territory, and capital are produced in relationship to the category of race.

[243] Iton, *In Search of the Black Fantastic*, 41–53.

[244] Mark Christian Thompson, *Anti-music: Jazz and Racial Blackness in German Thought Between the Wars* (New York: SUNY Press, 2018), 105.

[245] As with the problematic of "modern" art in general, this antinomic need for autonomy, as opposed to both direct political action and clarity of standpoint, does not discount the fact that, in the case of

of Black radicalism to the modernist concept of the autonomous work of art. For autonomous art is the other side to the ineffectual character of politics heretofore. It is the latter's scar. In this sense, free jazz and free atonality coalesce in the shared, dialectical repudiation of the manipulative personality's search for "calculated [musical] effects" in the audience.²⁴⁶ Against Antonin Artaud's cruelty, such a reduction, which treats the audience, not the inner movement of the artwork, as an object, forgets that these effects are "far from identical with the aesthetic experience of a work of art as such."²⁴⁷ Searching for stimuli-responses modeled on the marketing methodology of behaviorist psychology stimulates nothing. The weapons-grade propaganda tactics of the current aestheticized politics was implicit long before it became explicit in Cambridge Analytica. When these "effects" become the goal of either aesthetic production or philosophical criticism, they can never, therefore, be as pragmatic as the pragmatist's approach contends. The nonidentical is extinguished in the imperative to act. Music is not a means to an end. It is, rather, the critique of the means-ends logic that, as compulsion (*Zwang*), forgets the end. As Benjamin says, admonishing the patriarch with an eloquence that is Georg Christoph Tobler's, "to convince is unfruitful [*überzeugen ist unfruchtbar*]."²⁴⁸ Reconciliation would be conception without convincing or conquering.

Deferred Improvisation

The importance of Adorno's emphasis on the expelled as the source of authentic musical resistance cannot be overstated. This emphasis concentrates the sociopolitical dilemma that art expresses in micrological form without being able to change. There is no public in either the bourgeois or the post-bourgeois era. De Tocqueville's dream was stamped out long ago to the tune of marching

---

Ellison, there was arguably an "internalized racism" that stifled the possibility of forging pan-African solidarity. See Iton, *In Search of the Black Fantastic*, 53. See, also, T. W. Adorno, "Commitment," in *Aesthetics and Politics* (New York: Verso, 2007); "Engagement oder künstlicher Autonomie," in GS11 ed. Rolf Tiedemann (Frankfurt a.m.: Suhrkamp Verlag, 1972). To assume an unambivalent resistance to modernity in the Black expressive tradition, to leap hastily over the truth-content of Ellison's obstinacy concerning autonomous art, is to miss the dialectical antinomy itself, which long ago moved from the subjective category of taste modeled on the liberal stage of the market to the objective category of a "missed chance" in which bourgeois relations of production continually fetter the forces of production.

[246] Adorno, *Introduction to the Sociology of Music*, 4/GS14, 181.
[247] Ibid., 4/GS14, 181.
[248] Benjamin, *One-Way Street*, 446 (translation modified)/GS4, 87. Benjamin gives ironic advice to would-be Don Juans here with the title: "Für Männer."

battalions. The era of the spectacle is the era when the memory of the resistance to the bourgeois public sphere is obliterated. All of this is expressed in the inner-aesthetic developments of advanced art.[249] Abstract declarations of improvisation will not, therefore, suffice.[250] Unlike the apologist for the status quo who cannot, as Deleuze might say, envision emancipation as anything other than faithfulness to the golden chains of the representational model, that is, "inclusivity" in the administrative apparatus of the modern police state, Adorno argues that improvisation has not yet fully emerged, since its *organon* is still missing. This is why he maintains, in an equally neglected passage from the "Fetish-Character" essay, that a "better hour" may still strike for improvisation. "[I]nstead of prompt synchronization with pregiven material [*eher das prompte Schalten mit schon vorgegebenen Materialien*], the improvisatory displacement of things, as the sort of radical beginning that can only thrive under the protection of the unshaken world of things [*im Schutz der unerschütterten Dingwelt*]," could emerge.[251] This genuine "protection" is nothing other than the possibility of real political power subtending the co-enactment of experiments in the reconfiguration of the sensorium. It is, moreover, the truth-content of the protective, shudder-reducing function of the first lullaby, namely that an alternative form of security still awaits—one that prefigures a world beyond the prevailing territorialization process and itself emerges from the "worn out" and "overexposed" features of a music disenchanted in the process of mass production. With good reason, Adorno alludes to the fact that the prompt "synchronization" (*Schalten*) or forced "stepping in line" of pseudo-spontaneity is akin to the post-Weimar *Gleichschaltungsgesetzen* of the Nazi Party, in which the power of the total state was consolidated by brutally crushing all internal decent.[252] The lonely crowd shuns anyone who fails to get with the program. Ersatz warmth senses that spectatorship at the gathering conflagration will be the highest aesthetic pleasure. Conversely, Nietzsche laughed at *Parsifal*, and Deleuze attempted to locate the desacralizing indifference of pop music molecules.[253] Unearthing the

---

[249] This understanding of the inner-aesthetic developments of art is to be contrasted to Peter Bürger, *Theory of the Avant-garde*, trans. Michael Shaw (Minneapolis: University of Minnesota Press, 1984).

[250] For an example of this abstract conception of improvisation in which something "new" allegedly happens every performance, see George E. Lewis, "Improvised Music after 1950: Afrological and Eurological Perspectives," in *Audio Culture*, ed. Christoph Cox and Daniel Warner (New York: Continuum, 2010), 278.

[251] Adorno, "On the Fetish-Character in Music," 314 (translation modified)/*GS*14, 49.

[252] Franz Neumann, *Behemoth: The Structure and Practice of National Socialism, 1933-1944* (Chicago: Oxford University Press, 2009), 51–56; Victor Klemperer, *Language of the Third Reich* (New York: Continuum, 2006), 159–60.

[253] Deleuze and Guattari, *A Thousand Plateaus*, 346. For an example of this laughing critique of authority, see Isabelle Stengers, "The Cosmopolitical Proposal," in *Making Things Public*, ed. Bruno Latour and Peter Weibel (Cambridge, MA: MIT Press, 2005), 994–1003.

vital element of music from out of the debris of the reified world, saying what the commodities would say, if they could speak, is still, in this sense, the task. "Even discipline," continues Adorno, maintaining the need to resist the switched-on certainty of readymade formula, the "slick superficiality"[254] that actually falls in line with the flexible labor requisites of capitalist crisis, "[e]ven discipline [might] assume the expression of free solidarity, if freedom becomes its content."[255] If the educative command, which is today heteronomous and imposed from above, could become autonomous and freely chosen from below, improvisation might, with an unflappable institutional structure supporting it, finally leave the orbit of the law of labor: the ever-identical. Pleasure and asceticism, joy and self-denial, could still coalesce in a higher synthesis. Autonomous desire could become, as Adorno once put it in a dream note, "the martyr of happiness."[256] It could act for the sake of happiness by denying its possibility under the current conditions.[257] Even if every attempt to this point seems to have been the diametric opposite, namely a martyrdom to property and possession, sacrifice to the identity principle on which the unhappiness of civilization is based, this in no way forecloses the possibility of a sudden reversal, of an about-turn that, united with society, not opposed to it, could finally expropriate and rechannel the social and natural-historical force necessary to reverse the inertia of catastrophe. "Then history," as James Baldwin once aptly expressed it, sensing this same, immanent possibility of reconciliation, would "become a garment we can wear and share, and not a cloak in which to hide." Then, "[t]ime," he says, would "become a friend."[258]

Variations from the Bottom

Imagine a "band" of *jongleurs*. They have written a new song. It will not premiere on an album and then be part of the branding campaign called a "tour" where the "genius" front man plays it exactly as it sounds on the album (only worse), so that the consumer-tourists can say, as Benjamin noted with horror, that they were there to "experience" it. On the contrary, the work will premiere at a live performance. But imagine that it has not yet fully come to life, has not yet found

---

[254] Adorno, "Essay as Form," 5/*GS*11, 12.
[255] Adorno, "On the Fetish-Character in Music," 314 (translation modified)/*GS*14, 49.
[256] T. W. Adorno, *Dream Notes*, trans. Rodney Livingstone (Malden, MA: Polity Press, 2007), 45.
[257] Adorno, *Aesthetic Theory*, 13/*GS*7, 26: "For the sake of happiness, happiness [*Glück*] is renounced [*abgesagt*]."
[258] Baldwin, "Of the Sorrow Songs," 153.

its lasting form. For its form, which is a reference to the totality, both within the band's oeuvre and without the band's oeuvre (its placement within the history of music), will need to be worked out over a lifetime. Along the way, little phrases, transitional accents, melodic refrains will sediment in this new "song." The melodic line that emerges in a brief opening of a meticulously composed section will not always be that same line. In retrospect one will be stunned to find that the first iterations were, in fact, completely different, that the compulsion of the matter itself had not yet driven the work to its outermost expression. Importantly, this collective working out of the material, which takes a whole "summer tour" of live performances before it can congeal into place, extends to the next year and beyond, when instrumental and lyrical fragments will flash back up, when teases and quotes, minor riffs and "licks" from every conceivable moment, will point to different, virtual connections, linked to different, though fundamentally related, works. What is more, grasping the significance of this new emergence will require knowing not only the immanent development of the new work itself but the immanent development of every work in the band's five-hundred work repertoire, all of which have undergone the same, long-gestating, constellational shifts. Like a kaleidoscope, every instantiation, every singular monadic expression, whether of an instrumental or lyrical interval, whether explicated in this particular "show" (*Schauspiel*) or *the* Show that unifies all shows, will be integrally related to the whole.[259] In sublating its abstract opposition to the fairytale love of nature, the mythos of the epic journey returns in sincerity.[260] The fragmented universal is pieced together before it shatters once again in the downfall of its beautiful semblance. Even the cosmological element of electroacoustic music starts to open up, since here it can be said, without exaggeration, that the most minute textural and rhythmic blocks are amplified and repositioned without altering their temporal core. Each delicately selected or involuntarily discovered interval is, in other words, placed, as Charles Fourier's utopian vision promised, in a new, passionate series—a series that approximates the essence of the species: the fulfilled desire of every living creature. Like the sonata form tugging, after its death, on Michael Gordon's use of Sinatra's kitsch piano, or like Nero, whose murderous rage makes him, in the phalanstery, the greatest of butchers,[261] the virtual-real that was always present,

---

[259] This conception of *the* Show that unites all shows should be compared to Deleuze's conception of *the* Book that unites all books in Deleuze, *Proust and Signs*, 160.

[260] Benjamin, "The Storyteller," 157/GS2, 458.

[261] Elisabeth Lenk, "Introduction to the German Edition of Charles Fourier's The Theory of the Four Movements and the General Destinies," in *The Challenge of Surrealism: The Correspondence*

but not actualized, begins to shine forth.[262] With every minute, axial shift, every transposed series, the Jewish *theologoumenon* that, in the reconciled world, "all things would differ only a little from the way they are," becomes more and more palpable.[263] The firmament that suddenly opens up onto steppe in the developmental section of the first movement to Beethoven's *Violin Concerto in D* is contrasted to a play as light as the *onward* jaunt of a Vince Guaraldi promenade.[264] Transversals that were unthinkable just yesterday are activated. At the same time, it is all far more complicated than this,[265] because this description says nothing about the improvisational element on which so much of our phantasmatic band's vitality lives. Imagine if, beyond the limits of the sporadic alliance between, for example, Coltrane and Davis, that is, between the best living practitioners of their respective instruments, the members of our quartet were not only the best at their own instruments but had, in fact, been learning to listen to each other, humble each other, in tenderness, for their entire adult lives. Imagine that for, say, forty years, "under the protection of the unshaken world of things," they had been teaching each other how to hear the *dynamic contrast* between all of the parts, between each member's instrumental voice. With four instruments there's no room for ornamentation. As the rigidity of the identity principle begins to soften, conic loops within loops, fractally curving, contrapuntally spiraling down to the infinitesimally small and back up to the infinitely large, are heard. The equal spacing of the semitone no longer suffices. An ear attuned to the elemental and cosmological listens like the sight that sees the tree-crested openings, the breaks in the canopy where light juts through the weaving forest path of a moonlit evening. Imagine, still further, that these "voices" were machined by an almost infinite array of effects-rig modulation, samplings, and mastered stylistic variations, from old-time music, the blues, and the jest of a Gershwinian, rhapsodic show-tune to experimental jazz, ambient music, and the outright terror of industrial electronic noise. Would not these voices, by virtue of precisely this mediation between the extremes, become multiplicities of themselves, that is, brimming potencies that ebb and flow with and against the virtual totality of *Naturlauten*? Sober eyes (*nüchterne Augen*) and the mysteries converge in a new form of profane rites. Divine comedy and the

---

of *Theodor W. Adorno and Elisabeth Lenk*, trans. Susan H. Gillespie (Minneapolis: University of Minnesota Press, 2015), 200.

[262] Deleuze, *Difference and Repetition*, 208–14.
[263] Adorno, *Negative Dialectics*, 299/GS6, 294.
[264] Deleuze and Guattari, *A Thousand Plateaus*, 61–2.
[265] For an understanding of the use of the concept of "complication" here, see Deleuze's discussion of the Neoplatonist notion of the "birth of time" in Deleuze, *Proust and Signs*, 29–30.

horror of impending death reunite, preserving the mythical shudder before nature on a higher plane. The carnival at the end begins. Unlike nearly every example of commodity music, this lifetime of friendship, coupled with a tireless, borderline obsessive dedication to practice, to honing one's expressive and technical capacity, would be the precondition of actualizing real improvisation, that is, an improvisation that, refusing to spurn the concomitant need for prewritten, integral composition, embodies the dialectic between spontaneity and planning, instead of, with Cage, disposing of the latter on the basis of its allegedly heavy-handed, anthropocentric calculations. This backdrop would, furthermore, set in place the conditions for the possibility of premiering works that, although produced in old age, counted among the band's best, most youthful works. These works would, likewise, fit so nimbly, so "methodically unmethodically" into the ever-moving totality,[266] that it would be virtually impossible to understand what had taken place, as well as what still remained on the horizon, without them. The fleeting standstill before the transition to the next song, the clear channel of the Steinway that emerges from the engulfing, electroacoustic static, calms all anguish. *Tout à coup* a melody flashes up. How can it be so familiar? Like "interfolded cotyledons" or the earthy, *terra incognito* scent of the first books you read as a child, it is as though this melody from the present were your most intimate companion from the past.[267] So close is it that, even if it were literally produced or discovered at a late stage in your life, you can't help but remember it, like Platonic anamnesis, as the cradle song from your childhood, the song that mama sang to you as you lay nestled, rocking to and fro, in her lap. Thus the stage that ends all stages, the stage of co-implementation, is set. Thus the audience, whose rising and falling, hastening and slackening, tide is now, for the first time, in sync with the harmonic and rhythmic variations emanating from the band, can finally become the producer. A silence equal to the unanswered hopes of souls trapped in purgatory finally becomes contagious.[268] Static electricity, the crowd, and the becoming-rain of Leslie speakers blend together as Prometheus does with the rocks in Kafka's tale about the oblivion of the gods.[269] Now every performance is recorded, preserved, and—against the schizophrenic, commercial assault of the pan-radio spirit—held in common via an open access technology that is unfettered, in its turn, from the prevailing

---

[266] Adorno, "Essay as Form," 13/GS11, 21.
[267] Benjamin, "The Work of Art in the Age of Its Technological Reproducibility," 127/GS7, 368–9.
[268] Compare this to Proust's description of the Celtic belief concerning captive souls who are freed from the spell when properly named in Proust, *Remembrance of Things Past*, 47.
[269] Franz Kafka, "Prometheus," in *The Complete Stories*, ed. Nahum N. Glatzer (New York: Schocken Books), 432.

relations of production. Technology assists *la recherche*, instead of choking it out. Proust's indifference before death survives technical reproduction. Having canceled the patriarchal virility of old, an evil, becoming-serpent remedy for the blues sweeps back in, sidewinding 'round the Eden tale until its social roots are, at last, exposed for the nature-decay (*Naturverfallenheit*) they always were.[270] The false shelter of "happily ever after" gives way to a *resignation* as sweet as it is defiant, as divested of triumph as Goethe's melancholic "*verweile doch*." Here, then, the regulative task of "deliberately surrendering [. . .] to the chance of uncontrolled empiricism"[271] ceases to be the empty play of fetishization. Here, a congealed, second-nature capacity for improvisation on which all spontaneous political action must be modeled, lest it regress to pseudo-practice, begins to unfold. In the image of this experimental mode of production, we learn that the moment of recognizability only ever emerges in the now-time (*Jetztzeit*) of the latest performance. Like a Hindu *rāga* eternalizing the ephemerality of the seasons, what was discovered in this venue, on this date, during this "jam," is rearranged, again and again, is taken up and transformed, again and again. The discovery reverberates an unresolved past and only because it is inconsolably dedicated to rescuing that past from the wheel of fate does it also open onto an unknown future. Every development is a preservation of memory, each interval a resistance to the destruction of experience.

---

[270] Adorno, "Short Commentaries," 179 (translation modified)/*GS*11, 209.
[271] Adorno, "Transparencies on Film," 275 (translation modified)/*GS*10.1, 354.

Excursus III

Music after Auschwitz

It is now entirely possible that consonance may be reached only by passing through the most extreme dissonance.

—Marx, *Grundrisse*

The echo bespeaks a spell.

—Adorno, "Kierkegaard Once More"

Conatus

In Claude Lanzmann's 1985 documentary film *Shoah*, Filip Müller, survivor and *Sonderkommando* at Auschwitz, recounts his experience as an operator of the Birkenau crematoria. In crematoria II and III, after the zyklon crystals had been added and the lights from the gas chamber were turned off, the gas would, in Müller's retelling, first emerge from a ground-floor opening. Instinctively, blindly, the stronger would rise to the top, desperately evading the gas while crushing the skulls and limbs of the weak, the young, and the aged beneath them. Ten to fifteen minutes of this death-struggle was, in actuality, an eternity of torture. The ruthless, self-preservative drives sense that there is more air to breathe in hell at the summit of the chamber. It is impossible to conceive of an image of the natural-historical spell of domination appearing in a more sober light. Without sight or reason, brute force is unveiled as the "bad universal," the law of laws that underwrites every particular instantiation of law-setting and law-preserving, deterritorializing and reterritorializing, violence.[1] Trampling one's own children, abandoning them and everyone else, in order to steal the last breath of air from an encroaching adversary, triumphs as the first and last reflex. Excrement and blood pouring from every orifice of the body is all that can result from a nature that has, after Auschwitz, been revealed to be synonymous with

---

[1] Benjamin, "Critique of Violence," 243/*GS* 2.1, 190.

absolute punishment.[2] Like the response to the prisoner who was warned of the fate that would soon befall her and her comrades, who, upon informing them of their shared doom, is treated with as much coldness and mythical revenge as Cassandra was treated for her prophecy, everyone secretly knows that the sovereign victor at the top of the struggle will eventually roll out of the chamber no differently than the basalt, the blocks of stone, that his lifeless brothers and sisters have become. Everyone has, in short, seen the writing on the wall: whether inside or outside of the camp, whether inside or outside of the chamber, death is inescapable. There are only fluctuating degrees of reification. Even more terrifying, all knowledge of this fact appears to be utterly powerless before the blind repetition of nature. So-called life, the will to live—scarcely a consolation in the face of this suffocating pressure[3]—comes to the fore as a domination incapable of concealing that it, in truth, capitulated to the all-pervasive death-drive long ago.

Ontologization

In the face of catastrophe, art, which, like theology, once promised an escape from the misery of the empirical world, comes to diabolically parody Hegel's thesis concerning its end.[4] As the absolute is concretized, as the infinite becomes actual, art is increasingly impelled toward silence.[5] Who could go on making music in the face of the experience of the camps? Who could do so and not feel ashamed, not feel as though they were, in Adorno's terms, squeezing some kind of transcendent meaning out of the victim's fate?[6] The fact that these questions do not impinge upon the inner comportment of most artworks is evidence of the interminable triumph of the spell. It is in this respect—complete submission

---

[2] Compare this conception of punishment to Kant's claim that juridical punishment (*poena forensis*) can be distinguished from natural punishment (*poena naturalis*) by virtue of the alleged self-consciousness of the former. Immanuel Kant, "The Metaphysics of Morals," in *Practical Philosophy*, ed. Mary J. Gregor (New York: Cambridge University Press, 2009), 473. For more on the temporality of the natural-historical spell of punishment, see, also, Adorno, *Minima Moralia*, 166/GS4, 187.

[3] Adorno, *Negative Dialectics*, 262/GS6, 259–60: "Thus even concepts abstract enough to seem to approach invariance prove to be historic. An example is the concept of life. While life keeps reproducing itself under the prevailing conditions of unfreedom, its concept, by its own meaning, presupposes the possibility of things not yet included, of things yet to be experienced—and this possibility has been so far reduced that the word 'life' sounds by now like an empty consolation."

[4] Adorno, *Aesthetic Theory*, 32/GS7, 55.

[5] Ibid., 40/GS7, 66. Compare this tendency to Deleuze, "The Exhausted," in *Essays Critical and Clinical*, trans. Daniel W. Smith and Michael A. Greco (Minneapolis: University of Minnesota Press, 1997), 166. There, for example, Deleuze says of both Beethoven's and Beckett's works that they have intervals that are arranged by dissonant "holes of silence" or "unfathomable abysses of silence."

[6] Adorno, *Negative Dialectics*, 361/GS6, 354.

to all shudder suppressing forces—that one should understand the famous first lines of *Aesthetic Theory*. The guilt of Auschwitz is an *objective* guilt. Those who have escaped torture have more or less done so by accident, by *adaptation to the spell*, and should, by rights, have themselves been killed in the camps.[7] "It is self-evident," writes Adorno, in this vein, "that nothing concerning art is self-evident anymore, not its inner life, not its relation to the whole, not even its right to exist."[8] The antimony of modern art, that is, the fact that no clear path remains open to it, or the fact that it has become altogether questionable by virtue of its complicity in the history of domination, suggests that avoiding sanctimonious embarrassment is possible only by confronting this collective guilt directly.[9] Adorno, Benjamin, and Deleuze are all well aware of this contraction amid a seeming expansion, or this narrowing of the advanced path amid an apparent infinity of modern, *informelle* possibilities.[10] Understanding their answer to what Adorno calls the "radically darkened"[11] character of modern art brings into sharp relief the natural-historical constellation of the present moment, which has not, despite claims to the contrary, been fundamentally altered from the time of their respective writings. The overriding problem is that if a route outside of the eternal return of damnation is materially blocked, then insisting upon the inescapability of objective guilt appears to lapse into what should be avoided: the very subservience or masochism that results when one fails to call a "nature" that is trapped in the repetitions of punishment the "mythical spell," instead of calling it the "immutable truth."[12] The critique of the false, ontological need threatens to mirror precisely the fatalism of all ontological declarations.[13]

Infinite *Schuld*

Consider the problematic of infinite debt in Deleuze and Guattari's conception. Derived from Nietzsche, this debt just as much connotes guilt, since the German term is, of course, *Schuld*. Because it is predicated on the prehistory of production and exchange relations, *Schuld* also implies the metaphysical relationship to the past as such, that is, whether the past has been fulfilled or remains unfulfilled,

---

[7] Ibid., 363/GS6, 355.
[8] Adorno, *Aesthetic Theory*, 1 (translation modified)/GS7, 9.
[9] Améry, "Resentments," 72–3.
[10] Adorno, *Aesthetic Theory*, 1/GS7, 9.
[11] Ibid., 19/GS7, 35.
[12] Adorno, *Negative Dialectics*, 361/GS6, 354.
[13] Ibid., 92–3/GS6, 99–100.

whether it is realized or remains unredeemed. Deleuze and Guattari have, in this manner, supplemented Nietzsche's genealogy of the genesis of the Christianized, bad conscience by pointing to just how much capitalist production and circulation are its perfection, that is, the outermost expression of a process begun in the ancient form of despotism. This brings them remarkably close to Benjamin's early understanding of "Capitalism as Religion."[14] For Benjamin insists, against Max Weber, that "the Christianity of the Reformation period did not favor the growth of capitalism; instead it transformed itself into capitalism."[15] Once this parasitic process catches enough momentum, punishment ceases to be festive and starts to become vengeful.[16] Repayment is increasingly deferred, the internalization and spiritualization of the process of defeat, of sadistic revenge turning back upon itself, ensues and is ultimately completed when, in Deleuze and Guattari's terms, nothing can "slip away from the body of the despot" that has now metamorphosed into the fascist state of *ressentiment*.[17] The cult of cults subsumes everything in what Benjamin calls the *Verschuldung* process. There are no reference points outside of this ever-spreading guilt. Hence, the possibility of atonement collapses as well, and the only thing offered up in exchange for it is total destruction: the perverse pleasure of watching your own demise. This is what, in part, governs Deleuze and Guattari's ire for Freud and psychoanalysis. "It's not Oedipus that produces neurosis; it is neurosis—*that is, a desire that is already submissive and is searching to communicate its own submission*—that produces Oedipus."[18] Again, they are remarkably close to Benjamin, who himself says that "Freud's theory, too, belongs to the hegemony of the priests of this cult [of capitalism]."[19] A priest's psychology that kowtows to domination, instead of resisting it, begins to spread like a weed. Everyone is gradually tamed. Masochistic passivity becomes universal by projecting its own practical immobility onto all activity, all displays of innocent vitality. Taking the debtor's side in, for example, the debt jubilees of the past, so that an infinite, unpayable debt or taxation is consolidated all the more,[20] eventually gives way to the seemingly "pure availability" of the post-Bretton-Woods, "dematerialized" form

---

[14] Walter Benjamin, "Capitalism as Religion," in *Selected Writings*, vol. 1, ed. Michael W. Jennings (Cambridge, MA: Harvard University Press, 2003), 288–91; "Kapitalismus als Religion," in *Gesammelte Schriften*, vol. 6, ed. Rolf Tiedemann and Hermann Scheppenhäuser (Frankfurt a.m.: Suhrkamp Verlag, 1974), 100–3.

[15] Ibid., 290/*GS6*, 102.

[16] Deleuze and Guattari, *Anti-Oedipus*, 212.

[17] Ibid., 213.

[18] Deleuze and Guattari, *Kafka*, 10.

[19] Benjamin, "Capitalism as Religion," 289/*GS6*, 101.

[20] Deleuze and Guattari, *Anti-Oedipus*, 213.

of capital.²¹ This suggests that the debt and guilt of the ancient world was ideally infinite, but became, under the total cult, actually infinite, since Christianized capitalism and capitalized Christianity cannot possibly repay he who allegedly redeems all sin, all guilt, or he who makes all things possible: capital personified. "[C]an one credit that?" asks Nietzsche about the God who dies out of love for his debtor?²² No wonder there are no weekdays anymore. No wonder the "sacred pomp" of the feast day is now unending. When the state begins to tap into so-called deep-time, into a qualitatively different flow than that of the simple exchange on which human cognition is based, its control becomes total.²³ Like cholera spreading in water, an unproductively productive restlessness consumes everything.²⁴ In Deleuze and Guattari's emphatic summary,

> the hypnosis and the reign of images, the torpor they spread; the hatred of life and of all that is free, of all that passes and flows; the universal effusion of the death instinct; depression and guilt used as a means of contagion, the kiss of the Vampire: aren't you ashamed to be happy? follow my example, I won't let go before you say, "It's my fault," O ignoble contagion of the depressives, neurosis as the only illness consisting in making others ill; the permissive structure: let me deceive, rob, slaughter, kill! but in the name of the social order, and so daddy-mommy will be proud of me; the double direction given to *ressentiment*, the turning back against oneself, and the projection against the Other: the father is dead, it's my fault, who killed him? it's your fault, it's the Jews, the Arabs, the Chinese, all the resources of racism and segregation; the abject desire to be loved, the whimpering at not being loved enough, at not being "understood," concurrent with the reduction of sexuality to the "dirty little secret," this whole priest's psychology—there is not a single one of these tactics that does not find in Oedipus its land of milk and honey, its good provider. Nor is there a single one of these tactics that does not serve and develop in psychoanalysis, with the latter as the new avatar of the "ascetic ideal."²⁵

Neither music nor political struggle are possible without attempting to overcome this guilt-nexus, which now, in the capitalist era, expresses the life-denying, ascetic ideal in the form of the Oedipal triangle. Even much of the LGBTQ+ movement stops at the homonationalist end of marriage equality.²⁶

---

[21] Ibid., 229, 237.
[22] Nietzsche, *On the Genealogy of Morals*, 92.
[23] Maurizio Lazzarato, *The Making of Indebted Man: An Essay on the Neoliberal Condition* (Los Angeles, CA: Semiotext(e), 2012), 84–5.
[24] Adorno, *Minima Moralia*, 138/GS4, 155.
[25] Deleuze and Guattari, *Anti-Oedipus*, 268–9.
[26] Jasbir Puar, *Terrorist Assemblages: Homonationalism in Queer Times* (Durham, NC: Duke University Press, 2006).

The always repressed, unnamable thing has been decoded.²⁷ As much, then, as Deleuze and Guattari have pinpointed the precise problematic, as much as this is the capitalist guilt that weighs too much, that debilitates the will to power and becomes outright nihilism, they do not appear to recognize the implications of assuming that the "line of escape," the "head over heels and away," comedic exit, or the deterritorialized burrow in the milieu also, by definition, sacrifice the possibility of a universal, collective emancipation.²⁸ The successful breakout is, in truth, spoiled in the very attempt, since the line of flight is granted, in the end, by accident, or worse, by a self-deceptive "pseudo-individualization" and a minoritarian drive that remains just that: minoritarian and thus incapable of helping the hopeless ones, the weak, or those who lay prostrate, at the absolute bottom of the wreckage of civilization.²⁹ To Deleuze's affirmative gesture, Adorno retorts, with Primo Levi: Why you? How did you happen upon this reprieve, this breath of air? Whence this opening that you've laid hold of? Whence this hope, this feathery light step against the spirit of gravity? In Adorno's formulation:

> The sedentary man envies the nomadic existence, the quest for fresh pastures, and the green waggon is the house on wheels whose course follows the stars. Infantility, spellbound [*gebannt*] in aimless motion, to the haplessly restless, instantaneous urge [*Drang*] to continue surviving, stands in for the undistorted, for fulfillment, and yet excludes it, internally resembling the self-preservation from which it falsely promises deliverance. This is the circle of the bourgeois longing for the naive. What is soulless in those who, at the margins of culture, are daily forbidden self-determination, grace and agony at the same time, becomes the phantasmagoria of the soul for the well-provided-for [*Wohlbestallten*], who learned from culture to be ashamed of the soul. Love loses itself to the soulless as to the cipher of the ensouled, because the living are the theater of the desperate desire for salvation, which has its object only in what is lost: love arises in the soul first in its absence. Thus, precisely the expression of the eyes that are closest to those of the animal, the creaturely ones, remote from the reflection of the ego, is human. In the end, soul itself is the longing of the soulless for salvation [*die Sehnsucht des Unbeseelten nach Rettung*].³⁰

---

²⁷ Deleuze and Guattari, *Anti-Oedipus*, 153.
²⁸ Deleuze and Guattari, *Kafka*, 6.
²⁹ For an example of Adorno's frequent use of the concept of pseudo-individualization, see T. W. Adorno and Hanns Eisler, *Composing for the Films* (New York: Oxford University Press, 1947), 19; *Komposition für den Film*, in *Gesammelte Schriften*, vol. 15, ed. Rolf Tiedemann (Frankfurt a.m.: Suhrkamp Verlag, 1972), 27.
³⁰ Adorno, *Minima Moralia*, 170 (translation modified)/*GS4*, 191–2.

Perhaps Deleuze is not the subject of criticism here insofar as he repeatedly attempts to impugn this sedentary impulse. When he, similarly, avoids the naiveté of the bourgeoisie by directing his reader to the manner in which nomadic flight and war implicitly contain the appropriations or parasitification of the state, he nonetheless fails to hear the moment of falsehood, the historical limitation, of the Nietzschean spirit. No doubt, the threat of re-Oedipalization, of ensnaring oneself in the reterritorializations of the guilt-nexus, always lurks as a possibility for Deleuze.[31] Yet, demanding a second naiveté before its conditions of production have ripened, sanctioning the return to myth, in contrast to Kafka, who, according to Benjamin, did not succumb to such a temptation, is tantamount to what Ernst Bloch described as opting for the "disaster-line" (*Unheilslinie*) of German fascism.[32] "As soon as naiveté is taken up as a point of view, it no longer exists."[33] The philosopher does immeasurable harm by disavowing that he has always been the "well-provided-for," Deleuze and Guattari, no less than Adorno, none of whom ever struggled to find a meal. Even if the minstrel of the land displays a stunning elusiveness, indeed, an improvisational strength that far exceeds the reductive theory of neurosis through which the mommy-daddy-me circuit is powered, his escape is certainly not predicated on his happiness or his overflowing abundance of life.[34] "Underlying the prevalent health," writes Adorno, thinking of his good-spirited or happy-go-lucky contemporaries, "is death."[35] Romanticization of the marginalized, a stand-in, exoticized pleasure, is the projection of those who secretly know that neither option, the state or the house on wheels, delivers one from the restless chase of natural-history. Animal eyes evoke this truth of universal impotence with a sorrow proportionate to the false semblance of those "who burst with proofs of exuberant vitality."[36] In the end, both the first- and second-nature iterations of the self-preservative urge are antithetical to reconciliation, which would sublate such desperate movement or else betray its oath to happiness and humanity. The soul of the soulless, the

---

[31] Deleuze and Guattari, *Kafka*, 36.
[32] Walter Benjamin, "Franz Kafka: On the Tenth Anniversary of His Death," in *Selected Writings*, vol. 2.2, ed. Michael W. Jennings (Cambridge, MA: Harvard University Press, 2003), 794–818, 799; "Franz Kafka: Zur zehnten Wiederkehr seines Todestages," in *Gesammelte Schriften*, vol. 2, ed. Rolf Tiedemann and Hermann Scheppenhäuser (Frankfurt a.m.: Suhrkamp Verlag, 1974), 409–38, 415; Bloch, *The Principle of Hope*, 274.
[33] Adorno, *Aesthetic Theory*, 336/GS7, 500.
[34] For an examination of how, on the one hand, Deleuze's joyous affirmation has been appropriated by the forces of reaction, but, on the other hand, how Deleuze's thinking nonetheless contains a negativity that stubbornly resists the status quo, see Andrew Culp, *Dark Deleuze* (Minneapolis: University of Minnesota Press, 2016).
[35] Adorno, *Minima Moralia*, 59/GS4, 65.
[36] Ibid., 59/GS4, 65.

sigh of the oppressed, without whose redemption in music neither the escapee nor those left behind can ever taste satisfaction, is sacrificed in the name of the sound and healthy, practical frame of mind. Lip service, by contrast, to the schizophrenic force of unhealth, to the "powers of the false,"[37] or the alleged resistance to the "straightening" path,[38] hardly changes the fact that the line of flight of this allegedly non-normalized, vital path almost always lifts off by inadvertently stepping on the throats of its brothers and sisters. Head over heels flight is actually a headlong rush (*Sturz*) caught up in the larger, plummeting movement of the whole.[39] This is Kafka's *Trauer*, the universal condition. That some are dispensed from the toil of material labor and accordingly take pleasure, like Zarathustra, in their own spirit is the "unjust privilege" par excellence.[40] Everyone should enjoy and is, to be sure, capable of enjoying, *theoria*. This is why Nietzsche, who garners the greatest challenge, who follows this modern problematic of disenchantment to its nauseating extreme, does not pronounce the last word on art and music after Auschwitz. When he, for example, claims the following about the relationship between the particular and the whole, the individual and the cosmological totality, the spirit of Blanqui, the defeated revolutionary, hauntingly awaits him with a rebuttal:

> If we affirm one single moment, we thus affirm not only ourselves but all existence. For nothing is self-sufficient, neither in us ourselves nor in things: and if our soul has trembled with happiness and sounded like a harp string just once, all eternity was needed to produce this one event and in this single moment of affirmation all eternity was called good, redeemed, justified, and affirmed.[41]

The obverse of this statement is no less true. "Once more," after the camps, is simply obscene.[42] Silenus was closer to the truth all along.[43] As the leader of the communards unwittingly revealed from a prison cell some ten years before Nietzsche's explicit doctrine, the eternal return is, in reality, a vision of hell.[44] To say yes to life, after the absolute worst has not only taken place but been perpetuated uninterruptedly, is not a sign of strength, of an ethics that, despite it all, endures the hardship by looking it squarely in the face.[45] It is rather an

---

[37] Deleuze, *Cinema 2*, 126–55.
[38] Deleuze and Guattari, *A Thousand Plateaus*, 14.
[39] Benjamin, "Capitalism as Religion," 288/GS6, 100.
[40] Adorno, "Marginalia to Theory and Praxis," 267/GS10.2, 768.
[41] Cited from Adorno, "Essay as Form," 23/GS11, 33.
[42] Friedrich Nietzsche, *The Gay Science*, trans. Walter Kaufmann (New York: Vintage, 1974), 274.
[43] Friedrich Nietzsche, *The Birth of Tragedy and the Case of Wagner*, trans. Walter Kaufmann (New York: Vintage, 1967), 42.
[44] Benjamin, *The Arcades Project*, 25/GS5.1, 75.
[45] In a highly troubling moment from Deleuze, *Logic of Sense*, 169, the author similarly sides with Fortuna, the enemy of music, as if he were, like Marinetti, harmonizing with the satanic laughter

indication of the approaching universalization of schizophrenia, of a feebleness that has been swallowed up in the abyss and, beyond good and evil, forgotten the truth-content of the unity of apperception on which genuine *praxis* must be based.[46] The strength of identity is to be used to cast off identity.[47] It cannot be spurned in advance. Even if one supposed the cosmos to be infinite; even if, as a result, unimaginable pleasure and fulfillment exist somewhere in the universe, God would still be drawn into the web of guilt, as Benjamin insists in his rewriting of Zarathustra, for having sanctioned the unspeakable, for having allowed *Schuld* and despair to extend to the infinite. Not a single moment of affirmation, not a single musical note, can resound beautifully if it is paid for with torture, if the unnecessary suffering of others is its precondition.[48] In this sense, Benjamin illuminates the most advance philosophical and aesthetic path, the weak, "barely hoped for" moment that, as Müller himself once contemplated, refuses to go on living and, fulfilling the nihilistic *telos* of despair, instead opts for the line of collapse, for not leaving one's brothers and sister behind, until the god of persecution is truly dead.[49] Life without the prospect of the emancipation of all is not worthy of the name. And this prospect—as dubious as it is utopian for the Realpolitik ideology—is not merely a theological residue. If all of labor simultaneously followed the line of torpor or the line of collapse, the "barely hoped for,"[50] world-historical general strike would be realized, not overpowered in quietism, as the apologists of pseudo-practice declare with a finger-wagging arrogance that is always within an inch of taking a swing. The unproductive is the truth of productivity. *Décroissance* is the truth of growth.

---

of the camps and the trenches: "[Bousquet] apprehends the wound that he bears deep within his body in its eternal truth as a pure event. To the extent that events are actualized in us, they wait for us and invite us in. They signal us: 'My wound existed before me, I was born to embody it.' Either ethics makes no sense at all, or this is what it means and has nothing else to say: not to be unworthy of what happens to us." Contrast this affirmative conception of the wound to Eric Oberle, *Theodor Adorno and the Century of Negative Identity* (Stanford, CA: Stanford University Press, 2018), 29–70, where the wound is investigated in relationship to Adorno's concept of "negative identity." Oberle is helpful, if somewhat too psychologizing, in tracking the development of Adorno's theory of jazz. His claim that applying Adorno's postwar reading of Heine could overcome the narrowness of his prewar reading of jazz is a noteworthy approach. For if, in the German context, kitsch romanticism or Mahler's "intentionally false" notes were self-consciously incorporated into the critique of a wounded and nonidentical culture, then a parallel logic is almost certain to be at play in many of the vernacular forms of expression in the US context.

[46] This forgotten truth-content is bound up with what Adorno calls the memory of the empirical subject. Adorno, *Kant's Critique of Pure Reason*, trans. Rodney Livingstone (Stanford, CA: Stanford University Press, 2001), 176; *Kants Kritik der reinen Vernunft*, in *Nachgelassene Schriften, Abteilung IV*, vol. 4 (Frankfurt am Main: Verlag, 1995), 268.

[47] Adorno, *Negative Dialectics*, 277/GS6, 274.

[48] Cf. Ursula K. Le Guin, "The Ones Who Walk Away from Omelas," in *New Dimensions* 3, ed. Robert Silverberg (New York: Doubleday, 1973).

[49] In contrast to Nietzsche, Benjamin insists that God is not dead. See Benjamin, "Capitalism as Religion," 289/GS6, 101.

[50] Ibid., 289 (translation modified)/GS6, 101.

Der Ursprung des Übermenschen

Refusing to reverse course, as Benjamin says of both Zarathustra and Marx's conception of capitalism, means that an explosive intensification (*Steigerung*) is gathering, that the simple and compound interest powering both the concretizations of constant capital and its counterpart, the relative and absolute surplus value extraction of variable capital, is reaching its zenith.[51] How much more can nature, internal and external, take? Whether, under immense pressure, it will splinter, like a torture device, into an even more terrible, fascist calamity or produce real transformation via the recoil of the drives, that is, the self-reflective, political expropriation of the General Intellect, remains to be seen.[52] Even if it cannot, therefore, magically wish away the guilt of its semblance,[53] advanced music continues to gesture negatively to the overcoming of this human, all-too-human stalemate. There are no gradual steps, no straight lines of development from the human to the post-human, from capitalism to socialism. Nor is there a predetermined path that would, by redeeming the debt of the past, expressly answer the call of suffering and achieve the impossible: undoing the wrong of infinite torment.[54] In the real paradigm shifts, rehearsed in, for instance, the turntable fragments that puncture the work of musicians such as Otomo Yoshihide and Mutamassik, the bottom drops out, so to speak, from the temporal continuum: *natura facit saltum*.[55] The sudden interlude to the first movement of Beethoven's late *String Quartet in E flat* is perhaps the first instance of this in Western music. In contrast to Richard Strauss's bombastic chauvinism, Benjamin's canceled and preserved version of Zarathustra arrives, with a flash of lighting, to the texture of a sawtooth waveform that cracks open the heavens. Is the *Übermensch* signaled, along these zigzagging lines, in the post-human, electronic ears of Kaitlyn Aurelia Smith's music, in the wet, oceanic ambiance of Fennesz's *Agora*, or in the glitching, xylophone reverb of Tim Hecker's industrial naturescapes? Perhaps, more accurately, the first murmurs of the still absent *people* are heard in the phase alternating syntheses of Page McConnel's Yamaha CS-60, in a music that has finally been plugged into the cosmological energy of the stars, into the blackhole singularities of Mike Gordon's Eventide plug-ins, and the computer-chip fuzz of subatomic depths? Zarathustra, the communist promise

---

[51] Ibid., 289/*GS6*, 101–2.
[52] Adorno, *Negative Dialectics*, 346/*GS6*, 339.
[53] Adorno, *Aesthetic Theory*, 160/*GS7*, 240.
[54] Améry, "Resentments," 72.
[55] Benjamin, "Capitalism as Religion," 289/*GS6*, 101.

of redemption, then? Zarathustra, the figure of the electroacoustic transition, or better, the discontinuous leap (*Sprung*), to a second innocence (*Unschuld*)? Only if, to paraphrase Wolfgang Hilbig's melancholic lament, he can find a way to lock arms with others and, ipso facto, begin transforming, begin taking up, the debt that has hitherto been impossible to bear: the mass grave of bodies and languages, the mass grave of mass movements and subjugated-knowledges, of hopes and resignations forgotten, of eons of accumulated dead matter, of the tree of taboos whose shadow shrouds every memory in darkness, to the point at which the line between the living and the dead, between nature-decay and societal-rot, becomes virtually indiscernible.[56] Only if the subject of history is, in brief, driven *through* the *Verschuldung* process, rather than *away* from it;[57] only if the mimetic absorption *in* and the concomitant drive to sublate the unbearable noise *of* nature prevails over the current process of inoculation, of fallaciously withstanding the intolerable by deferring the inevitable confrontation a little while longer. In mimetically becoming like the hardened and alienated, in taking up the *Schuld*, the dead-labor of the vanquished through which law-preserving catastrophe is perpetuated, music implicitly begins to ask: What is the sound of interpellation? What is the sound of the state of emergency? Little by little, it discovers that which experimental film discovered a century ago, that which music began flirting with in, for example, the sorrowful, *flâneur* wonderings of Eric Satie's piano works and, later, the deranged nursery rhymes of Nurse with Wound. It discovers, that is to say, the blood-soaked farce and the gallows humor of a surrealism barred from premature celebration.[58] Not only do chimneys and fireflies start to blend with cigarette ends and city lights to rearrange the images of the collective unconscious.[59] Not only do shooting stars and airplane trails begin to light up the path of music. The tonal range of what has, for so many, signified nothing other than punishment, the shudder inducing fright of the YHAAVALE Police Siren, is also taken up, canceled, and preserved by an experimentation that refuses to turn away from this technological variation in the aural dialectic of natural-historical domination. In this sense, electroacoustic music acts, as both Nietzsche and Marx promised, for the sake of the consonance that must, as yet,

---

[56] Wolfgang Hilbig, *Old Rendering Plant*, trans. Isabel Fargo Cole (San Francisco: Two Lines Press, 2017), 70–7.
[57] This irreversible passing through is also implied in what Benjamin calls the method of nihilism in Walter Benjamin, "Theological-Political Fragment," in *Selected Writings*, vol. 3, ed. Michael W. Jennings (Cambridge, MA: Harvard University Press, 2003), 306; "Theologisch-Politisches Fragment," in *Gesammelte Schriften*, vol. 2, ed. Rolf Tiedemann and Hermann Scheppenhäuser (Frankfurt a.m.: Suhrkamp Verlag, 1974), 204.
[58] Benjamin, "Surrealism," 216/GS2, 307.
[59] Deleuze, *Cinema 2*, 57.

be withheld. A glimpse of a world beyond the sacrifice of human and nonhuman animals flits past in a regulative pursuit that promises to be "on par with [its] instrument"[60] and, in so doing, promises to keep open, in Benjamin's words, the prospect of one day "responding to the new technological possibilities with a new social order."[61] The poison already contains the healing antidote.

The Categorical Imperative of Music

Assuming, as one must, that there are no easy answers for the critical theory and practice of music today, no forthcoming solutions to the antinomy of the present guilt-nexus, one can nonetheless glean something of the, so to speak, vague outline within which critical music might still be possible. The categorical imperative of musical form would have to be an imperative to make music as if it were repaying in equal measure the survivor's guilt of those who have, on the one hand, been spared and, on the other, gone on "living" by refusing to admit, in repression, precisely this sacrificial precondition of their temporary security. Social labor has always been reproduced via the objective expulsion of the powerless and a corresponding subjective disavowal of the manner in which this very expulsion is the collective condition for the possibility of accumulated "wealth," that is, relative, class-based safety. The composer as producer would have to be compelled, then, to make music as if she were living, as Adorno once put it, the insane wish of someone who failed to escape the camps, whether these are understood as Warsaw, Gaza, or El Paso, Texas.[62] This would, furthermore, mean composing music that acts as if it could be the grounds of disenchantment, as if it could exorcise the demons of the past. So long as the reconfiguration of social reality via *praxis* is, in truth, the only basis of repayment (*Vergeltung*),[63] art will, of course, fall short of the goal. This immanent impossibility, which artworks must, with a bad conscience, deny, lest they acquiesce to reification, is the unresolved lineage of their omnipotent fantasy. Yet, artworks can and have on many occasions become conscious of the guilt-relation within which they are enmeshed. In, for instance, the basalt tombstones of Joseph Beuys's *The End*

---

[60] Walter Benjamin, "Little History of Photography," in *Selected Writings*, vol. 2.2, ed. Michael W. Jennings (Cambridge, MA: Harvard University Press, 2003), 507–30, 514; "Kleine Geschichte der Photographie," in *Gesammelte Schriften*, vol. 2, ed. Rolf Tiedemann and Hermann Scheppenhäuser (Frankfurt a.m.: Suhrkamp Verlag, 1974), 368–85, 374.
[61] Benjamin, *Arcades Project*, 26/GS5.1, 76.
[62] Adorno, *Negative Dialectics*, 363/GS6, 356.
[63] Ibid., 363 (translation modified)/GS6, 356.

of the Twentieth Century, or the protruding texture of the flowers that, as ashen as the smoke of the crematoria, blend with the barbed wire of Anselm Kiefer's paintings, the subject of art reflects the fact that a stolen supply of air is what, in actuality, nourishes the vitality of the work in the first place. What affirmative culture calls "life" appears, in works such as these, as the unimpeded march of death. Ferdinand Kürnberger gives the lie to Deleuze's false optimism.

Little Hans's Lullaby

Analytically speaking, the task of driving music to the point of self-consciousness appears in an especially acute light when the minute difference between Adorno's and Deleuze's perspective on the famous case of Little Hans is examined. Recall that for Deleuze, Herbert Graf's "truly political option" consists in his chance to become horse and courageously flee to the street, where he once witnessed the horrific, traumatizing collapse.[64] Instead of continuing to play the imitative game of the family imposed upon him by Freud's imputation of a neurosis caused by castration anxiety or sibling rivalry, becoming-horse is, for Deleuze and Guattari, a kind of schizophrenic rerouting of the flow of desire that purportedly avoids Freud's straightening, normative violence. This is, to express it succinctly, an exemplary case of "schizophrenia without the schizophrenic."[65] The potential for a nonrepresentational becoming-animal is missed by psychoanalysis, then, and this, according to the authors of *A Thousand Plateaus*, has frighteningly reactionary political consequences.[66] In territorializing desire from within the narrow circuits of the fascist state-machine, it actually fuels the explosive revenge fantasies that, for the sake of the victims, the imperative of art aims to calm. Overflow is seldom on the side of a transformative politics. Adorno, who only alludes to Graf's case, parallels this warning against what he, in his essay on Kafka, refers to as the archaic spell of the family, that is, the socially necessary complicity of the bourgeois household in the reproduction of the at once totalitarian and prehistoric state.[67] But he also amplifies a resonance that likely eludes the non-German speaker. He does this by discussing a lullaby that

---

[64] Deleuze and Guattari, *A Thousand Plateaus*, 14.
[65] Gilles Deleuze and Félix Guattari, "La synthèse disjonctive," *L'arc* 43, special issue on Pierre Klossowski (Aix-en-Provence: Duponchelle, 1970): 56.
[66] Deleuze and Guattari, *A Thousand Plateaus*, 259.
[67] T. W. Adorno, "Notes on Kafka," in *Prisms*, trans. Samuel Weber and Shierry Weber Nicholsen (Cambridge, MA: MIT Press, 1984), 263; "Aufzeichnungen zu Kafka," in *Gesammelte Schriften*, vol. 10.1, ed. Rolf Tiedemann (Frankfurt a.m.: Suhrkamp Verlag, 1972), 276–7.

almost every German speaker knows from their youth, namely *Hänschen klein*. Just as Deleuze and Guattari encourage a route that discourages conventionality, Adorno seeks to show the offensive character of the standardized ditty, in this case, the predigested familiarity of a melody whose imperfect cadence directly calls for the "symmetrical fulfillment" of a perfect cadence.[68] To reified consciousness, "Little Hans / went alone [*Hänschen klein/Ging allein*]" already implies the next verse, "out into the wide world [*In die weite Welt hinein*]," and the masochistic lonely crowd is ready, with the rage of the brownshirts, to pounce on anyone who might upset this "appealing" (*sympathisch*) anticipation of the ever-identical.[69] At the same time, beyond Deleuze and Guattari's analysis, Adorno extracts from this Biedermeier period tune the truth-content of the lullaby as such. Hans, he says, "does not go out into the wide world at all, because he has always been entirely alone."[70] This insight cannot be taken for granted, even by the strongest, most autonomous or separatist community, for it is based on a material contradiction, on a blockage that objectively limits the flow of everyone's movement. The escape to the street is just as perilous as the return home when mother recognizes you with a "Grüß dich gott." A twice-removed parody of 1936, anarchist rebellion under the current social formation is more infantile than Fabrice's attempt in *The Charterhouse of Parma* to storm out into canon fire and become a hero.[71] When war becomes a farcical repetition of the tragedy that once was, suicide and opiate addiction are all that can reasonably be expected from repatriation. Hans is alone, and no homecoming or rebellious flight, allegedly having escaped its dependency on the past, social labor of others, will suffice to fill the void. In this context, the functionless function of advanced music—the only help—converges with the critico-philosophical task of exposing the lie of pseudo-praxis. This is part of what Adorno detects in Schoenberg's music, especially his early work, *Erwartung*. In the same way as a collective debt weighs on every last one of us, so a collective loneliness, which is "that of city dwellers who no longer know each other,"[72] contracts to the point of crystallizing an entire style. Music can only be adequate to the universal intolerability of the lonely condition by wishing to silence any work, including itself, that would deny this fact. Deleuze's essay on Beckett, which claims that art eventually, in a parallel fashion, aims to *exhaust* all possibilities, comes closer to the emphatic

---

[68] Adorno, *Aesthetics*, 192/*NS*3, 305.
[69] Ibid., 193/*NS*3, 307.
[70] Ibid., 192/*NS*3, 306.
[71] Stendhal, *The Charterhouse of Parma*, trans. Richard Howard (New York: Modern Library, 2000).
[72] Adorno, *Philosophy of New Music*, 41 (translation modified)/*GS*12, 51.

nature of Adorno's critique than his work with Guattari.⁷³ The "Beloved, Beloved, morning is coming" from measure 389 of *Erwartung* harkens to more than the sun-rising ship of redemption in *Tristan*. It also harkens to the self-preservative vow of the lullaby's own dawn. Utterly alienated, "[t]housands of people march past," as though you are caught in a time-lapse video that cannot be slowed.⁷⁴ The "Be still," which self-reflection was supposed to impart to the knowledge of a temporary captivity, illuminates, in Schoenberg's music, an imprisonment that is, in truth, as old as Socrates's dissatisfactory consolation.⁷⁵ "Nature," as Adorno describes it in the concluding lines of the *Naturgeschichte* fragment of *Negative Dialectics*, "becomes the irresistible allegory of imprisonment [*Gleichnis der Gefangenschaft*]."⁷⁶ The material ground that would calm the nerves before impending sleep is still absent. The sun has yet to rise on a new day. Without resolving the contradiction, the "absolute monad" of the work of art, which is a windowless expression of the absolute despair of the totality, thus embodies, in Adorno's words, "resistance to spurious socialization," but also "a willingness to endure even worse."⁷⁷ It will not, in other words, abide the false reconciliation between monad and totality, individual and collective. A preestablished *disharmony* blocks any premature claim to have overcome the lonely condition.⁷⁸ This is why even the dissonant expression of music fails or, forgetting its genesis, eventually hardens into abstract dissonance.⁷⁹ Pointing out the false choice between the lonely street and the lonely charnel house of the bourgeois family alerts domination, which knows nothing but blind force, that you have not yet been defeated. The strong are weak, in this sense, for having endured what seemed like the worst.⁸⁰ Their survival provokes a response that will almost certainly be even more horrifying than the last iteration of law-preserving violence. "And how comfortless," writes Adorno, in a similar context, "is the thought that the sickness of the normal does not necessarily imply as its opposite the health of the sick, but that the latter usually only present, in a different way, the schema of the same disaster."⁸¹ Neither art nor theory can resolve the contradiction.

---

[73] Deleuze, "The Exhausted," 170.
[74] Adorno, *Philosophy of New Music*, 41/GS12, 51.
[75] Ibid., 41/GS12, 51.
[76] Adorno, *Negative Dialectics*, 358 (translation modified)/GS6, 351.
[77] Adorno, *Philosophy of New Music*, 41/GS12, 52.
[78] Adorno, "Short Commentaries," 177/GS11, 206.
[79] Adorno, *Aesthetic Theory*, 15/GS7, 30.
[80] Cf. Primo Levi, "Shame," in *The Drowned and the Saved*, trans. Raymond Rosenthal (New York: Vintage, 1989), 82.
[81] Adorno, *Minima Moralia*, 60 (translation modified)/GS4, 65.

The Most Advanced

The culture industry is the name of this willingness to endure more suffering. Günther Anders once described it as Promethean shame, a concept that is intimately related to the interiorization of *Schuld*. He, more specifically, understood this stage in the composition of capital as a stage in which the body is forced to stretch itself beyond the "human" threshold in a series of disciplinary tests concerning what is and is not bearable.[82] Ashamed before the engineering efficiency of the machine, before its artificial superiority, "humans" flee to the camp of the machine, unflinchingly accepting their status as appendages. They know that they can never measure up, can never be as well polished as the second-nature, GPS precision with which the war economy reproduces the system as a whole. If the rate of exploitation can never abate, then nature will have to bear the compounding intensifications of surplus value extraction through which it flows. The objective compulsion of a music that would live up to both the victim's torment and her corresponding dream—that no one, under any circumstance, shall be subjected to torture again—might, therefore, be described as the task of becoming a dialectical composer. Transgressing the limit hitherto posited by capital by exposing its own limit recommences as the guiding impulse. By this nothing more is meant than that music is compelled, for the sake of its own concept, to search for the next "syntheses," the advanced developments that are only now becoming recognizable. To renounce this goal, which is virtually the stated program of contemporary philosophy, having long since consigned dialectics to the dustbin of history, is to do nothing short of abandoning the attempt to harness the substantial element of art's form: its voice of suffering.[83] The emancipatory means cannot possibly be the same today as they were yesterday. Nor, by implication, can the means of convalescence, the basis of the proletariat's power.[84] Peter Bürger's and Arthur Danto's similar theses on the impossibility of bindingly distinguishing the "most advanced" (*fortgeschrittenste*) truth of modern artworks from their regressive counterparts prove to be wide of the mark.[85] Critical philosophical reflection is not only required to assess the balance of forces through which labor might successfully launch a counterattack against capital; it is required and, indeed,

---

[82] Anders, "On Promethean Shame," 41.
[83] Adorno, *Aesthetic Theory*, 260/GS7, 386–7.
[84] Benjamin, *One-Way Street*, 487/GS4, 148.
[85] Bürger, *Theory of the Avant-garde*; Arthur C. Danto, *After the End of Art: Contemporary Art and the Pale of History* (Princeton, NJ: Princeton University Press, 1997).

quite capable of elucidating the political complicity in the neutral, liberal, or "anything goes" position, whether of the political or musical-formal variety.[86] Above all others, Michael Gordon's music embodies this dialectical imperative, which, stated differently, amounts to the only route through which one can legitimately keep faith with the task of critique. Although there are a wide range of solutions that could all justifiably be called dialectical, the force of both theory and aesthetic comportment depends, as Adorno says, on illuminating "the contours of a burned-out prehistory with the glow of the latest disaster in order to perceive the parallel that exists between them."[87] He could just as well be referring to Gordon's music, which unremittingly critiques and rescues the myth through which disaster is perpetuated, which never tires of unearthing the rational kernel to the mystical shell of his predecessors' music, and which finds expression, unlike the works of so many of his contemporaries, in and through mastering the most advanced technical means.

Aeon and Chronos

As is so often the case with so many present-day composers, most egregiously Hans Zimmer, whose music often resembles the feature film trailer music of Paul Dinletir and Kevin Rix's unabashedly named "audiomachine," Gordon spent his early years of composition trying to, so to speak, rock-and-roll-ify art-music. This is clearly at work in several of the Bang on a Can productions with David Lang and Julia Wolfe, as well as in the early work, *Trance*, for the Icebreaker Ensemble, where a set of conspicuously Reichian, post-minimalist, electronic guitars, cellos, and violins drive the development with a heavy-handed, clanking repetition that affords the listener none of the overtone resonance constitutive of more mature works such as *Rushes* and *"8"*. Electronification is obtrusive in the former attempts, but not in the sense of upsetting the norms of listening, rather, in the sense of giving the audience exactly what it wants: the familiar tone of chic, amplified, rockstar instruments.[88] A similar false need is at play in segments

---

[86] One indication of both theory and aesthetic practice failing to embody this critical reflection is what Adorno calls the "slackening" or "loss" of tension (*Spannungsverlust*) of the work. See, for example, Adorno, *Aesthetic Theory*, 53/GS7, 85.

[87] Adorno, "Reflections on Class Theory," 95/GS8, 375.

[88] This consumer demand to not be bothered with anything that might intrude upon listening conventions is paralleled in Adorno and Eisler's discussion of the prejudice regarding how film music should not be heard or should not intrude upon the primary function of film, namely providing optical pleasure. Adorno and Eisler, *Composing for the Films*, 9–12/GS15, 19–21.

of Gordon's work for the Ensemble Resonanz, *Weather*, where a "drum-and-bass" studio modification lends the allegro interval of the orchestral second movement the veneer of fashionability, of being up-to-date and hip enough to meet the consumption demands of the beat. If the late 1990s pressures of state austerity, privatization, and the apparent decline in the patronage of the nation's "cultural treasures" did not cause panic about the viability of "serious music" among every student of music history, the pan-radio assault of the culture industry was enough to discipline taste into obediently identifying with exchange-value. Like staging Shakespeare in updated, imperial garb, as if that did not hallow out the substance of the early modern constellation, choosing indiscriminately from a grab-bag of styles, each of which was formed in a disparate, historical climate, gave the appearance of freedom. Jimi Hendrix combined with the minimalism of the Kronos Quartet and autumnal adagio of Vivaldi seemed like the antidote that was needed. But this was a caricature of *musique informelle*, which demands that all possibilities are, on the contrary, possibilities by virtue of an immanent necessity, a compulsion (*Nötigung*) that irresistibly compels the next development. Such confusion was likely grounded in the fact that the catastrophe seemed to be taking place on the periphery, conveniently off the omnipresent screen of the culture industry. The euphoria of the "postmodern" economic boom and the fall of the iron curtain slackened the tension—suffering unresolved—from which integral music springs. Hence, the best that one can say of music like this is that it abstractly incorporates previously alien instruments and textures, as well as exoticized cultural forms, instead of reciprocally constituting them on the basis of their own plane of consistency. Incorporation amounts to compromise, that is, capitalist subsumption, when an immanent force is not the source of the need to reconfigure or expand the points that, as it were, comprise the musical constellation. Fidelity to form, to following out technique, wherever it might take you, teaches this truth. A painstaking dedication to practice, in fact, taught Gordon precisely this dialectical lesson of only following those impulses that search for the hidden "language within the language" of form,[89] the missed chance or "inconspicuous spot" that, to paraphrase Benjamin's theory of the photographic aura, is the future nestled in the long-forgotten past, the future waiting to be rediscovered.[90] With time and, arguably, within the immanent unfolding of *Weather* itself, Gordon came to realize that the unfulfilled hope sedimented in form is never revealed unless

---

[89] Deleuze, "Life and Literature," 5.
[90] Benjamin, "Little History of Photography," 510/*GS2*, 369.

form itself is pushed to the edge of comprehensibility. "The dialectic moves by way of extremes."[91] Everything else conforms to the empty play, the abstract need, of the new. Despite the undialectical residue of the second movement, *Weather*, which was composed in 1997, already on the whole shows a dialectical subtlety that, at times, escapes even one of the so-called fathers of electroacoustic music, namely Karlheinz Stockhausen. Take, for example, Stockhausen's celebrated *Helicopter Quartet*. The primary gesture of this work is, for all intents and purposes, on the side of the advance of enlightenment. A music that fails to address the noise of industry and permanent war would inevitably betray its immanent pursuit of happiness; it would flatly regress to myth by disavowing its conditions of production. And yet, the string instruments in this work stand over and against the recorded sounds of the helicopter. An abstract, indifferent relation between the contrasting "voices" prevails. Just as, on another plane, George Russell's electronic surge stands over and against his jazz ensemble in *Electric Sonata for Souls Loved*, Stockhausen fails to sublate, to constitute reciprocally, the previously one-sided relationship. Unlike Pimmon, who makes an active instruments of the noisy effect, who blends the entire *tableau* of musical textures, so that a glitching monitor is indistinguishable from a muscle spasm or concussion, the noise of the helicopters is foisted heteronomously upon the traditional instruments.[92] Their machinic thrumming remains a separate track on an 8-track analogue recorder cleansed of any imbrication with the other tracks. The traditional instruments have not, then, come to reflect the noise that is latent within them. In contrast, the state of emergency that is conjured up from the siren movement of *Weather* drives music further. It parts ways with the limitations of both Gordon's partner, David Lang, and his teacher, Martin Bresnick, each of whom still takes solace in the, so to speak, heartfelt sojourn to the countryside, instead of reflecting the industrial wasteland of the present. This means that the limits of minimalism are finally being driven *through* the noise that Reich and Glass, Nyman and Bryars, could only deflect. A minor,

---

[91] Adorno, *Minima Moralia*, 86/GS4, 94.
[92] The historical limits of an earlier stage in the dialectic between forces and relations of production are revealed in Adorno's analysis of music too. In 1967 he, for example, could still maintain that Stockhausen's experimentations made clear that the tonal range of the electroacoustic did not, as was initially hoped, extend the tonal range of the traditional, unamplified orchestra. This was true at the time, insofar as attempts to combine these two planes of musical color faltered. But, since that time, the gap in the continuum between abstractly distinguished planes of sound has been overcome dialectically, the "integral orchestra" has been realized. As was likely already evident in Boulez, but is certainly present in an array of contemporary film scores, as well as the filtered reverb effects of, for instance, Ashley Bathgate's and Zoë Keating's cello performances, the electroacoustic and the previously "homogeneous" orchestra are no longer, in critical works, oppositional in the same way. See Adorno, "Art and the Arts," 382–3/GS10.1, 448.

digitally elongated piano note resonates before it is abruptly sucked up, as it were, in the transitional refrains of the first movement. These minor, bass echoes are unobtrusive, however. In keeping with this subtlety, the rain recording that inaugurates the first movement—no doubt, as abstract as Stockhausen's helicopter or Francisco López's insects—is transformed, by the fourth movement, into an abstract machine. This, paradoxically, constitutes its concretion and immanence.[93] Thus the hovering, background, static fuzz and the hovering, background, industrial generator, neither of which are noticed *as* background. No one would dare say, "ah-ha, that's rain; ah-ha, that's a piece of industry." In fact, the most dialectical moments of this work are so attuned to the play between identity and nonidentity that the "how beautiful" moment before the sublimity of nature-beauty (*Naturschöne*) returns in the most-mediated, synthetic presentation of art-beauty (*Kunstschöne*).[94] No plush landscapes or mountaintops, no crashing waves, mighty rivers, or hurricanes are directly presented, and yet nature speaks all the more eloquently in their absence. The nonrepresentational, technical mastery of form impels the soloist virtuosity of the past to sink down into the dynamic movement of the whole, so that no instrument is more important than the next, so that nature-sounds become indistinguishable from the social products and instruments of civilization. A fleeting space between nature and society, between the machine and the nonintentionality of the so-called organic, opens up in, of all places, the studio. The echo of a barely audible, electronic turn of the pitch-bend-wheel feels like the soft winter breeze that, from nothing, wafts by in Werther's forlorn diary entry.[95] The watery vapor of this same breeze is evoked as well. But this is possible only via the power of negation, at once conceptual and nonconceptual, via, that is, the outright withdrawal of the original rain recording and all of the visual associations that attend it. Pointillist fluttering, microtonal sprinklings, fill the floating, electroacoustic space and are critically juxtaposed to the momentous rhythm of the strings. The animating compulsion powering the dialectic of natural-history finds an outlet precisely because nature is remembered in the nonsensuous similarity between what was and what is. At one end, the extreme of prehistorical,

---

[93] This sense of the concretion of the so-called abstract machine or, in Marx's terms, this "real abstraction" of the more developed stage of capitalism is perhaps best expounded in Deleuze and Guattari, *Kafka*, 48, 86–8. Eventually the abstraction of the transcendental law (of value) no longer stands outside of the concrete, as in the despotic stage of justice, but rather "diffuses into" it. This real subsumption of all immanence and this immanence of all real subsumption not only unfolds in *The Trial*, as Deleuze and Guattari argue, but also in the history of music.

[94] Adorno, *Aesthetic Theory*, 69/GS7, 108.

[95] Johann Wolfgang von Goethe, *The Sufferings of Young Werther*, trans. Stanley Corngold (New York: W.W. Norton and Company, 2012), 68–9.

uncorrupted nature—probably only ever a nostalgic projection—endowed with biodiversity, a self-regenerating metabolism (*Stoffwechsel*), and an almost infinite array of playful, evolutionary variations.[96] At the other end, the extreme of total reification, of electricity surging through every layer, silicone clogging every membrane, atrophying every dendrite, no less than every rhizomatic vein, river channel, or passageway of the nutrient depleted, urbanized globe. Growing tauter by the second, each extreme incessantly pulls at the other until, all at once, in an ephemeral snapshot, the beholder of advanced music looks up at the divided sky to see, on this chance occasion, a jet airplane slowly crossing over the white glow reflection of the sun on the moon. Sure that she, like the beholder, must be stirred by the scene, Artemis disappoints as only she can. For she remains as silent and unmoved as she was 4 billion years ago, as silent and unmoved as she was amid the bombardments, historical and celestial, that have never stopped wreaking havoc upon the surface of the earth. Thus the momentary standstill in the face of the self-preservative bustle. Thus the resignation before the natural-historical technology of death reaches its apex and then descends, irresistibly, to the flight path of a ballistic projectile. With every meteor and bomb, an echo as deafeningly mute as the crash of uncounted coils that Aeon is said to have sloughed off resounds.[97] The time signature of Chronos seems, by contrast, to be as uniform as the red-light flash of distant radio towers and passing satellites. Like the "fixed element" whose "high note hovers for two measures" above the silent beat, the static indifference to the dynamic chaos surrounding it gives the lie to the dominion of historical time.[98] Deleuze's filmic, "motionless at a great pace," is realized in an autonomous music that, holding fast to these polar extremes, reinvigorates the aural and visual, natural and technological, movement of the dialectic.[99] In the image of unfulfilled nature, the musical wish of the optical unconscious dawns. Its mute gesture says: One day another age will come to pass. One day the dominion of war will cease to be.

---

[96] Massumi, *What Animals Teach Us about Politics*, 13. For a look at how the concept of metabolism (*Stoffwechsel*) figures in the theory of social ecology, see J. B. Foster, "Marx's Theory of Metabolic Rift: Classical Foundations for Environmental Sociology," *American Journal of Sociology* 143 (September 1999): 366–405.

[97] Deleuze and Guattari, *A Thousand Plateaus*, 261–2. In an attempt to avoid dialectics, Deleuze and Guattari assert that Chronos and Aeon work on two qualitatively different planes. This aphorism, on the contrary, insists upon the dialectically constituted nature of these allegedly discrete forms of temporality.

[98] Deleuze, "Boulez, Proust, and Time," 72.

[99] Deleuze, *Cinema 2*, 59. In opposition to what Benjamin describes as the vacuous debates concerning the legitimacy of "photography-as-art," this construction aims to consider the natural-historical significance of "art-as-photography" or "art-as-film." It, in other words, suggests that the critical understanding of the natural history of music must, despite the acoustic primacy of music, be grasped as the history of the dialectical image.

Involuntary Reproduction

It is not accidental that a decisive turning point in Gordon's oeuvre proceeded from catastrophic events. Nor is it surprising that what resulted was a form that, at times, concerns the becoming-child of music and, at others, sharpens the aural problem-nexus (*Problemzusammenhang*) of the state of emergency.[100] The looping siren from "Weather Three," which makes a fugue of this emergency warning by differentiating each "voice" in a lower or higher octave from the original, points the way forward. The poison becomes a counter-poison in this movement, as the higher-register pitch is stretched to the entrancing, repetitive limit. Beethoven's angelic longing is recapitulated with each extension, but now it bears within itself the negativity of its soaring flight. It knows that it cannot wish away, with a magical wand, the danger from which it flees. The technique that was perhaps first experimented with in Gordon's earlier *Industry* and *Potassium*, namely using electronic tempo changes to alter the tonal landscape, anticipates works like *Rewriting Beethoven's Seventh Symphony* and *The Sad Park* from the first decade of the volatile twenty-first century. In using this technique to unfurl the, so to speak, thread of a note within a cello's note-cluster, Gordon was already illuminating the chemical breakdown implicit in the instruments of the era of handcraft. Fuzz box distortion, as well as the repetition of major and minor chords *sliding* into atonality, likewise suggested that there was no turning back anymore, that music would have to turn *toward* the catastrophe, *toward* the decaying sounds of mechanical reproduction, or else confess its allegiance to reactionary nostalgia. In *Rewriting*, the first phrase of Beethoven's *poco sostenuto* loops continuously. This reminds one of the jutting, almost shrill, loops of the string instruments from *Clouded Yellow*. As if incapable of getting off the ground, incapable of modulating to C and F major like the original score, in Gordon's hands, Beethoven is turned, bit by bit, against himself. A repudiation of the positive dialectic, of the gapless continuum of the march of freedom, supervenes. Only the skeletal remains of the apotheosis of dance endure the *Vergänglichkeit* of nature. Similarly, in *The Sad Park*, a recording of a child's turn of phrase, "two evil planes, broke," is slowed down, as in Alvin Lucier's *I am Sitting in a Room*, and passed through filters to reveal, with each repetition, an inner resonance of terror in the barely articulate, innocent tone of dismay vis-à-vis the crumbling Twin Towers. When Kluge said of Leonard Warren that there was a metallic core to his voice, he was, without knowing it, touching upon the

---

[100] Adorno, *Aesthetic Theory*, 358/*GS7*, 532.

natural-historical dialectic of song that Gordon's music unveils.[101] This metallic core, which comprises the virtual resonance of mechanical reproduction, is internal to, and detachable from, every voice. In the case of *The Sad Park*, as each loop curves back in upon itself, a melodic voice tries to escape the curse of the new within which Hans and every unborn child is trapped. It seems to be a soprano or maybe a thousand shards of Clara Rockmore's theremin.[102] In *"8"*, it is a humming, Gouldian baritone or maybe the wisdom of your grandfather's voice. And in *Light Is Calling* it is a moaning children's choir. Perfume- and cologne-scented guests from faraway lands, these involuntary melodies assuage the fairytale presentiment that a kidnapper lurks around the corner.[103] Paralleling Alain Resnais's unforgettable image of Japanese children halted from the onward procession and primped by adults in the impossible attempt to remember, through representation, the bombing of Hiroshima, humankind's unconscious despair over its reproductive labor finally becomes conscious. The "wish to live on," projected onto the child, "the chimera of the never known thing," was always allied with death.[104] This is not the external audio sample, then, that is so ominously weaved into the concluding moments of "Weather Four," the muffled orders of the bomber command. This is the voice within the voice of the overtone that is finally being released and antiphonally echoed in both the instrument and the effect. Still, Gordon's "unconscious self-consciousness"[105] of the involuntary moment arguably only truly comes into its own in works such as *Timber*, written for amplified simantras, and *Rushes*, written for seven bassoons. In both of these works, which are ostensibly limited by the monochromatic range of their chosen instruments, heavy-handed form drops away, as it were, no longer appearing to impose its technique, the made, upon the immanent, textural movement, the not made.[106] Gordon follows John Adams but then supersedes him. Thousands upon thousands of rapid-fire, percussive repetitions are layered one upon the other. This divisionist procedure—Seurat without a corresponding image—gives rise to floating overtones never before heard in music, not even György Ligeti's. Without anticipation, it is as though these overtones then, of their own volition, produce hidden, singing melodies. But these phantom voices released

---

[101] Alexander Kluge and Gerhard Richter, *Dispatches from Moments of Calm*, trans. Nathaniel McBride (New York: Seagull Books, 2016), 23.
[102] For an analysis that, in examining Rockmore's music, troubles the traditional, masculine origin stories of electronic music, see Tara Rodgers, *Pink Noise: Women on Electronic Music and Sound* (Durham, NC: Duke University Press, 2010), 8–10.
[103] Adorno, *Minima Moralia*, 177–8/GS4, 199–201.
[104] Ibid., 238/GS4, 270.
[105] Adorno, *Aesthetic Theory*, 8/GS7, 19.
[106] Ibid., 131/GS7, 199.

from purgatory are not part of the graphic notation. They are discovered in the performance itself.[107] This music rushes, it ebbs and flows, like nonintentional nature. It communicates as Thoreau's telegraph harp does. Every pore and fiber of wood swells with an electric current, as if it were played by the elemental and cosmological winds of a tenth, long-forgotten Muse.[108] Upon first listening to *Rushes* without knowledge of the score, one is convinced that there must be flutes, saxophones, and even double-basses accompanying the bassoons. Not so. One instrument smoothly becomes another instrument, as if the music were not composed at all, as if the bassoon contained the hopes of all the other instruments within itself. Without offering a single visual cue, the most refined expression of Gordon's music plays on the similarity between the reed of the instrument and the reedy growth of the forest, on the subway metal that vibrates, in Gordon's own words, mournfully and the orgiastic, low-down growl of ducks and bullfrogs. Even the high-pitched singing of chorus frogs and power-drill repetition of American toad calls adorn the brackish water that flows through the estuaries of Michael Gordon's industrial naturescape.

Indifferenzpunkt

On the hottest day of summer, the Paleokastritsa Harbour of Corfu, Greece, where Odysseus is said to have disembarked, fills the visitor of this myth-enshrouded waterfront with a sensation like few others. The depth of Ionian Sea runs so deep that months of the sun's sweltering, equator heat are incapable of warming the water above its constant, nearly frozen state. For millennia, the Corfu Jews, precariously fluctuating, as elsewhere in Europe, between equal rights, ghettoization, and blood libel pogroms, must have found in these waters a singular feeling of absolution, a glimpse of another world that the persecuted know intimately, and that, by virtue of the extreme contrast in temperature, leaves the swimmer feeling that she is on the verge of being baptized into the utopian transfiguration of the body. If there is any merit to Nietzsche's description of the guiltless gaiety of the southern hemisphere, one finds its justification here. In

---

[107] This involuntary discovery parallels Marie Thompson's attempt to give a Spinozan-Deleuzian account of sonic materiality that avoids anthropomorphic intervention in the works of Alvin Lucier, Okkyung Lee, and Yasunao Tone. Thompson, "Experimental Music and the Question of What a Body Can Do," in *Musical Encounters with Deleuze and Guattari* (New York: Bloomsbury, 2017), 149–68.

[108] Henry David Thoreau, "A Telegraph Harp," in *Poems for the Millennium*, vol. 3, ed. Jerome Rothenberg and Jeffrey C. Robinson (Los Angeles: University of California Press, 2009), 723–4.

June of 1944, when the German Armed Forces had, by all accounts, already lost the war, the Gestapo rounded up the roughly 2,000 Romaniote Jews living on the island of Corfu and deported them to the Auschwitz-Birkenau death camp. Their journey on the *Sonderzüge*, which lasted eighteen days, consisted of freight cars with one latrine and one tauntingly sado-masochistic bucket of water. So as to make room for upwards of 150 passengers per freight, each passenger was forced to keep their hands raised in the air for the entire trip. The hell of this longest of train journeys to Auschwitz is incomprehensible. The hallucinatory descent into madness and bodily exhaustion that Primo Levi describes from Fossoli was, by comparison, six days. Almost every passenger perished en route. When, on this same summer day, the descendants of these tortured souls visit the memorial sites of Auschwitz and Dachau, Treblinka and Buchenwald, they discover an infernal truth. Perhaps only Samuel Beckett's work has registered it, for it exceeds the documentary form of testimony.[109] Block 11 of Auschwitz and the bunker at Dachau, where the unspeakable happened daily, are both, without exaggeration, eerily frigged places. The summer heat literally fails to penetrate the walls, although it is all the more present in its absence. It is as if nature knows that, like the desolate rendering plants of Wolfgang Hilbig's prose, nothing dependent on the warmth and light of the heliotropic cosmos should grow here anymore. If this does not drive art and theory, to say nothing of *praxis*, to despair, the implication is that the same contrast in temperature that, in one instance, stands for utopia, in the next, stands for hell. Only the smallest, molecular link determines their difference. The closer one sinks to the bottom, the more the coldness of the *Untergang* points negatively to the warmth of the *gradus ad parnassum*. As Adorno describes Beckett's *Endgame*, this means that, after Auschwitz,

> the imageless image of death is one of indifference [*Indifferenz*]. In it the distinction between absolute domination, the hell in which time is completely banished into space [*in den Raum gebannt ist*], in which absolutely nothing changes any more, and the messianic state, in which everything would be in its right place, vanishes. The ultimate absurdity is that the peacefulness of the void and that of reconciliation cannot be distinguished from one another.[110]

Becoming appears to negate itself precisely because, under absolute domination, it no longer becomes anything other than what is. The possibilities that remain for art, which, as subject, reflects the possibilities that remain for life, are thus

---

[109] Adorno, *Aesthetic Theory*, 32/*GS*7, 55.
[110] Adorno, "Trying to Understand *Endgame*," 274 (translation modified)/*GS*11, 321.

narrowed in the midst of what reified consciousness takes to be an infinity of "anything goes" opportunities. "The space between discursive barbarism and poetic euphemism that remains to artworks," continues Adorno, along these lines, "is scarcely larger than the indifference-point [*Indifferenzpunkt*] into which Beckett burrowed."[111] Adorno could hardly anticipate Deleuze more directly than in this formulation. The minimal difference *is* the minimal difference of molecular becoming, the fleeting, barely decipherable moment just prior to identity and differentiation. It resembles the infinitesimally small, almost hallucinatory moment between waking-life and passing into sleep, or the moment of Dostoevskian epilepsy that, vis-à-vis the "moment of danger" of the firing squad, slows time and space to a virtual crawl. In both cases, all the senses are momentarily heightened and the synesthesia of the prehistorical sensorium is momentarily reignited. Today, however, suspending the space between these moments appears to be so thoroughly tabooed that, as a parody of actual fulfillment, nature seems to have become identical to itself. This apparent blockage, which suggests that one state can no longer flow into the other, constitutes the *Nullpunkt* of the subject itself, the shuddering moment that first stirs the subject to awaken and confront the Old Testament adage: "dust thou shalt become."[112] Yet, torture is torture because it feels like it will go on forever, because the helping hand of humanity has completely abandoned the persecuted. As the subject increasingly becomes object and cannot, therefore, like both Gracchus and the bourgeoisie, die, so the longing for the negative other, the refuge of *Tod und Verklärung*, increases. The problem, then, is that the recoil of warmth into coldness, or the moment when the howling wind ceases to hound because it has somehow grown cold in the midst of the scorching heat, seems to have been altogether eliminated from experience. The lullaby *Abgesang* that unexpectedly emerges after the cello recapitulation to the third movement of Brahms's *Piano Concerto in B-flat* appears to have fallen into oblivion. This is because the return to the land of childhood is all but impossible after the torturous destruction of memory. For Beckett and Hilbig, who reflect this historical phenomenon in literature, just as Schoenberg and Penderecki do in music, the only recourse is to translate this missed chance of nonidentity into filth and excrement.[113] Of

---

[111] Adorno, *Aesthetic Theory*, 32/GS7, 55. For further discussion of this dialectic between utopia and hell, see Anna-Verena Nosthoff, "Beckett, Adorno and the Hope for Nothingness as Something: Meditations on Theology in the Age of Its Impossibility," *Critical Research on Religion* 6, no. 1 (2018): 35–53.

[112] Adorno, "Trying to Understand *Endgame*," 274 /GS11, 321. Deleuze too uses this concept of the "degree zero" in, for instance, *Cinema 2*, 62, in order to illustrate the infinitesimal moment when the sensory-motor activity of the movement-image gives way to the pure situations of the time-image.

[113] Ibid., 274/GS11, 321.

course, in a certain sense, the subject senses this, its hollowness, all along. But it fails to conceptualize it, fails to see itself as a reaction formation. Modern art, and especially music, given its *sinnlich übersinnliche* essence, presents this ongoing failure of self-conscious recognition. It attempts to reactivate the "mimetic, pre-individual moment [*mimetisch-vorindividuellen Moments*],"[114] the repression of which negates the possibility of one day ascending to the second reflection of our ontological transience. The near impossibility of successfully capturing what Deleuze, resonating with Adorno, calls the "indiscernibility" between the actual and the virtual, or the "indiscernibility" between the self and its other, likely accounts for why the abstract negation of the pain in which the subject is presently suffused usurps the painstakingly slow movement and comparatively weak intensity of the concept.[115] Pointing to the missed chance, to the virtual otherness that was actually immanent to the torturous moment all along, rubs salt in the wound of those whose suffering is so great that nothingness feels like the only liberation.

Autumn Death

With good reason, both Adorno and Deleuze describe this minimal difference between utopia and hell, between messianic fulfillment and death, as constituting the ideas, if not the *Idee*, of art.[116] The "veritable Ideas" of the writer's "fiction" and, by implication, the musician's music are heard, Deleuze argues, "in the interstices of language, in its intervals,"[117] that is, prior to their outright conceptualization and, for that reason, all the more dependent on it. These ideas are based, in other words, on the nonconceptuality built into conceptuality, the quivering moment built into the fixating or reifying determination. "[T]ouched by the other,"[118] linked in a circuit to the virtual, one is inexorably driven outside of one's monadological confinement. As immanently transcendent moments,

---

[114] Adorno, *Aesthetic Theory*, 42 (translation modified)/*GS7*, 69. Although never characterizing them as mimetic because of his traditional conception of mimesis, Deleuze shares this same emphasis on the transformative potential of pre-individual sensations in, for example, Deleuze, *Logic of Sense*, 102.
[115] Deleuze, *Cinema 2*, 69; Deleuze, *Kafka*, 48.
[116] This similarity prevails, despite the fact that, for Nietzschean reasons, Deleuze will not countenance Adorno's conception of this idea as the promise of the reconciliation of nature, that is, the end of war.
[117] Deleuze, "Life and Literature," 5.
[118] Adorno, *Aesthetic Theory*, 331/*GS7*, 489–90: "That shudder in which subjectivity stirs [*sich regt*] without yet being subjectivity is the act of being touched by the other [*Anderen Angerührtsein*]. Aesthetic comportment assimilates itself to [*bildet sich an*] that other rather than subordinating it [*sich untertan zu machen*]. Such a constitutive relation of the subject to objectivity in aesthetic comportment joins [*vermählt*] eros and knowledge [*Erkenntnis*]."

these ideas come to the fore "like an eternity," Deleuze continues, "that can only be revealed in becoming."[119] In this Benjaminian sense of ephemerality at a standstill, Adorno and Deleuze both locate the *Indifferenzbegriff* of desire. Adorno, not incidentally, associates it with the ambivalent drives of the Kantian will.[120] In antagonistic society this will is both free and unfree simultaneously. Counterpart to the minimal difference, it of necessity misrecognizes the minimal similarity, that is, the oscillation and affinity between the intelligible ego and the empirical ego from which it is extrapolated. Each moment of the negating spirit, that is, each moment of determining and differentiating, of wresting itself from the amorphous mass of nature and, therefore, rising above it, is paid for at the price of harming the heteronomous on which it lives. Hence, the absurdity of the present consists not simply, as Adorno maintains, in the fact that the peace of the void becomes indistinguishable from the peace of reconciliation. It also consists in the fact that recording the victim's death throes—those of Proust no less than those of memory itself—is maniacally repressed at every moment of history.[121] As the, so to speak, micrological correlate to the macrological standstill at the threshold of a blackhole, theory has yet to determine whether the allegedly utopian moment of the brain's so-called electrical gamma surge immediately prior to slipping into death would, for the victim of torture, become the opposite, namely an eternity of torment. Myth would, as Charlie Brooker has shown, then be a more terrifying punishment of the innocent for the sins of the guilty than any document of culture has hitherto conceived: a bad infinity without end, instead of the fulfilled time in which the temporality of the intramundane is sublated into the temporality of supramundane. Over and over again, day after day, the last will and testament bequeathed by the victim is breached. The death rattle, in which the phosphorescence of rotting corpses resembles, as Benjamin noted, the emerging and changing colors of autumn, in which the child locked away in the wearied adult pleas for protection one last time, is neither glimpsed nor heard.[122] All is submerged in the gray barrenness of decolored (*entfärbt*) history: eternal winter. The last, lullaby gesture that suspends the furious conclusion of Bartók's *String Quartet No. 5* with a "*con indifferenza*" has no audience. The

---

[119] Deleuze, "Life and Literature," 5.
[120] Adorno, *Negative Dialectics*, 294 /GS6, 294.
[121] Adorno, "Trying to Understand *Endgame*," 275. See, also, Adorno, *Aesthetic Theory*, 113/GS7, 171: "Artworks bear expression not where they communicate the subject, but rather where they reverberate with the primal-history [*Urgeschichte*] of subjectivity." "This is the affinity of the artwork to the subject and it endures because this primal-history survives in the subject and recommences in every moment of history."
[122] Walter Benjamin, "Zur Phantasie, fr 89," in *Gesammelte Schriften*, vol. 6, ed. Rolf Tiedemann and Hermann Scheppenhäuser (Frankfurt a.m.: Suhrkamp Verlag, 1974), 121–2.

rainbow colors that, similarly, emerge *tout à coup* from the tension between the back-and-forth, "empirical time" of the arpeggiating piano and the hovering, "angelic time" of the tremolo violin from the concluding bars to the seventh movement of Messiaen's *Quatuor pour la fin du Temps* fall on deaf ears. There will be no respite for the prisoners of war. For no such moment of *Indifferenz*, no such moment of escape from the eternity of the self-same, is permitted by the positivist spirit of domination.

Decasia: Part 1

Only the pre-artistic have contempt for Adorno's claim that "every work [of art] is the mortal enemy of the other."[123] The *agon*, undoubtedly a prefiguration of the historical materialist's call to force the *real* civil war, offends liberal sensibilities.[124] Avoiding the revenge fantasies that the sight of suffering generates for regressive consciousness, Michael Gordon's magnum opus, *Decasia*, performs the annihilation of its adversary by inconsolably immersing itself in this suffering. This constitutes its law of form, which might also be described as the embodiment of Adorno's dictum that "there is tenderness in the coarsest demand."[125] From the first bars, originally performed alongside Bill Morrison's multimedia experimental film about the decay of the aura, but doubtless standing alone as an autonomous construction, the critique and rescue of the past is manifestly at play. The rusted, junkyard brake drum echoes the electronic rattling and jingling from Xenakis's *La Légende d'Eer*. From the beginning, the beholder learns that, as Morrison's introductory image of Sufi whirling attests, seizing the *Indifferenzpunkt* that would distinguish human beings turning-in-circles from old film reels doing the same is extraordinarily difficult. Whether striving to become one with the harmony of the spheres, which both movements, living-labor and dead-labor, resemble, amounts to unity with God or unity with downright terror is likewise undecidable. And so the minimalist repetition of Part 1 ensues. An orchestra mistuned, sometimes an eighth higher, sometimes an eighth lower, from its in-tuned counterparts emerges from the cobwebs and the dust, the mottled celluloid and the hissing resonance of abandonment. Unable to pick up speed, the monotony of the first five minutes of this introductory

---

[123] Adorno, *Aesthetic Theory*, 211/*GS7*, 313–14.
[124] Walter Benjamin, "On the Concept of History," 392/*GS1.2*, 697; Benjamin, "Theories of German Fascism," 321/*GS3*, 250.
[125] Adorno, *Minima Moralia*, 154/*GS4*, 176.

sequence lends Part 1 a sense of catastrophe that is catastrophic precisely because, as Adorno once said of Beckett's work, it never takes place.[126] The simplicity of the pitch-wheel half-steps encourages the listener to regress to a childlike song. She cannot help but sing along with the vibraphones and detuned pianos, even if there is a kind of desperate moaning to their circular movement. All of this changes abruptly when the slow-looping, shrill strings, whose repetition will come to play an imperative role, enter at 5:47. An *onward*, ambivalent like never before in music rings out. One knows that a journey is ahead. One knows that one will have to endure something of immense proportion. When, in due course, the violins finally begin to wind down like the winding reeling they mimetically emulate, it feels as though the slow decay of experience is, contrary to the concomitant, epic feeling, nearing its end. But you have, in truth, only just begun. The melancholy of the lower register summons its opposite: the high-pitched lament of the machine evoked by the three flutes. No one could deny that these mistuned flutes signal the "all aboard" train whistle of a heinous trip to come. A creaturely wailing merges with the howling of the machine. Are these laments human or animal? Are they machinic or Dicken's melancholy mad elephants? They appear to be accompanied by a flashing lantern, by the sinister illumination of the will-o'-the-wisp. Each sustained cry imitates the same turning-in-circles previously heard in the strings. As Part 1 closes, the churning junkyard brake momentarily relents. Time is thus suspended. Will help come? Will the dignity of art, which "enrobes two measures of a Beethoven quartet snatched up from between the murky stream" of monotony, intervene?[127]

Decasia: Part 2

The percussive entrance of the electric guitar and the seemingly unending, now-amplified sobbing of the atonal flutes give the answer as Part 2 begins. Dignity is dead.[128] Nothing accessible, not even a fragment of the damaged pastiche, seems salvageable. Nonetheless, the whole orchestra steadily gathers momentum under the guidance of the simple, repetitive rhythm. The entrance of the bass guitar thickens what still felt somewhat flimsy just moments ago. The entrance of the trombones at 2:36 is decisive. Morrison is especially sensitive when he decides to pair this emergence with the first mournful glance—the

---

[126] Adorno, *Aesthetic Theory*, 154/*GS7*, 231.
[127] Ibid., 39/*GS7*, 65.
[128] Cf. Agamben, *Remnants of Auschwitz*, 55–81.

auratic stare of the dead—of the furisode-clad Japanese woman. Living-labor remains trapped in dead-labor and will soon be forgotten forever as it follows out the *Fluchtpunkt* of history. These trombone loops are at once carnivalesque and, like the scherzo from Beethoven's *Eroica Symphony*, becoming conscious of their bombast. When they finally drop away, another standstill results. Impending departure to another land—to nowhere—is signaled by the non-pulsed floating. In no time it will feel, as Gordon himself has described it, as though the music were about to ascend to unity with five-hundred choirs of singing angels. Cage's *Four2* is multiplied to the nth power. How can the horror that subsequently unfolds after this temporary pause be so entwined with bliss? First, the flutes become one with a sampled, AC/DC-converted power supply. They are supported by the driving, stringed downbeat. Then, suddenly, high-pitched cries reach distances never before reached in music. This is a shrieking terror more horrifying than Penderecki's *De Natura Sonoris No 2*. Only the stars are witness to the unbearable helplessness of being packed into freight cars like so many specimen. The delusions of cosmological music are critiqued, as if music were imploring: "leave possibilities unused, instead of storming under a confused compulsion to the conquest of strange stars"; attend to the suffering nature that is here, before you, now.[129] And yet, disobeying this imperative, you want to become completely immersed in the mechanical rattle and hissing reverb, for all the voices of the past are stored up in them. All of the missed melodies and broken cries, the stones in the throat of the desperate, call you. Mozart's dream is, as Jean-Luc Godard has shown, forever locked within *notre musique de génocide*.[130] These are the lost voices of the forgotten and hopeless ones, human and nonhuman, those for the sake of whom one is given hope. Ten thousand iridescent lights glitter off the gossamer-laced landscape of this music. The universal dependence of all moments on all other moments—a "millionfold web" (*millionenfältiges Gespinst*) of simultaneity—indicts causality itself as the epistemological double of domination.[131] Without noticing it, another rhythm has been gathering momentum all along. When, in the course of Part 2, the horns finally cry out from this rhythm, one discovers that it is a train that has become

---

[129] Adorno, *Minima Moralia*, 156/GS4, 177.
[130] Just as Godard's technique gives voice to the old in the new, the genocide in Mozart, and the Mozart in genocide, so Gordon and his friends give voice to the missed chance via a process of remixing each other's music. Unlike the commodity form, however, in which preserving the fetish of the new is the *modus operandi*, these composers embody the repudiation of private property as they search for the deterritorializing virtuality that was, in truth, always stored up in their common property but not yet recognized. David Harrington's and Bill Frisell's respective remixes of Gordon's *Clouded Yellow* are exemplary of this critique of the exchange-value of the remix.
[131] Adorno, *Negative Dialectics*, 267–8/GS6, 264–5.

Sprachähnlich.[132] Only its language is not Honegger's, Bailey's, or even Ellington's. It is not Schaefer's train, Poulenc's, or Nyman's jaunty train that is speaking here. This is the train from Corfu. But it is more than that too. This is the train that reveals the false promise of every escape train—the train of the future that is already casting a shadow on the present. As the horns continue to resound in tension with the sampled, found-sounds of flanging and chugging train wheels, it is as though the train were itself protesting against its complicity in genocide. As Baudelaire once said of the "mute language [*langue muette*]" of the "out-of-work [*désoeuvré*] and homesick [*nostalgique*]" ships of the Paris harbor, these horns similarly ask: "when do we depart for happiness?"[133] Becoming-animal and becoming-machine coalesce in a cacophonous repudiation of all tradition. Importantly, the cheap, programmatic trick of Kraftwerk's *Trans Europa Express*, or worse, Villa-Lobos's *The Little Train of the Caipira*, is avoided here, since the French horns blend into an imperceptible unity with the Leslie S-3K chimes, and the crotales reverb becomes nonsensuously similar to the winds that flutter from beyond the mountain. As the horn screams and the slapping and clacking metal continue to be driven forward by the thumping repetition of the bass drums and tam-tams, all the earth swells with a *frisson*. A bass rumbles, as Thoreau says, with the thunderous snort and smoke-breathing nostrils of an iron horse.[134] As the intervals between the horn notes shorten, one after another, the bottom of the whole orchestra, except for the higher register, unexpectedly drops out. There the music hovers, calm before the storm, for an entire minute, without any distinct time signature. This is something akin to the resonance that remains after an eardrum has ruptured. The subject is unbearably weak now. It wants to *resign*. It cannot find its bearings anymore. Will it finally be permitted to sleep?

Decasia: Part 3

An infinitesimally small pause suggests that the answer is yes. But within a microinterval of that same pause, the roar of the train's trundling bass comes right

---

[132] Adorno, *Aesthetic Theory*, 112/GS7, 171. Adorno's frequent use of the concept of *Sprachähnlichkeit* evokes Benjamin's sense of the language of things and the mute, nonintentional language of nature. There is an inherent musicality to this non-communicative, mimetic language. See, also, T. W. Adorno, "Music and Language: A Fragment," in *Quasi una Fantasia: Essays on Modern Music*, trans. Rodney Livingstone (New York: Verso, 1998), 1–6; "Fragment über Musik und Sprache," in *Gesammelte Schriften*, vol. 16.2, ed. Rolf Tiedemann (Frankfurt a.m.: Suhrkamp Verlag, 1972), 251–6.

[133] Charles Baudelaire, *Intimate Journals*, trans. Christopher Isherwood (Mineola, NY: Dover Publications 2006), 40.

[134] Henry David Thoreau, *Walden* (New York: Oxford University Press, 1999), 106.

back to begin Part 3. You have not, in fact, escaped into the dark real of night, into the death that the strident flutes foretold. There is no escape. The simple wish, to be done with it, has been denied. As the sorrowful railway journey (*traurige Eisenbahnfahrt*)[135] sets off for nowhere once again, it does not take long for the horizon to open from the dismal fog in a way that was previously impossible. The same moon that shines this evening once shined through the cracks of the freight car on the way to Auschwitz. After approximately thirty more seconds of the harrowing introduction, the overwhelming momentum finally gives way to something light, as a more distinct electric guitar now takes the rhythmic lead. Shortly thereafter the snare drum becomes increasingly prominent. Once again, the adversary is reduced to embarrassment over this superior presentation. The blues and jazz percussion, even the extraordinary silences conjured by Art Blakey or the pyramid dragging momentum of Jon Fishman's floor toms, are comparatively too affirmative. Ravel's *Bolero* blushes over the ensnaring spell of this repetition. With each electric bass downbeat, another *onward* is announced, although it is equally ambivalent. Again and again, one is called to survive, to endure. And yet, one starts to believe that perhaps doing so is possible, since all of the wind instruments and brass from before have been sublimated into something more manageable in this movement. This manageability determines the semblance (*Schein*) of reconciliation of the work as a whole. Even the barely noticeable tempo shifts that sigh a melancholic sigh do not, at this point, feel like they will necessarily eclipse you. Chimes and jingles become pleasant as the angelic choir from the distance is teased again. The clenched hand that has been clenched from the primordial origin onward unclenches. Again the orchestra falls away, leaving only the higher register. The rapid-fire flute repetitions, which anticipate the theme and variations from the coming movement, are a soft caress. Their string accompaniment passes through a *flanger* effect. This renders it other-worldly, dizzying. While the flanging strings float, it feels like a soprano voice is intermittently punctuating the flute notes, turning them inside out, as it were, or trying to arrest the songlike element before the final decay of their enveloping arc. It would not be inaccurate to say that these quickened repetitions harken to the playfulness of *Till Eulenspiegels lustige Streiche*, which was, no doubt, perversely played in the Nazi quarters of the camps. Animal observation looking in on the calamity is ambivalently evoked. A becoming-bird, good-spiritedness emerges for a moment. Every creature is consoled by the *falsetto* of the maternal voice. This suspended temporality goes on for more

---

[135] Benjamin, "Surrealism," 210/*GS2*, 300.

than a minute, until, not unsurprisingly, Part 4 begins, as its predecessors began, with a bang.

Decasia: Part 4

And so the drive of the guitar and vibraphones once again ensues. It will circulate like the rounded character of the whole work for some time. An intentional monotony that recollects the conclusion to Part 1 of John Adam's *Harmonielehre* prevails at this point. More importantly, the monophonic, percussive repetitions of the whole orchestra are now drawn, as it were, to the center by the whole-note repetitions of those old Wagnerian and Brucknerian horns. The difference is that now the train horns have a more distinct, amplified and electroacoustic resonance to them. It is as if they have recoiled into a qualitatively new era of natural-history—one that has canceled and preserved, deterritorialized and reterritorialized, the echo of the previous generation. This lighter, cityscape trek, which is not wholly dissimilar from the terrifying inanity of Gordon's *Dystopia*, continues for four and a half minutes with minor variations. It must inevitably end. We know that we have opened up onto new terrain when the dominant loop, as old as the siren from *Weather*, returns. Although reminiscent of Part 1, now this stringed loop bears an even closer likeness to something like a winding, electronic clock that is set to explode an atomic bomb. The countdown approaches zero, the *Nullpunkt* of the Capitalocene. In dialectical contrast, each high-pitched sustain in the strings summons the *Indifferenz* that constitutes the movement of the whole, namely the "smallest link" between messianic fulfillment and the longing for death, between angelic self-relinquishment and the downfall into the hallucinatory, Muselmann bottom. After roughly six minutes into this part of Gordon's masterpiece, the listener is reminded of what has already occurred. The tortured have the smell of the concrete chamber within which they were tortured seared into their memory. The wailing flutes once again begin rising. The dissonance mounts. Ligeti's suffocating traffic jam is recalled. The mistuned rhizome of woodwinds and brass starts to drown out, via Gordon's amplifying technique, the center that was heretofore holding the movement together. Bombed out enclaves are all that remain. In a truly striking turn of events, the flutes give way to a melodic line in the basses and cellos that sounds like something out of the scherzo movement of the *Ninth Symphony* right before the marvelous bassoon solo intervenes with its characteristic, Schillerian play. Here, the bass line is repeated and, soon enough, folds in upon itself, so that it cannot, anticipating Gordon's later *Rewriting*, get off the ground and cannot, moreover, maintain its playful triumph. Europe sounds a final lament before its greatest achievement is reduced to rubble. That this Beethovian quote could emerge, of all places, at this moment, after more than thirty minutes of virtually nonstop atonality, is astonishing. Whereas musicians were arguably too quick to move beyond the implications of Cage's *Concerto for Prepared Piano and Chamber Orchestra*, in which no melodic or harmonic repetitions are permitted, Gordon finds the, so to speak, solution insofar as he refuses to give you a melodic refrain until you have passed through the most profound struggle, until you have, in other words, passed through what appears to be the complete dissolution of the melody and the song-like shelter on which it is based. In *Beijing Harmony*, one of Gordon's most important works, Gordon not only—in contrast to this renunciation—dissolves the line between nature and society, hearing the deterritorialized echo of the former in the latter as it bounces off of the Echo Wall of the Temple of Heaven, he rescues the breathtakingly delicate flute solos from Beethoven's *Ninth* and Brahms's *Symphony No. 1*. He does this by, of all methods, filtering what seems like a theme from *Francesca da Rimini* through a reverb effect. This gives the impression that ten thousand flutes are answering one another in the *wanwu*, that is, the infinite chaos, of being. In this way, Gordon approximates the master of cinema, Godard, who likewise rescues Tchaikovsky from one of Dante's rings of hell, the eternal kitsch of the commodity form, by ripping his *Symphony No. 6 in B minor* out of its original contexts and placing the farewell horns from the first movement within a new, contemporary context. Thus a train appears for Godard as well. Having failed to realize that the Muslim genocide is identical to the Jewish genocide, it inevitably departs for Paradise.[136] If this echoing coda is the only possible affirmation left to music and film, the refusal, on the one hand, to leave the danger behind and the need, on the other, to swear off all affirmation differentiates *Decasia* from almost every other work. Its obstinance should be thought alongside the other extreme of Godard's symphonic form, namely the earth-shattering reverberation of the *note commune* piano refrain from *Film Socialisme*. Such an ungrievable state, which resembles the haunting repetition of Stockhausen's *Klavierstück IX* and the motionless despair of Hans Otte's *Buch der Klänge IV*, gives rise, as *Decasia* continues, to more horns and even a few more punctuations from either Eulenspiegel's clarinet or Ligeti's macabre clowns. They fail to pick up the pace or complete their melodic line as well. This is musical debris. After once

---

[136] Jean-Luc Godard, *Notre musique* (Paris: Avventura Films, 2004).

again being driven along by the layered electronic and acoustic basses, a series of never-completed, intermittent call and response notes are articulated by the flutes and clarinets. The music has now explicitly regressed. There is something fundamentally infantile, something akin to a nursery rhyme, in the simplicity of these repetitions. Kluge once gave voice to a similar becoming-child siren-song in the filtered cries that warn the salvage-operators from his *Der Grosse Verhau* of impending bombs. In a passing moment, the only authentic protest to false authority that exists sounds its alarm: "[a]ccumulation of wealth at one pole is [. . .] at the same time accumulation of misery, the torment of labour, slavery, ignorance, brutalization and moral degradation at the opposite pole."[137] The course of the world goes on, while humanity is reduced to babbling. One is reminded of Adorno's claim that the triad "animal/fool/clown" is an indispensable layer of modern art.[138] This triad is soaked in blood now. Yet, nobody seems to notice, until once again the bass-drive falls away. The listener is suspended once again. The Beethovian bass line returns and almost completes itself, even though the contrasting, arrhythmic, air-dispensing smokestacks of the cacophonous wind instruments make keeping pace with it virtually impossible. There are screams because bodies are caught in the gears of industry. No one is laughing at Chaplin, however.[139] There is nothing left to laugh at.[140] Before returning one more time to the bass theme and variation that was introduced in Part 3, Part 4 circles for a few more measures in that old monotony. The Wagnerian, death-camp horns then return again, before the punctuated drop-off technique marks the transition to the penultimate movement, Part 5.

Decasia: Part 5

The incomplete, broken-off melody that characterized both the strings and the woodwinds from the previous movement might well have comprised an actual melody, instead of fragmented *Klangfarbenmelodie*, if the instruments were not mistuned or if humanity had not, by analogy, begun its anti-technological dissent into barbarism. Such a failure is exemplified in this brief movement. The music floats interminably, without direction. The resonance of the mismatched notes might even be said to have a kind of wind-chime effect without the wind.

---

[137] Alexander Kluge, *The Big Mess* (West Germany: Kairos-Film, 1968); Marx, *Capital*, 799.
[138] Adorno, *Aesthetic Theory*, 119/GS7, 182.
[139] Adorno and Horkheimer, *Dialectic of Enlightenment*, 119/GS3, 171.
[140] T. W. Adorno, "Notes on Beckett," *Journal of Beckett Studies* 19, no. 2 (2010): 157–78, 159.

"Martyred instruments," they are like Odradek, who laughs without any lungs.[141] The journey is going to start up again in no time. On this occasion it might even be setting sail for the *unchanging sea*. And so the horns announce departure. The unity of apperception is, of course, all but annihilated at this point. After the world-historical assault, it is difficult to remember what these horns long ago summoned, the future or the past. This breach in the barrier against explosive stimuli, the radical disjunction between experience and the totality that forms it, paralyzes temporality. For, as Adorno puts it, "each shock that is not absorbed inwardly, is a ferment of future destruction."[142] When the inwardly reverberating, pizzicato heartstrings can no longer double the hammering thirds of the B-flat minor orchestra as they do in the decrescendo of the coda to the first movement of Brahms's *Symphony No. 1 in C minor*; when, by implication, the memory trace of the similar coda from the first movement of the *Ninth Symphony* is obliterated, and interiority cannot therefore perform its softening, pillow-like transformation of the initial assault into a reconciling echo, this indicates that the mimetic shock absorber and, with it, the experience that could alone heal the wound, is nearing complete dissolution. The breathtaking silence that, following this same inward path, accentuates the transition from the sorrow of the first movement of Beethoven's late *String Quartet No. 14 in C-sharp Minor* to the celebratory dance of the second movement is impossible without the sublimating power of memory. Differentiated repetition appeases. This is why Adorno contrasts the flat exteriority of jazz with the ponderous depth of Beethoven without thereby recognizing that jazz performs the truth of the false interior after that interior has exploded.[143] Gordon knows all of this, of course, if only unconsciously. *Decasia* has an immense depth in a certain sense, but unlike its nineteenth-century forebears, it is not the depth of the subject. For another four and a half minutes we wait and wait. Luckily, the pain of this delay seems different from before. As the fifth, interlude movement of *Decasia* comes to a close, the beholder is transported back to the looping strings that first entered in the middle of Part 1.

Decasia: Part 6

The beginning of Part 6 emphatically declares that there is no escaping the spell anymore. Will you sing with the moaning vibraphones that rest beneath

---

[141] Deleuze and Guattari, *Kafka*, 6.
[142] Adorno, *Minima Moralia*, 54/*GS4*, 60.
[143] Adorno, *Aesthetic Theory*, 116/*GS7*, 177.

the loop this time around? Is it possible to rest content with being one of the millions upon millions of voices whose corresponding visage beseechingly asks the audience, in Morrison's film, to rescue them from a torment that was once felt, but later forgotten, as the shudder before the dogcatcher's van and the rat clubbing ego-ideal?[144] History's answer to the manic gaze of the suffering creature is simple. Without ever convincing itself, it says: they are "only animals."[145] The loops start piling up like the piling corpses of history. The palpitating hum of airplane propellers hovers from above. Bombs drop with a descending whistle. Our Sufi friend is no more. Permanent war is upon us. Accumulation *is* extinction. There's no differentiating the siren's warning call from the creaturely cry of desperation. As the loops sound increasingly like chimpanzee calls from the trees, and one, accordingly, realizes that it is not simply the ape who looks mournfully like he wants to be human,[146] but the humans themselves who want to be so, a clumsy rock-and-roll band continues to play in the background, as if nothing had happened. Unlike in Kluge's visual and aural decontextualization of the rock band from *Der Grosse Verhau*, the tongue of kitsch has not been untied here.[147] The unfulfilled melodies, the recapitulations from Part 1, sound increasingly like the digits from Ryoji Ikeda's or İlhan Mimaroğlu's music, which are plugged into an algorithmic computation. The rising conflagration cannot, so it seems, be stopped in the age of informatics.[148] When the bass guitar enters back in at the 8-minute mark, and the bass drums rumble with the lower strings and tubas, one thing becomes evident: every living species is implicated in this *Grundbass*. This is the return of what Benjamin describes as the intoxication (*Rausch*) of the ancient world, which was forgotten, in modernity, with the exclusive emphasis on the optical connection to nature. The consequence of this forgetting, which is tantamount to forgetting the communal, already meant, in Benjamin's lifetime, that "human multitudes, gases, electrical forces were hurled into the open country, high-frequency currents coursed through the landscape, new constellations rose in the sky, aerial space and ocean depths thundered with propellers, and everywhere sacrificial shafts were dug in Mother Earth." It already meant, in the First World War, that "this immense wooing of the cosmos was enacted for the first time on a planetary scale."[149] Gordon's work

---

[144] Adorno, *Negative Dialectics*, 366/GS6, 359.
[145] Adorno, *Minima Moralia*, 105/GS4, 116.
[146] Adorno, *Aesthetic Theory*, 113/GS7, 172.
[147] T. W. Adorno, *Mahler: A Musical Physiognomy*, trans. Edmund Jephcott (Chicago: University of Chicago Press, 1992), 39; *Mahler Eine Musikalische Physiognomik, in Gesammelte Schriften*, vol. 13, ed. Rolf Tiedemann (Frankfurt a.m.: Suhrkamp Verlag, 1972), 189.
[148] Deleuze, *Cinema 2*, 270–1.
[149] Benjamin, *One-Way Street*, 486–7/GS4, 147–8.

turns this at once cosmological and terrestrial calamity into music. But there's no consolation in it, and certainly not, à la the fascist futurists of the last century, any affirmation to be wrung out of the noise. This is, rather, the unconscious remembrance of the sorrow of nature. Now, however, in the final moments, the negativity of experience has lost its vigor. Now, the mass begins to congeal. The machinery slowly grinds to a halt. As if it were the final breath of the aura, one last loop from Michael Gordon's *Decasia* escapes the mechanical clatter before unceremoniously trailing off, like everything else, into the termless night of history.

Bibliography

Abel, Mark. *Groove: An Aesthetic of Measured Time*. Boston, MA: Brill, 2014.
Adams, Jason Michael. "The King's Two Faces: Michael Jackson, the Postracial Presidency and the 'Curious Concept of Non-white.'" In *Deleuze and Race*, 168–89. Edinburgh: Edinburgh University Press, 2013.
Adorno, Theodor W. "The Actuality of Philosophy." Translated by Benjamin Snow. *Telos* 31 (Spring 1977): 120–33.
Adorno, Theodor W. *Aesthetic Theory*. Translated by Robert Hullot-Kentor. Minneapolis: University of Minnesota Press, 1997.
Adorno, Theodor W. *Aesthetics*. Translated by Wieland Hoban. Medford, MA: Polity Press, 2018.
Adorno, Theodor W. *Äesthetische Theorie*. In *Gesammelte Schriften*. Vol. 7, edited by Rolf Tiedemann. Frankfurt a.m.: Suhrkamp Verlag, 1972.
Adorno, Theodor W. *Against Epistemology: A Metacritique*. Translated by Willis Domingo. Malden, MA: Polity Press, 2013.
Adorno, Theodor W. "The Aging of the New Music." In *Essays on Music*, edited by Richard Leppert, 181–202. Los Angeles: University of California Press, 2002.
Adorno, Theodor W. "Aktualität der Philosophie." In *Gesammelte Schriften*. Vol. 1, edited by Rolf Tiedemann, 325–44. Frankfurt a.m.: Suhrkamp Verlag, 1972.
Adorno, Theodor W. *Alban Berg: Master of the Smallest Link*. Translated by Christopher Hailey and Juliane Brand. Cambridge: Cambridge University Press, 1994.
Adorno, Theodor W. "Art and the Arts." In *Can One Live after Auschwitz?* edited by Rolf Tiedemann. Stanford, CA: Stanford University Press, 2003.
Adorno, Theodor W. *Ästhetik*. In *Nachgelassene Schriften, Abteilung IV*. Vol. 3, edited by Rolf Tiedemann. Frankfurt am Main: Verlag, 1994.
Adorno, Theodor W. "Aufzeichnungen zu Kafka." In *Gesammelte Schriften*. Vol. 10.1, edited by Rolf Tiedemann. Frankfurt a.m.: Suhrkamp Verlag, 1972.
Adorno, Theodor W. "Bach Defended against his Devotees." In *Prisms*. Translated by Samuel Weber and Shierry Weber. Cambridge, MA: MIT Press, 1984.
Adorno, Theodor W. "Bach gegen seine Liebhaber verteidigt." In *Gesammelte Schriften*. Vol. 10.1, edited by Rolf Tiedemann. Frankfurt a.m.: Suhrkamp Verlag, 1972.
Adorno, Theodor W. *Beethoven: The Philosophy of Music*. Translated by Edmund Jephcott, edited by Rolf Tiedemann. Stanford, CA: Stanford University Press, 1998.
Adorno, Theodor W. *Beethoven: Philosophie der Musik*. In *Nachgelassenen Schriften*. Vol 1. Frankfurt am Main: Verlag, 1994.
Adorno, Theodor W. "Beethoven's Late Style." In *Can One Live after Auschwitz*, edited by Rolf Tiedemann. Stanford, CA: Stanford University Press, 2003.

Adorno, Theodor W. *Berg: Der Meister des kleinsten Übergangs*. In *Gesammelte Schriften*. Vol. 13, edited by Rolf Tiedemann. Frankfurt a.m.: Suhrkamp Verlag, 1972.

Adorno, Theodor W. *Can One Live after Auschwitz?: A Philosophical Reader*. Translated by Rodney Livingstone and Others, edited by Rolf Tiedemann. Stanford, CA: Stanford University Press, 2003.

Adorno, Theodor W. "Commitment." In *Aesthetics and Politics*. New York: Verso, 2007.

Adorno, Theodor W. *Critical Models: Interventions and Catchwords*. Translated by Henry W. Pickford. New York: Columbia University Press, 2005.

Adorno, Theodor W. "Cultural Criticism and Society." In *Prisms*. Translated by Samuel Weber and Shierry Weber Nicholsen. Cambridge, MA: MIT Press, 1984.

Adorno, Theodor W. *Current of Music: Elements of a Radio Theory*. Translated by Robert Hullot-Kentor. Malden, MA: Polity Press, 2009.

Adorno, Theodor W. "Das Altern der Neuen Musik." In *Gesammelte Schriften*. Vol. 14, edited by Rolf Tiedemann, 143–67. Frankfurt a.m.: Suhrkamp Verlag, 1972.

Adorno, Theodor W. "Democratic Leadership and Mass Manipulation." In *Gesammelte Schriften*. Vol. 20, edited by Rolf Tiedemann, 267–86. Frankfurt a.m.: Suhrkamp Verlag, 1972.

Adorno, Theodor W. "Der Essay als Form." In *Gesammelte Schriften*. Vol. 11, edited by Rolf Tiedemann. Frankfurt a.m.: Suhrkamp Verlag, 1972.

Adorno, Theodor W. "Die Idee der Naturgeschichte." In *Gesammelte Schriften*. Vol. 1, edited by Rolf Tiedemann, 345–65. Frankfurt a.m.: Suhrkamp Verlag, 1972.

Adorno, Theodor W. "Die Kunst und die Künste." In *Gesammelte Schriften*. Vol. 11.1, edited by Rolf Tiedemann. Frankfurt a.m.: Suhrkamp Verlag, 1972.

Adorno, Theodor W. *Dream Notes*. Translated by Rodney Livingstone. Malden, MA: Polity Press, 2007.

Adorno, Theodor W. *Drei Studien zu Hegel*. In *Gesammelte Schriften*. Vol. 1, edited by Rolf Tiedemann. Frankfurt a.m.: Suhrkamp Verlag, 1972.

Adorno, Theodor W. "Education after Auschwitz." In *Can One Live after Auschwitz?*, edited by Rolf Tiedemann. Stanford, CA: Stanford University Press, 2003.

Adorno, Theodor W. "Einleitung zu Benjamins Schriften." In *Gesammelte Schriften*. Vol. 11, edited by Rolf Tiedemann. Frankfurt a.m.: Suhrkamp Verlag, 1972.

Adorno, Theodor W. *Einleitung in die Musiksoziologie*. In *Gesammelte Schriften*. Vol. 14, edited by Rolf Tiedemann. Frankfurt a.m.: Suhrkamp Verlag, 1972.

Adorno, Theodor W. "Engagement oder künstlicher Autonomie." In *Gesammelte Schriften*. Vol. 11, edited by Rolf Tiedemann. Frankfurt a.m.: Suhrkamp Verlag, 1972.

Adorno, Theodor W. "Erziehung nach Auschwitz." In *Gesammelte Schriften*. Vol. 10.2, edited by Rolf Tiedemann. Frankfurt a.m.: Suhrkamp Verlag, 1972.

Adorno, Theodor W. "Essay as Form." In *Notes to Literature*. Vol. 1, edited by Rolf Tiedemann. New York: Columbia University Press, 1992.

Adorno, Theodor W. "Filmtransparente." In *Gesammelte Schriften*. Vol. 10.1, edited by Rolf Tiedemann. Frankfurt a.m.: Suhrkamp Verlag, 1972.

Adorno, Theodor W. "Fortschritt." In *Gesammelte Schriften*. Vol. 10.2, edited by Rolf Tiedemann. Frankfurt a.m.: Suhrkamp Verlag, 1972.

Adorno, Theodor W. "Fragment über Musik und Sprache." In *Gesammelte Schriften*. Vol. 16, edited by Rolf Tiedemann. Frankfurt a.m.: Suhrkamp Verlag, 1972.

Adorno, Theodor W. "The Function of Counterpoint in New Music." In *Sound Figures*. Translated by Rodney Livingstone, 123–44. Stanford, CA: Stanford University Press, 1999.

Adorno, Theodor W. *Gesammelte Schriften*. 20 volumes. Edited by Rolf Tiedemann. Frankfurt a.m.: Suhrkamp Verlag, 1972.

Adorno, Theodor W. *Hegel: Three Studies*. Translated by Shierry Weber Nicholsen. Cambridge, MA: MIT Press, 1993.

Adorno, Theodor W. "The Idea of Natural History." Translated by Robert Hullot-Kentor. *Telos* 60 (Summer 1984): 111–24.

Adorno, Theodor W. "Introduction to Benjamin's *Schriften*." In *Notes to Literature*. Vol. 2. Translated by Shierry Weber Nicholsen. New York: Columbia University Press, 1992.

Adorno, Theodor W. *An Introduction to Dialectics*. Translated by Nicholas Walker. Malden, MA: Polity Press, 2017.

Adorno, Theodor W. *Introduction to the Sociology of Music*. Translated by E. B. Ashton. New York: Continuum, 1976.

Adorno, Theodor W. "Is Art Lighthearted?" In *Notes to Literature*. Vol. 2. Translated by Shierry Weber Nicholsen, edited by Rolf Tiedemann. New York: Columbia University Press, 1992.

Adorno, Theodor W. "Ist die Kunst heiter?" In *Gesammelte Schriften*. Vol. 11, edited by Rolf Tiedemann, 599–608. Frankfurt a.m.: Suhrkamp Verlag, 1972.

Adorno, Theodor W. *Kant's Critique of Pure Reason*. Translated by Rodney Livingstone, edited by Rolf Tiedemann. Stanford, CA: Stanford University Press, 2001.

Adorno, Theodor W. *Kants Kritik der reinen Vernunft*. In *Nachgelassenen Schriften*. Vol. 4, edited by Rolf Tiedemann. Frankfurt am Main: Verlag, 1995.

Adorno, Theodor W. "Kierkegaard noch einmal." In *Gesammelte Schriften*. Vol. 2, edited by Rolf Tiedemann, 239–58. Frankfurt a.m.: Suhrkamp Verlag, 1972.

Adorno, Theodor W. "Kierkegaard once More." *Telos* 174 (Spring 2016): 57–74.

Adorno, Theodor W. "Kleine Proust-Kommentare." In *Gesammelte Schriften*. Vol. 11, edited by Rolf Tiedemann. Frankfurt a.m.: Suhrkamp Verlag, 1972.

Adorno, Theodor W. *Kranichsteiner Vorlesungen*. In *Nachgelassene Schriften, Abteilung IV*. Vol. 17, edited by Klaus Reichert and Michael Schwarz. Berlin: Suhrkamp, 2014.

Adorno, Theodor W. "Kritik des Musikanten." In *Gesammelte Schriften*. Vol. 14, edited by Rolf Tiedemann, 67–107. Frankfurt a.m.: Suhrkamp Verlag, 1972.

Adorno, Theodor W. "Kulturkritik und Gesellschaft." In *Gesammelte Schriften*. Vol. 10, edited by Rolf Tiedemann. Frankfurt a.m.: Suhrkamp Verlag, 1972.

Adorno, Theodor W. "Late Capitalism or Industrial Society?: The Fundamental Question of the Present Structure of Society." In *Can One Live after Auschwitz?: A*

Philosophical Reader, edited by Rolf Tiedemann, 111–25. Stanford, CA: Stanford University Press, 2003.

Adorno, Theodor W. *Mahler: A Musical Physiognomy*. Translated by Edmund Jephcott. Chicago: University of Chicago Press, 1992.

Adorno, Theodor W. *Mahler Eine Musikalische Physiognomik*. In *Gesammelte Schriften*. Vol. 13, edited by Rolf Tiedemann. Frankfurt a.m.: Suhrkamp Verlag, 1972.

Adorno, Theodor W. "Marginalia on Mahler." In *Essays on Music*, edited by Richard Leppert. Los Angeles: University of California Press, 2002.

Adorno, Theodor W. "Marginalia to Theory and Praxis." In *Critical Models: Interventions and Catchwords*. Translated by Henry W. Pickford. New York: Columbia University Press, 2005.

Adorno, Theodor W. "Marginalien zu Mahler." In *Gesammelte Schriften*. Vol. 18, edited by Rolf Tiedemann. Frankfurt a.m.: Suhrkamp Verlag, 1972.

Adorno, Theodor W. "Marginalien zur Theorie und Praxis." In *Gesammelte Schriften*. Vol. 10.2, edited by Rolf Tiedemann. Frankfurt a.m.: Suhrkamp Verlag, 1972.

Adorno, Theodor W. "The Meaning of Working through the Past." In *Can One Live after Auschwitz?: A Philosophical Reader*, edited by Rolf Tiedemann. Stanford, CA: Stanford University Press, 2003.

Adorno, Theodor W. *Metaphysics: Concept and Problems*. Translated by Edmund Jephcott, edited by Rolf Tiedemann. Stanford, CA: Stanford University Press, 2001.

Adorno, Theodor W. *Metaphysik: Begriff und Probleme*. In *Nachgelassenen Schriften*. Vol. 14, edited by Rolf Tiedemann. Frankfurt am Main: Verlag, 1998.

Adorno, Theodor W. *Minima Moralia: Reflections from Damaged Life*. Translated by E. F. N. Jephcott. New York: Verso, 2005.

Adorno, Theodor W. *Minima Moralia: Reflexionen aus dem beschädigten Leben*. In *Gesammelte Schriften*. Vol. 4, edited by Rolf Tiedemann. Frankfurt a.m.: Suhrkamp Verlag, 1972.

Adorno, Theodor W. "Music and Language: A Fragment." In *Quasi una Fantasia: Essays on Modern Music*. Translated by Rodney Livingstone, 1–6. New York: Verso, 1998.

Adorno, Theodor W. "The Natural History of the Theatre." In *Quasi Una Fantasia: Essays on Modern Music*. Translated by Rodney Livingstone. New York: Verso, 1998.

Adorno, Theodor W. "Naturgeschichte des Theaters." In *Gesammelte Schriften*. Vo. 16, edited by Rolf Tiedemann. Frankfurt a.m.: Suhrkamp Verlag, 1972.

Adorno, Theodor W. *Negative Dialectics*. Translated by E. B. Ashton. New York: Continuum, 1973.

Adorno, Theodor W. *Negativ Dialektik*. In *Gesammelte Schriften*. Vol. 6, edited by Rolf Tiedemann. Frankfurt a.m.: Suhrkamp Verlag, 1972.

Adorno, Theodor W. "Notes on Beckett." *Journal of Beckett Studies* 19, no. 2 (2010): 157–78.

Adorno, Theodor W. "Notes on Kafka." In *Prisms*. Translated by Samuel Weber and Shierry Weber Nicholsen Cambridge, MA: MIT Press, 1984.

Adorno, Theodor W. *Notes to Literature*. 2 volumes. Translated by Shierry Weber Nicholsen, edited by Rolf Tiedemann. New York: Columbia University Press, 1992.

Adorno, Theodor W. *Noten zur Literatur*. In *Gesammelte Schriften*. Vol. 11, edited by Rolf Tiedemann. Frankfurt a.m.: Suhrkamp Verlag, 1972.

Adorno, Theodor W. "On the Fetish-Character in Music and the Regression of Listening." In *Essays on Music*. Translated by Susan H. Gillespie, edited by Richard Leppert. Los Angeles, CA: University of California Press, 2002.

Adorno, Theodor W. "On Jazz." In *Essays on Music*, edited by Richard Leppert. Los Angeles: University of California Press, 2002.

Adorno, Theodor W. "On Some Relationships between Music and Painting." *The Musical Quarterly* 79, no. 1 (Spring, 1995): 66–79.

Adorno, Theodor W. "On Subject and Object." In *Critical Models: Interventions and Catchwords*. Translated by Henry W. Pickford. New York: Columbia University Press, 2005.

Adorno, Theodor W. "Parataxis: On Hölderlin's Late Poetry." In *Notes to Literature*. Vol. 2. Translated by Shierry Weber Nicholsen. New York: Columbia University Press, 1992.

Adorno, Theodor W. "Parataxis: Zur späten Lyrik Hölderlins." In *Gesammelte Schriften*. Vol. 11, edited by Rolf Tiedemann. Frankfurt a.m.: Suhrkamp Verlag, 1972.

Adorno, Theodor W. "Perrenial Fashion—Jazz." In *Prisms*. Translated by Samuel Weber and Shierry Weber Nicholsen. Cambridge, MA: MIT Press, 1984.

Adorno, Theodor W. *Philosophie der neuen Musik*. In *Gesammelte Schriften*. Vol. 12, edited by Rolf Tiedemann. Frankfurt a.m.: Suhrkamp Verlag, 1972.

Adorno, Theodor W. *Philosophy of New Music*. Translated by Robert Hullot-Kentor. Minneapolis: University of Minnesota Press, 2006.

Adorno, Theodor W. *Prisms*. Translated by Samuel Weber and Shierry Weber. Cambridge, MA: MIT Press, 1990.

Adorno, Theodor W. "Progress." In *Critical Models: Interventions and Catchwords*. Translated by Henry W. Pickford. New York: Columbia University Press, 2005.

Adorno, Theodor W. *Quasi una Fantasia: Essays on Modern Music*. Translated by Rodney Livingstone. New York: Verso, 1998.

Adorno, Theodor W. "Reflections on Class Theory." In *Can One Live after Auschwitz?*, edited by Rolf Tiedemann Stanford, CA: Stanford University Press, 2003.

Adorno, Theodor W. "Reflexion zur Klassentheorie." In *Gesammelte Schriften*. Vol. 8, edited by Rolf Tiedemann. Frankfurt a.m.: Suhrkamp Verlag, 1972.

Adorno, Theodor W. "Resignation." In *Critical Models: Interventions and Catchwords*. Translated by Henry W. Pickford, 289–93. New York: Columbia University Press, 2005.

Adorno, Theodor W. "Resignation." In *Gesammelte Schriften*. Vol. 10.2, edited by Rolf Tiedemann, 794–9. Frankfurt a.m.: Suhrkamp Verlag, 1972.

Adorno, Theodor W. "Spätkapitalismus oder Industriegesellschaft?" In *Gesammelte Schriften*. Vol. 6, edited by Rolf Tiedemann, 354–72. Frankfurt a.m.: Suhrkamp Verlag, 1972.

Adorno, Theodor W. "Spatstil Beethovens." In *Gesammelte Schriften*. Vol. 17, edited by Rolf Tiedemann. Frankfurt a.m.: Suhrkamp Verlag, 1972.

Adorno, Theodor W. "Short Commentaries on Proust." In *Notes to Literature*. Vol. 2. Translated by Shierry Weber Nicholsen, edited by Rolf Tiedemann. New York: Columbia University Press, 1992.

Adorno, Theodor W. *Towards a Theory of Musical Reproduction: Notes, A Draft, and Two Schemata*. Translated by Wieland Hoban. Malden, MA: Polity, 2006.

Adorno, Theodor W. "Transparencies on Film." In *The Continental Philosophy of Film Reader*, edited by Joseph Westfall. New York: Bloomsbury, 2018.

Adorno, Theodor W. "Trying to Understand *Endgame*." In *Notes to Literature*. Vol. 1. Translated by Shierry Weber Nicholsen, edited by Rolf Tiedemann. New York: Columbia University Press, 1992.

Adorno, Theodor W. "Über den Fetischcharakter in der Musik und die Regression des Hörens." In *Gesammelte Schriften*. Vol. 14, edited by Rolf Tiedemann. Frankfurt a.m.: Suhrkamp Verlag, 1972.

Adorno, Theodor W. "Über einige Relationen zwischen Musik und Malerei." In *Gesammelte Schriften*. Vol. 16, edited by Rolf Tiedemann. Frankfurt a.m.: Suhrkamp Verlag, 1972.

Adorno, Theodor W. "Über Jazz." In *Gesammelte Schriften*. Vol. 17, edited by Rolf Tiedemann. Frankfurt a.m.: Suhrkamp Verlag, 1972.

Adorno, Theodor W. "Vers une musique informelle." In *Gesammelte Schriften*. Vol. 16, edited by Rolf Tiedemann. Frankfurt a.m.: Suhrkamp Verlag, 1972.

Adorno, Theodor W. "Vers une musique informelle." In *Quasi una Fantasia: Essays on Modern Music*. Translated by Rodney Livingstone. New York: Verso, 1998.

Adorno, Theodor W. "Versuch, das Endspiel zu verstehen." In *Gesammelte Schriften*. Vol. 11, edited by Rolf Tiedemann, 281–324. Frankfurt a.m.: Suhrkamp Verlag, 1972.

Adorno, Theodor W. "Was bedeutet: Aufarbeitung der Vergangenheit." In *Gesammelte Schriften*. Vol. 10, edited by Rolf Tiedemann, 555–73. Frankfurt a.m.: Suhrkamp Verlag, 1972.

Adorno, Theodor W. "What National Socialism Has Done to the Arts." In *Essays on Music*, edited by Richard Leppert. Los Angeles: University of California Press, 2002.

Adorno, Theodor W. "Zeitlose Mode—Zum Jazz." In *Gesammelte Schriften*. Vol. 10.1, edited by Rolf Tiedemann. Frankfurt a.m.: Suhrkamp Verlag, 1972.

Adorno, Theodor W. *Zu einer Theorie der musikalischen Reproduktion: Aufzeichnungen, ein Entwurf und zwei Schemata*. In *Nachgelassene Schriften, Abteilung I*. Vol. 2, edited by Henri Lonitz Frankfurt am Main: Verlag, 2005.

Adorno, Theodor W. "Zu Subjekt und Objekt." In *Gesammelte Schriften*. Vol. 10.2, edited by Rolf Tiedemann, 741–58. Frankfurt a.m.: Suhrkamp Verlag, 1972.

Adorno, Theodor W. *Zur Metakritik der Erkenntnistheorie*. In *Gesammelte Schriften*. Vol. 5, edited by Rolf Tiedemann. Frankfurt a.m.: Suhrkamp Verlag, 1972.

Adorno, Theodor W. and Hanns Eisler. *Composing for the Films*. New York: Oxford University Press, 1947.

Adorno, Theodor W. and Hanns Eisler. *Komposition für den Film*. In *Gesammelte Schriften*. Vol. 15, edited by Rolf Tiedemann. Frankfurt a.m.: Suhrkamp Verlag, 1972.

Adorno, Theodor W. and Max Horkheimer. *Dialectic of Enlightenment: Philosophical Fragments*. Translated by Edmund Jephcott, edited by Gunzelin Schmid Noerr. Stanford, CA: Stanford University Press, 2002.

Adorno, Theodor W. and Max Horkheimer. *Dialektik der Aufklärung: Philosophische Fragmente*. In *Gesammelte Schriften*. Vol. 3, edited by Rolf Tiedemann. Frankfurt a.m.: Suhrkamp Verlag, 1972.

Adorno, Theodor W. and Max Horkheimer. "Society." In *German Sociology*, edited by Uta Gerhhardt. New York: Continuum, 1988.

Adorno, Theodor W. and Walter Benjamin. *The Complete Correspondence, 1928–1940*. Translated by Nicholas Walker, edited by Henri Lonitz. Cambridge, MA: Harvard University Press, 1999.

Agamben, Giorgio. *Homo Sacer: Sovereign Power and Bare Life*. Translated by Daniel Heller-Roazen. Stanford, CA: Stanford University Press, 1998.

Agamben, Giorgio. *Remnants of Auschwitz*. Translated by Daniel Heller-Roazen. New York: Zone Books, 1999.

Althusser, Louis. *The Humanist Controversy and Other Texts*. Translated by G. M. Goshgarian. New York: Verso, 2003.

Althusser, Louis. *Reading Capital*. Translated by Ben Brewster. New York: Verso, 2009.

Améry, Jean. "Resentments." In *At the Mind's Limits*. Translated by Sidney Rosenfeld and Stella P. Rosenfeld. Bloomington: Indiana University Press, 1980.

Améry, Jean. "Torture." In *At the Mind's Limits*. Translated by Sidney Rosenfeld and Stella P. Rosenfeld. Bloomington: Indiana University Press, 1980.

Anders, Günther. *Die Antiquiertheit des Menschen, Bd. I: Über die Seele im Zeitalter der zweiten industriellen Revolution*. München: C.H. Beck Verlag, 2002.

Anders, Günther. "On Promethean Shame." In *Prometheanism: Technology, Digital Culture, and Human Obsolescence*, edited by Christopher John Müller. New York: Rowman & Littlefield, 2016.

Anderson, Paul Allen. *Deep River: Music and Memory in Harlem Renaissance Thought*. Durham, NC: Duke University Press, 2001.

Attali, Jacques. *Noise: The Political Economy of Music*. Translated by Brian Massumi Minneapolis: University of Minnesota Press, 1985.

Badiou, Alain. *Deleuze: The Clamor of Being*. Translated by Louise Burchill. Minneapolis: University of Minnesota Press, 1999.

Baker, Jr., Houston A. *Blues, Ideology, and Afro-American Literature: A Vernacular Theory*. Chicago: University of Chicago Press.

Baldwin, James. *Go Tell It on the Mountain*. New York: Vintage Books, 1980.

Baldwin, James. "Of the Sorrow Songs: The Cross of Redemption." In *The Cross of Redemption: Uncollected Writings*, edited by Randall Kenan. New York: Vintage Books, 2010.

Baldwin, James. "Sonny's Blues." In *Going to Meet the Man*. New York: Vintage Books, 1993.

Baldwin, James. "The White Man's Guilt." In *Collected Essays*, edited by Toni Morrison. New York: Library of America, 1998.

Barthe, Roland. "The Bourgeois Art of Song." In *Mythologies*. Translated by Richard Howard and Annette Lavers. New York: Hill and Wang, 2012.

Baudelaire, Charles. *Intimate Journals*. Translated by Christopher Isherwood. Mineola, NY: Dover Publications 2006.

Beckett, Samuel. *Endgame & Act Without Words*. New York: Grove Press, 1958.

Beckett, Samuel. *How It Is*. Translated by Samuel Beckett. New York: Grove Press, 1964.

Benjamin, Walter. "Anmerkungen zu 'Über den Begriff der Geschichte.'" In *Gesammelte Schriften*. Vol. 1.3, edited by Rolf Tiedemann and Hermann Scheppenhäuser, 1230–40. Frankfurt a.m.: Suhrkamp Verlag, 1974.

Benjamin, Walter. *The Arcades Project*. Translated by Howard Eiland and Kevin McLaughlin. Cambridge, MA: Harvard University Press, 1999.

Benjamin, Walter. "Capitalism as Religion." In *Selected Writings*, Vol. 1, edited by Michael W. Jennings, 288–91. Cambridge, MA: Harvard University Press, 2003.

Benjamin, Walter. *The Concept of Criticism in German Romanticism*. In *Selected Writings*, Vol. 1, edited by Michael W. Jennings, 116–200. Cambridge, MA: Harvard University Press, 2003.

Benjamin, Walter. "Critique of Violence." In *Selected Writings*, Vol. 1, edited by Michael W. Jennings, 236–52. Cambridge, MA: Harvard University Press, 2003.

Benjamin, Walter. "Das Kunstwerk im Zeitalter seiner technischen Reproduzierbarkeit: Dritte Fassung." In *Gesammelte Schriften*. Vol. 1.2, edited by Rolf Tiedemann and Hermann Scheppenhäuser, 471–508. Frankfurt a.m.: Suhrkamp Verlag, 1974.

Benjamin, Walter. "Das Kunstwerk im Zeitalter seiner technischen Reproduzierbarkeit: Zweite Fassung." In *Gesammelte Schriften*. Vol. 7.1, edited by Rolf Tiedemann and Hermann Scheppenhäuser, 350–84. Frankfurt a.m.: Suhrkamp Verlag, 1974.

Benjamin, Walter. *Der Begriff der Kunstkritik in der deutschen Romantik*. In *Gesammelte Schriften*. Vol. 1.1, edited by Rolf Tiedemann and Hermann Scheppenhäuser, 7–122. Frankfurt a.m.: Suhrkamp Verlag, 1974.

Benjamin, Walter. "Der Erzähler: Betrachtungen zum Werke Nikolai Lesskows." In *Gesammelte Schriften*. Vol. 2.2, edited by Rolf Tiedemann and Hermann Scheppenhäuser, 438–65. Frankfurt a.m.: Suhrkamp Verlag, 1974.

Benjamin, Walter. "Der Sürrealismus." In *Gesammelte Schriften*. Vol. 2.1, edited by Rolf Tiedemann and Hermann Scheppenhäuser, 295–310. Frankfurt a.m.: Suhrkamp Verlag, 1974.

Benjamin, Walter. "Die Bedeutung der Sprache in Trauerspiel und Tragödie." In *Gesammelte Schriften*. Vol. 2.1, edited by Rolf Tiedemann and Hermann Scheppenhäuser, 137–40. Frankfurt a.m.: Suhrkamp Verlag, 1974.

Benjamin, Walter. "'Die Rückschritte der Poesie,' von Carl Gustav Jochmann." In *Gesammelte Schriften*. Vol. 1, edited by Rolf Tiedemann and Hermann Scheppenhäuser, 572–98. Frankfurt a.m.: Suhrkamp Verlag, 1974.

Benjamin, Walter. "Dream Kitsch: Gloss on Surrealism." In *Selected Writings*. Vol. 2.1, edited by Michael W. Jennings, 3–5. Cambridge, MA: Harvard University Press, 2003.

Benjamin, Walter. *Einbahnstraße*. In *Gesammelte Schriften*. Vol. 4, edited by Rolf Tiedemann and Hermann Scheppenhäuser. Frankfurt a.m.: Suhrkamp Verlag, 1974.

Benjamin, Walter. "Fate and Character." In *Selected Writings*. Vol. 1, edited by Michael W. Jennings, 201–6. Cambridge, MA: Harvard University Press, 2003.

Benjamin, Walter. "Franz Kafka: On the Tenth Anniversary of His Death." In *Selected Writings*. Vol. 2.2, edited by Michael W. Jennings, Cambridge, 794–818. MA: Harvard University Press, 2003.

Benjamin, Walter. "Franz Kafka: Zur zehnten Wiederkehr seines Todestages." In *Gesammelte Schriften*. Vol. 2, edited by Rolf Tiedemann and Hermann Scheppenhäuser, 409–38. Frankfurt a.m.: Suhrkamp Verlag, 1974.

Benjamin, Walter. *Gesammelte Schriften*. 7 volumes. Edited by Rolf Tiedemann and Hermann Scheppenhäuser. Frankfurt a.m.: Suhrkamp Verlag, 1974.

Benjamin, Walter. "Kapitalismus als Religion." In *Gesammelte Schriften*. Vol. 6, edited by Rolf Tiedemann and Hermann Scheppenhäuser, 100–3. Frankfurt a.m.: Suhrkamp Verlag, 1974.

Benjamin, Walter. "Karl Kraus." In *Gesammelte Schriften*. Vol. 2.1, edited by Rolf Tiedemann and Hermann Scheppenhäuser, 334–67. Frankfurt a.m.: Suhrkamp Verlag, 1974.

Benjamin, Walter. "Karl Kraus." In *Selected Writings*, Vol. 2.2, edited by Michael W. Jennings, 433–58. Cambridge, MA: Harvard University Press, 2003.

Benjamin, Walter. "Kleine Geschichte der Photographie." In *Gesammelte Schriften*. Vol. 2, edited by Rolf Tiedemann and Hermann Scheppenhäuser, 368–85. Frankfurt a.m.: Suhrkamp Verlag, 1974.

Benjamin, Walter. "Kurze Schatten (II)." In *Gesammelte Schriften*. Vol. 4, edited by Rolf Tiedemann and Hermann Scheppenhäuser, 425–28. Frankfurt a.m.: Suhrkamp Verlag, 1974.

Benjamin, Walter. "Little History of Photography." In *Selected Writings*. Vol. 2.2, edited by Michael W. Jennings, 507–30. Cambridge, MA: Harvard University Press, 2003.

Benjamin, Walter. "The Metaphysics of Youth." In *Selected Writings*. Vol. 1. edited by Michael W. Jennings, 6–17. Cambridge, MA: Harvard University Press, 2003.

Benjamin, Walter. "Metaphysik der Jugend." In *Gesammelte Schriften*. Vol. 2, edited by Rolf Tiedemann and Hermann Scheppenhäuser, 91–104. Frankfurt a.m.: Suhrkamp Verlag, 1974.

Benjamin, Walter. "On the Concept of History." In *Selected Writings*, Vol. 4, edited by Michael W. Jennings, 389–400. Cambridge, MA: Harvard University Press, 2003.

Benjamin, Walter. "On Language as Such and on the Language of Man." In *Selected Writings*. Vol. 1, edited by Michael W. Jennings, 62–74. Cambridge, MA: Harvard University Press, 2003.

Benjamin, Walter. "On the Mimetic Faculty." In *Selected Writings*, Vol. 2.2, edited by Michael W. Jennings, 720–22. Cambridge, MA: Harvard University Press, 2003.

Benjamin, Walter. *One-Way Street*. In *Selected Writings*. Vol. 1, edited by Michael W. Jennings. Cambridge, MA: Harvard University Press, 2003.

Benjamin, Walter. *The Origin of German Tragic Drama*. Translated by John Osborne. New York: Verso, 1998.

Benjamin, Walter. "Paralipomena to 'On the Concept of History.'" In *Selected Writings*. Vol. 4, edited by Michael W. Jennings, 401–11. Cambridge, MA: Harvard University Press, 2003.

Benjamin, Walter. "'The Regression of Poetry,' by Carl Gustav Jochmann." In *Selected Writings*. Vol. 4, edited by Michael W. Jennings, 356–80. Cambridge, MA: Harvard University Press, 2003.

Benjamin, Walter. "The Role of Language in *Trauerspiel* and Tragedy." In *Selected Writings*. Vol. 1, edited by Michael W. Jennings, 59–61. Cambridge, MA: Harvard University Press, 2003.

Benjamin, Walter. "Schicksal und Charakter." In *Gesammelte Schriften*. Vol. 2.1, edited by Rolf Tiedemann and Hermann Scheppenhäuser, 171–9. Frankfurt a.m.: Suhrkamp Verlag, 1974.

Benjamin, Walter. *Selected Writings*. 4 volumes. Edited by Michael W. Jennings. Cambridge, MA: Harvard University Press, 2003.

Benjamin, Walter. "Short Shadows (II)." In *Selected Writings*. Vol. 2.2, edited by Michael W. Jennings, 699–702. Cambridge, MA: Harvard University Press, 2003.

Benjamin, Walter. "The Storyteller: Observations on the Works of Nikolai Leskov." In *Selected Writings*. Vol. 3, edited by Michael W. Jennings, 143–66. Cambridge, MA: Harvard University Press, 2003.

Benjamin, Walter. "Surrealism." In *Selected Writings*. Vol. 2.1, edited by Michael W. Jennings, 207–21. Cambridge, MA: Harvard University Press, 2003.

Benjamin, Walter. "Theological-Political Fragment." In *Selected Writings*. Vol. 3, edited by Michael W. Jennings, 306. Cambridge, MA: Harvard University Press, 2003.

Benjamin, Walter. "Theologisch-Politisches Fragment." In *Gesammelte Schriften*. Vol. 2, edited by Rolf Tiedemann and Hermann Scheppenhäuser, 204. Frankfurt a.m.: Suhrkamp Verlag, 1974.

Benjamin, Walter. "Theorien des deutschen Faschismus." In *Gesammelte Schriften*. Vol. 3, edited by Rolf Tiedemann and Hermann Scheppenhäuser, 238–50. Frankfurt a.m.: Suhrkamp Verlag, 1974.

Benjamin, Walter. "Theories of German Fascism." In *Selected Writings*. Vol. 2.1, edited by Michael W. Jennings, 312–21. Cambridge, MA: Harvard University Press, 2003.

Benjamin, Walter. "Traumkitsch." In *Gesammelte Schriften*. Vol. 2, edited by Rolf Tiedemann and Hermann Scheppenhäuser, 620–2. Frankfurt a.m.: Suhrkamp Verlag, 1974.

Benjamin, Walter. "Über das mimetische Vermögen." In *Gesammelte Schriften*. Vol. 2.1, edited by Rolf Tiedemann and Hermann Scheppenhäuser, 210–13. Frankfurt a.m.: Suhrkamp Verlag, 1974.

Benjamin, Walter. "Über den Begriff der Geschichte." In *Gesammelte Schriften*. Vol. 1.2, edited by Rolf Tiedemann and Hermann Scheppenhäuser, 691–706. Frankfurt a.m.: Suhrkamp Verlag, 1974.

Benjamin, Walter. "Über Sprache überhaupt und über die Sprache des Menschen." In *Gesammelte Schriften*. Vol. 2.1, edited by Rolf Tiedemann and Hermann Scheppenhäuser, 140–57. Frankfurt a.m.: Suhrkamp Verlag, 1974.

Benjamin, Walter. *Ursprung des deutschen Trauerspiels*. In *Gesammelte Schriften*. Vol. 1.1, edited by Rolf Tiedemann and Hermann Scheppenhäuser, 203–430. Frankfurt a.m.: Suhrkamp Verlag, 1974.

Benjamin, Walter. "The Work of Art in the Age of Its Technological Reproducibility: Second Version." In *Selected Writings*. Vol. 3, edited by Michael W. Jennings, 101–33. Cambridge, MA: Harvard University Press, 2003.

Benjamin, Walter. "The Work of Art in the Age of Its Technological Reproducibility: Third Version." In *Selected Writings*. Vol. 4, edited by Michael W. Jennings, 251–83. Cambridge, MA: Harvard University Press, 2003.

Benjamin, Walter. "Zur Kritik der Gewalt." In *Gesammelte Schriften*. Vol. 2.1, edited by Rolf Tiedemann and Hermann Scheppenhäuser, 179–203. Frankfurt a.m.: Suhrkamp Verlag, 1974.

Benjamin, Walter. "Zur Phantasie, fr 89." In *Gesammelte Schriften*. Vol. 6, edited by Rolf Tiedemann and Hermann Scheppenhäuser, 121–2. Frankfurt a.m.: Suhrkamp Verlag, 1974.

Bensmaïa, Réda. "The Kafka Effect." In *Kafka: Toward a Minor Literature*. Translated by Terry Cochran, ix–xxi. Minneapolis: University of Minnesota Press, 1986.

Bhabha, Homi K. *The Location of Culture*. New York: Routledge, 1994.

Bignall, Simone and Paul Patton. *Deleuze and the Postcolonial*. Edinburgh: Edinburgh University Press, 2010.

Bloch, Ernst. *The Principle of Hope*. Vol. 1. Translated by Neville Plaice, et al. Cambridge, MA: MIT Press, 1995.

Bloch, Ernst. *The Spirit of Utopia*. Translated by Anthony A. Nassar. Stanford, CA: Stanford University Press, 2000.

Braidotti, Rosi. *The Posthuman*. Malden, MA: Polity Press, 2013.

Bryant, Levi, et al. "Towards a Speculative Philosophy." In *The Speculative Turn: Continental Materialism and Realism*, edited by Levi Bryant, Nick Srnicek, and Graham Harman. Melbourne: re.press, 2011.

Bürger, Peter. *Theory of the Avant-garde*. Translated by Michael Shaw. Minneapolis: University of Minnesota Press, 1984.

Caillois, Roger. "Mimicry and Legendary Psychasthenia." October 31 (Winter, 1984): 16–32.

Calarco, Mathew. *Thinking Through Animals: Identity, Difference, Indistinction*. Stanford, CA: Stanford University Press, 2015.

Campbell, Edward. *Music after Deleuze*. New York: Bloomsbury, 2013.

Canetti, Elias. *Crowds and Power*. Translated by Carol Stewart. New York: Farrar, Straus and Giroux, 1984.
Cascone, Kim. "The Aesthetics of Failure: 'Post-Digital' Tendencies in Contemporary Computer Music." In *Audio Culture*, edited by Christoph Cox and Daniel Warner, 392–98. New York: Continuum, 2010.
Colebrook, Claire. *Deleuze: A Guide for the Perplexed*. New York: Continuum, 2006.
Cook, Deborah. *Adorno, Foucault and the Critique of the West*. New York: Verso, 2018.
Cook, Deborah. *Adorno on Nature*. New York: Routledge, 2014.
Culp, Andrew. *Dark Deleuze*. Minneapolis: University of Minnesota Press, 2016.
Cutler, Chris. "Plunderphonia." In *Audio Culture*, edited by Christoph Cox and Daniel Warner New York: Continuum, 2010.
Danto, Arthur C. *After the End of Art: Contemporary Art and the Pale of History*. Princeton, NJ: Princeton University Press, 1997.
Davis, Angela. *Are Prisons Obsolete?* New York: Seven Stories Press, 2003.
Davis, Angela. *Blues Legacies and Black Feminism: Gertrude "Ma" Rainey, Bessie Smith, and Billie Holiday*. New York: Vintage, 1998.
Davis, Angela. "From the Prison of Slavery to the Slavery of Prison: Frederick Douglass and the Convict Leasing System." In *The Angela Y. Davis Reader*, edited by Joy James, 74–95. Malden, MA: Blackwell Publishers, 1998.
Davis, Mike. *Ecology of Fear: Los Angeles and the Imagination of Disaster*. New York: Metropolitan Books, 1998.
Deleuze, Gilles. *Bergsonism*. Translated by Barbara Habberjam. New York: Zone Books, 2006.
Deleuze, Gilles. "Boulez, Proust, and Time: 'Occupying without Counting.'" *Angelaki* 3, no. 2 (1998): 69–74.
Deleuze, Gilles. *Cinema 1: The Movement-Image*. Translated by Hugh Tomlinson and Barbara Habberjam Minneapolis: University of Minnesota Press, 1986.
Deleuze, Gilles. *Cinema 2: The Time-Image*. Translated by Hugh Tomlinson and Robert Galeta. Minneapolis: University of Minnesota Press, 1991.
Deleuze, Gilles. *Difference and Repetition*. Translated by Paul Patton. New York: Continuum, 1997.
Deleuze, Gilles. "The Exhausted." In *Essays Critical and Clinical*. Translated by Daniel W. Smith and Michael A. Greco. Minneapolis: University of Minnesota Press, 1997.
Deleuze, Gilles. *The Fold: Leibniz and the Baroque*. Translated by Tom Conley. Minneapolis: University of Minnesota Press, 1993.
Deleuze, Gilles. "Life and Literature." In *Essays Critical and Clinical*. Translated by Daniel W. Smith and Michael A. Greco. Minneapolis: University of Minnesota Press, 1997.
Deleuze, Gilles. *The Logic of Sense*. Translated by Mark Lester. New York: Columbia University Press, 1990.
Deleuze, Gilles. "Making Inaudible Forces Audible." In *Two Regimes of Madness: Texts and Interviews 1975–1995*, edited by David Lapoujade, 156–60. Cambridge, MA: MIT Semiotext(e), 2006.

Deleuze, Gilles. *Negotiations*. Translated by Martin Joughin. New York: Columbia University Press, 1995.

Deleuze, Gilles. *Nietzsche and Philosophy*. Translated by Hugh Tomlinson. New York: Columbia University Press, 1983.

Deleuze, Gilles. "Postscript on the Societies of Control." October 59 (Winter, 1992): 3–7.

Deleuze, Gilles. *Proust and Signs*. Translated by Richard Howard. Minneapolis: University of Minnesota Press, 2000.

Deleuze, Gilles. *Spinoza: Practical Philosophy*. Translated by Robert Hurley. San Francisco: City Light Books, 1988.

Deleuze, Gilles and Félix Guattari. *Anti-Oedipus: Capitalism and Schizophrenia*. Translated by Robert Hurley, Mark Seem, and Helen R. Lane. London: Continuum, 1983.

Deleuze, Gilles and Félix Guattari. *Kafka: Toward a Minor Literature*. Translated by Dana Polan. Minneapolis: University of Minnesota Press.

Deleuze, Gilles and Félix Guattari. "La synthèse disjonctive." *L'arc* 43, special issue on Pierre Klossowski (Aix-en-Provence: Duponchelle, 1970): 56.

Deleuze, Gilles and Félix Guattari. *A Thousand Plateaus: Capitalism and Schizophrenia*. Translated by Brian Massumi. London: Continuum, 2004.

Deleuze, Gilles and Félix Guattari. *What Is Philosophy?* Translated by Hugh Tomlinson and Graham Burchell. New York: Columbia University Press, 1996.

Derrida, Jacques. "Force of Law: The 'Mystical Foundation of Authority.'" In *Acts of Religion*. Translated by Mary Quaintance, 228–98. New York: Routlege, 2002.

Döblin, Alfred. "Materialism, A Fable." In *Bright Magic: Stories*. Translated by Damion Searls New York: New York Review Books, 2016.

Dolar, Mladen. *A Voice and Nothing More*. Cambridge, MA: MIT Press, 2006.

Du Bois, W. E. B. *The Souls of Black Folk*. New York: Oxford University Press, 2017.

Dumas, Henry. "Will the Circle be Unbroken?" In *Echo Tree: The Collected Short Fiction of Henry Dumas*, edited by Eugene B. Redmond. Minneapolis: Coffee House Press, 2003.

Eshun, Kodwo. "Further Considerations on Afrofuturism." *The New Centennial Review* 3, no. 2 (Summer, 2003): 287–302.

Eshun, Kodwo. *More Brilliant than the Sun*. London: Quartet Books Limited, 1998.

Fanon, Frantz. *Black Skin, White Masks*. Translated by Charles Lam Markmann. New York: Grove Press, 1967.

Fanon, Frantz. *The Wretched of the Earth*. Translated by Richard Philcox. New York: Grove Press, 2004.

Faulkner, William. *The Sound and the Fury*. New York: Vintage International, 1990.

Floyd, Jr., Samuel A. *The Power of Black Music: Interpreting Its History from Africa to the United States*. New York: Oxford University Press, 1995.

Foster, J. B. "Marx's Theory of Metabolic Rift: Classical Foundations for Environmental Sociology." *American Journal of Sociology* 143 (September 1999): 366–405.

Foster, Roger. *The Recovery of Experience*. Albany: State University of New York Press, 2007.

Gallope, Michael. *Deep Refrains: Music, Philosophy, and the Ineffable*. Chicago: University of Chicago Press, 2017.

Gayraud, Agnès. *Dialectic of Pop*. Translated by Robin Mackay, et al. Windsor Quarry: Urbanomic Media, 2019.

Gilbert, Jeremy. "Becoming-Music: The Rhizomatic Moment of Improvisation." In *Deleuze and Music*, edited by Ian Buchanan and Marcel Swiboda. Edinburgh: Edinburgh University Press, 2004.

Gilroy, Paul. *The Black Atlantic: Modernity and Double Consciousness*. Cambridge, MA: Harvard University Press, 1993.

Glissant, Édouard. *Caribbean Discourse: Selected Essays*. Translated by J. Michael Dash. Charlottesville: University Press of Virginia, 1989.

Godard, Jean-Luc. *Notre musique*. Paris: Avventura Films, 2004.

Goethe, Johann Wolfgang von. *The Sufferings of Young Werther*. Translated by Stanley Corngold. New York: W.W. Norton and Company, 2012.

Gould, Glenn. "The Prospects of Recording." In *Audio Culture*, edited by Christoph Cox and Daniel Warner, 115–26. New York: Continuum, 2010.

Gracyk, Theodore. "Adorno, Jazz, and the Aesthetics of Popular Music." *Musical Quarterly* 76, no. 4 (1992): 526–42.

Grosz, Elizabeth. "Deleuze, Ruyer and Becoming-Brain: The Music of Life's Temporality." *Parrhesia* 15 (2012): 1–13.

Habermas, Jürgen. *The Theory of Communicative Action: Reason and the Rationalization of Society*. 2 volumes. Translated by Thomas McCarthy. Boston: Beacon Press, 1984.

Haraway, Donna. "A Cyborg Manifesto: Science, Technology, and Socialist-Feminism in the Late Twentieth Century." In *Simians, Cyborgs and Women: The Reinvention of Nature*, 149–81. New York: Routledge, 1991.

Haraway, Donna. *Staying with the Trouble: Making Kin in the Chthulucene*. Durham, NC: Duke University Press, 2016.

Hartman, Saidiya. *Scenes of Subjection: Terror, Slavery, and Self-Making in Nineteenth-Century America*. New York: Oxford University Press.

Hegel, G. W. F. *Phenomenology of Spirit*. Translated by A. V. Miller. New York: Oxford University Press, 1977.

Hegel, G. W. F. *Science of Logic*. Translated by A. V. Miller. Atlantic Highlands, NJ: Humanities Press International, 1969.

Higgins, Sean. "A Deleuzian Noise/Excavating the Body of Abstract Sound." In *Sounding the Virtual: Gilles Deleuze and the Theory and Philosophy of Music*, edited by Brian Hulse and Nick Nesbitt. Burlington, VT: Ashgate, 2010.

Hilbig, Wolfgang. *Old Rendering Plant*. Translated by Isabel Fargo Cole. San Francisco: Two Lines Press, 2017.

Horkheimer, Max. *Dawn and Decline*. Translated by Michael Shaw. New York: The Seabury Press, 1978.

Horkheimer, Max. *Eclipse of Reason*. New York: Oxford University Press, 1947.

Horne, Gerald. *Paul Robeson: The Artist as Revolutionary*. London: Pluto Press, 2016.

Hughes, Langston. "The Negro Speaks of Rivers." In *The Collected Poems of Langston Hughes*, editedy by Arnold Rampersad and David Roessell. New York: Vincatage Classics—Random House, 1995.

Huhn, Tom. "Kant, Adorno, and the Social Opacity of the Aesthetic." In *The Semblance of Subjectivity: Essays in Adorno's Aesthetic Theory*, edited by Tom Huhn and Lambert Zuidervaart, 237-58. Cambridge, MA: MIT Press, 1997.

Husserl, Edmund. *The Phenomenology of Internal Time-Consciousness*. Translated by James S. Churchill. Bloomington: Indiana University Press, 1964.

Irigaray, Luce. "Women on the Market." In *This Sex Which Is Not One*. Translated by Catherine Porter. New York: Cornell University Press, 1985.

Iton, Richard. *In Search of the Black Fantastic: Politics and Popular Culture in the Post-Civil Right Era*. New York: Oxford University Press.

James, C. L. R. *Black Jacobins: Toussaint L'Ouverture and the San Domingo Revolution*. New York: Vintage Books.

James, Robin. "Neoliberal Noise: Attali, Foucault, and the Biopolitics of the Uncool." *Culture, Theory and Critique* 55, no. 2 (2014): 138-58.

James, Robin. *Resilience and Melancholy: Pop Music, Feminism, Neoliberalism*. Winchester: Zero Books, 2015.

Jameson, Fredric. *Postmodernism, or, The Cultural Logic of Late Capitalism*. Durham, NC: Duke University Press, 1991.

Johnston, Adrian. "For a Thoughtful Ontology: Hegel's Immanent Critique of Spinoza." In *Adventures in Transcendental Materialism*. Edinburgh: Edinburgh University Press, 2014.

Jones, Leroi (Amiri Baraka). *Blues People: The Negro Experience in White America and the Music that Developed from It*. New York: Morrow Quill, 1963.

Kafka, Franz, "Prometheus." In *The Complete Stories*, edited by Nahum N. Glatzer. New York: Schocken Books.

Kahn, Douglas. *Noise, Water, Meat: A History of Sound in the Arts*. Cambridge, MA: MIT Press, 1999.

Kant, Immanuel. *Critique of the Power of Judgment*. Translated by Paul Guyer and Eric Matthews. New York: Cambridge University Press, 2000.

Kant, Immanuel. *Critique of Pure Reason*. Translated by Paul Guyer and Allen W. Wood. New York: Cambridge University Press, 1998.

Kant, Immanuel. *Grounding for the Metaphysics of Morals*. Translated by James W. Ellington. Indianapolis: Hackett Publishing, 1993.

Kant, Immanuel. "The Metaphysics of Morals." In *Practical Philosophy*, edited by Mary J. Gregor. New York: Cambridge University Press, 2009.

Kant, Immanuel. *Prolegomena to Any Future Metaphysics*. Translated by Paul Carus. Indianapolis, IN: Hackett Publishing, 1977.

Kant, Immanuel. *Prolegomena zu einer jeden künftigen Metaphysik*, in *Sammtliche Werke*, Band 3. Edited by J. H. Kirchmann. Leipzig: L Heimann's Verlag, 1876.

Kiloh, Kathy. "Towards an Ethical Politics: T.W. Adorno and Aesthetic Self-relinquishment." *Philosophy and Social Criticism* 43, no. 6 (2017): 571-98.

Klemperer, Victor. *Language of the Third Reich*. New York: Continuum, 2006.

Kluge, Alexander. *Artist Under the Big Top: Perplexed*. West Germany: Kairos-Film, 1968.

Kluge, Alexander. *The Big Mess*. West Germany: Kairos-Film, 1968.

Kluge, Alexander and Gerhard Richter. *Dispatches from Moments of Calm*. Translated by Nathaniel McBride. New York: Seagull Books, 2016.

Kracauer, Siegfried. "The Mass Ornament." Translated by Barbara Correll and Jack Zipes, *New German Critique* 5 (Spring 1975): 67–76.

Kramer, Sina. *Excluded Within: The (Un)Intelligibility of Radical Political Actors*. New York: Oxford University Press, 2017.

Kristeva, Julia. *Melanie Klein*. Translated by Ross Guberman. New York: Columbia University Press, 2001.

Kristeva, Julia. *The Power of Horror: An Essay on Abjection*. Translated by Leon S. Roudiez. New York: Columbia University Press, 1982.

Lazzarato, Maurizio. *The Making of Indebted Man: An Essay on the Neoliberal Condition*. Los Angeles, CA: Semiotext(e), 2012.

Lee, Jr., Richard A. *The Thought of Matter: Materialism, Conceptuality, and the Transcendence of Immanence*. New York: Roman and Littlefield, 2016.

Le Guin, Ursula K. "The Ones Who Walk Away from Omelas." In *New Dimensions* 3, edited by Robert Silverberg. New York: Doubleday, 1973.

Lem, Stanislaw. *One Human Minute*. Translated by Catherine S. Leach. New York: Harvest Book, 1986.

Lenk, Elisabeth. "Introduction to the German Edition of Charles Fourier's The Theory of the Four Movements and the General Destinies." In *The Challenge of Surrealism: The Correspondence of Theodor W. Adorno and Elisabeth Lenk*. Translated by Susan H. Gillespie. Minneapolis: University of Minnesota Press, 2015.

Leppert, Richard. "'Commentary' to 'Music and Mass Culture.'" In *Essays on Music*, edited by Richard Leppert, 327–72. Los Angeles: University of California Press, 2002.

Levi, Primo. "Shame." In *The Drowned and the Saved*. Translated by Raymond Rosenthal. New York: Vintage, 1989.

Levi, Primo. *Survival in Auschwitz*. Translated by Stuart Woolf. New York: Simon & Schuster, 1986.

Lewis, George E. "Improvised Music after 1950: Afrological and Eurological Perspectives." In *Audio Culture*, edited by Christoph Cox and Daniel Warner. New York: Continuum, 2010.

López, Francisco. "Profound Listening and Environmental Sound Matter." In *Audio Culture*, edited by Christoph Cox and Daniel Warner. New York: Continuum, 2010.

Löwenthal, Leo. "Terror's Atomization of Man." *Commentary: A Jewish Review* 1 (1945/1946): 1–8.

Lowney, John. *Jazz Internationalism: Literary Afro-modernism and the Cultural Politics of Black Music*. Urbana: University of Illinois Press, 2017.

Lukács, Georg. *History and Class Consciousness: Studies in Marxist Dialectics.* Cambridge, MA: MIT Press, 1971.

Mann, Thomas. *Doctor Faustus: The Life of the German Composer Adrian Leverkühn as Told by a Friend.* Translated by H. T. Lowe-Porter. New York: Vintage Books, 1948.

Marcuse, Herbert. "The Affirmative Character of Culture." In *Art and Liberation*, edited by Douglas Kellner. New York: Routledge, 2007.

Marcuse, Herbert. *Eros and Civilization: A Philosophical Inquiry into Freud.* Boston, MA: Beacon Press, 1966.

Marx, Karl. *Capital: A Critique of Political Economy.* Vol. 1. Translated by Ben Fowkes. New York: Vintage Books, 1977.

Marx, Karl. *Capital: A Critique of Political Economy.* Vol. 2. Translated by David Fernbach. New York: Penguin Books, 1978.

Marx, Karl. "Contribution to the Critique of Hegel's *Philosophy of Right*: Introduction." In *Collected Works*. Vol. 3, edited by James S. Allen, et al., 175–87. New York: International Publishers, 1975.

Marx, Karl. "The Eighteenth Brumaire of Louis Bonaparte." In *Collected Works*. Vol. 11, edited. James S. Allen, et al. New York: International Publishers, 1975.

Marx, Karl. *Grundrisse: Foundation of the Critique of Political Economy.* Translated by Martin Nicolaus New York: Penguin Books, 1973.

Marx, Karl. "Private Property and Communism." In *Collected Works*. Vol. 3, edited by James S. Allen, et al., 293–305. New York: International Publishers, 1975.

Marx, Karl. "Results of the Immediate Process of Production." In *Capital*. Vol. 1. Translated by Ben Fowkes. New York: Vintage Books, 1977.

Massumi, Brian. *What Animals Teach Us about Politics.* Durham, NC: Duke University Press, 2014.

Maupassant, Guy de. *Aflout.* Translated by Douglas Parmée. New York: NYRB Classics, 2008.

McBrien, Justin. "Accumulating Extinction: Planetary Catastrophism in the Necrocene." In *Anthropocene or Capitalocene*, edited by Jason W. Moore, 116–37. Oakland, CA: PM Press, 2016.

McClary, Susan. *Conventional Wisdom: The Content of Musical Form.* Berkeley: University of California Press, 2000.

McKittrick, Katherine and Sylvia Wynter. *Sylvia Wynter: On Being Human as Praxis.* Durham, NC: Duke University Press, 2015.

Meillassoux, Quentin. *After Finitude: An Essay on the Necessity of Contingency.* Translated by Ray Brassier. New York: Continuum, 2008.

Melhem, D. H. "Revolution: The Constancy of Change." In *Conversations with Amiri Baraka*, edited by Charlie Reilly. Jackson: University Press of Mississippi, 1994.

Moore, Jason. *Capitalism in the Web of Life.* New York: Verso, 2015.

Morgan, Alastair. "A Preponderance of Objects: Critical Theory and the Turn to the Object." *Adorno Studies* 1, no. 1 (2017): 13–30.

Morris, William. *News from Nowhere and Other Writings.* New York: Penguin Books, 2004.

Morrison, Toni. *Song of Solomon*. New York: Vintage, 1977.
Moten, Fred. *Black and Blur: Consent not to be a Single Being*. Durham, NC: Duke University Press, 2017.
Moten, Fred. *In the Break: The Aesthetics of the Black Radical Tradition*. Minneapolis: University of Minnesota Press, 2003.
Mowitt, John. "The Sound of Music in the Era of Its Electronic Reproducibility." In *The Sound Studies Reader*, edited by Jonathan Sterne, 213–24. New York: Routledge, 2012.
Murray, Albert. *Stomping the Blues*. Boston, MA: Da Capo Press, 1989.
Murray, Albert. *Train Whistle Guitar*. New York: Vintage Books, 1974.
Neal, Mark Anthony. *What the Music Said: Black Popular Music and Black Public Culture*. New York: Routledge, 1999.
Nealon, Jeffrey. *Post-Postmodernism: or, The Cultural Logic of Just-in-Time Capitalism* Stanford, CA: Stanford University Press, 2012.
Nesbitt, Nick. "Critique and Clinique: From Sounding Bodies to the Musical Event." In *Sounding the Virtual: Gilles Deleuze and the Theory and Philosophy of Music*, edited by Brian Hulse and Nick Nesbitt, 159–80. Burlington, VT: Ashgate, 2010.
Nesbitt, Nick. "Deleuze, Adorno, and the Composition of Musical Multiplicity." In *Deleuze and Music*, edited by Ian Buchanan and Marcel Swiboda. Edinburgh: Edinburgh University Press, 2004.
Nesbitt, Nick. "The Expulsion of the Negative: Deleuze, Adorno, and the Ethics of Internal Difference." *Substance*, 34, no. 107 (2005): 75–97.
Neumann, Franz. *Behemoth: The Structure and Practice of National Socialism, 1933–1944*. Chicago: Oxford University Press, 2009.
Nietzsche, Friedrich. *The Birth of Tragedy and the Case of Wagner*. Translated by Walter Kaufmann. New York: Vintage Books, 1967.
Nietzsche, Friedrich. *The Gay Science*. Translated by Walter Kaufmann. New York: Vintage, 1974.
Nietzsche, Friedrich. *Twilight of the Idols, The Anti-Christ, Ecce Homo, and Other Writings*. Translated by Judith Norman. New York: Cambridge University Press, 2005.
Nosthoff, Anna-Verena. "Beckett, Adorno and the Hope for Nothingness as Something: Meditations on Theology in the Age of Its Impossibility." *Critical Research on Religion* 6, no. 1 (2018): 35–53.
Noys, Benjamin. *Malign Velocities: Accelerationism and Capitalism*. Winchester: Zero Books, 2014.
Oberle, Eric. *Theodor Adorno and the Century of Negative Identity*. Stanford, CA: Stanford University Press, 2018.
Okiji, Fumi. *Jazz as Critique: Adorno and Black Expression Revisited*. Stanford, CA: Stanford University Press, 2018.
Paddison, Max. *Adorno's Aesthetics of Music*. New York: Cambridge University Press, 1993.

Palmer, Robert. *Deep Blues: A Musical and Cultural History of the Mississippi Delta*. New York: Penguin Books, 1982.
Patterson, Orlando. *Slavery and Social Death: A Comparative Study*. Cambridge, MA: Harvard University Press, 1985.
Patton, Paul and John Protevi, et al. *Between Deleuze and Derrida*. New York: Continuum, 2003.
Pickford, Henry W. *The Sense of Semblance: Philosophical Analyses of Holocaust Art*. New York: Fordham University Press, 2013.
Pinto, Samantha. *Difficult Diasporas: The Transnational Feminist Aesthetic of the Black Atlantic* New York: New York University Press, 2013.
Proust, Marcel. *Remembrance of Things Past*. Vol. 1. Translated by C. K. Scott Moncrieff and Terence Kilmartin. New York: Vintage Books, 1982.
Proust, Marcel. *Remembrance of Things Past*. Vol. 2. Translated by C. K. Scott Moncrieff. London: Wordworth Editions, 2006.
Puar, Jasbir K. *The Right to Maim: Debility, Capacity, Disability*. Durham, NC: Duke University Press, 2017.
Puar, Jasbir K. *Terrorist Assemblages: Homonationalism in Queer Times*. Durham, NC: Duke University Press, 2006.
Pynchon, Thomas. *Gravity's Rainbow*. New York: Penguin Books, 1973.
Rancière, Jacques. "The Aesthetic Revolution and Its Outcomes." In *Dissensus*. Translated by Steven Corcoran. New York: Continuum, 2010.
Rancière, Jacques. *Aesthetics and Its Discontents*. Translated by Steven Corcoran. Malden, MA: Polity, 2009.
Robinson, Cedric. *Black Marxism: The Making of the Black Radical Tradition*. Chapel Hill: University of North Carolina Press, 2000.
Rodgers, Tara. *Pink Noise: Women on Electronic Music and Sound*. Durham, NC: Duke University Press, 2010.
Rose, Tricia. *Black Noise: Rap Music and Black Culture in Contemporary America*. Hanover, NH: Wesleyan University Press, 1994.
Rusert, Britt. *Fugitive Science: Empiricism and Freedom in Early African American Culture*. New York: New York University Press, 2017.
Rzewski, Frederic. "Little Bangs: A Nihilist Theory of Improvisation." In *Audio Culture*, edited by Christoph Cox and Daniel Warner. New York: Continuum, 2010.
Safatle, Vladimir. "Mirrors Without Images: Mimesis and Recognition in Lacan and Adorno." *Radical Philosophy* no. 139 (September/October 2006): 9–19.
Said, Edward. *On Late Style: Music and Literature Against the Grain*. New York: Vintage Books, 2007.
Scarry, Elaine. *Body in Pain: The Making and Unmaking of the World*. New York: Oxford University Press, 1985.
Schafer, R. Murray. *The Soundscape: Our Sonic Environment and the Tuning of the World*. Rochester, VT: Destiny Books, 1994.

Schwarz, Boris. "Joseph Joachim and the Genesis of Brahms's Violin Concerto." *The Musical Quarterly* LXIX, no. 4 (October 1983): 503–26.
Smith, Daniel W. "'A Life of Pure Immanence': Deleuze's 'Critique et Clinique' Project." In *Essays Critical and Clinical*. Translated by Daniel W. Smith and Michael A. Greco, xli–xlv. Minneapolis: University of Minnesota Press, 1997.
Spivak, Gayatri. "Can the Subaltern Speak?" In *Marxism and the Interpretation of Culture*, edited by Cary Nelson and Lawrence Grossberg. Chicago: University of Illinois Press, 1988.
Stendhal, *The Charterhouse of Parma*. Translated by Richard Howard. New York: Modern Library, 2000.
Stengers, Isabelle. "The Cosmopolitical Proposal." In *Making Things Public*, edited by Bruno Latour and Peter Weibel, 994–1003. Cambridge, MA: MIT Press, 2005.
Subotnik, Rose. "Toward a Deconstruction of Structural Listening: A Critique of Schoenberg, Adorno, and Stravinsky." In *Deconstructive Variations: Music and Reason in Western Society*. Minneapolis: University of Minnesota Press, 1996.
Sutherland, Kestin. "The Poetics of *Capital*." In *Capitalism: Concept, Idea, Image*. London: CRMEP Books, 2019.
Swiboda, Marcel. "Cosmic Strategies: The Electric Experiments of Miles Davis." In *Deleuze and Music*, edited by Ian Buchanan and Marcel Swiboda. Edinburgh: Edinburgh University Press, 2004.
Thomas, Greg. "Afro-Blue Notes: The Death of Afro-pessimism (2.0)?" *Theory & Event* 21, no. 1 (January 2018): 282–317.
Thompson, Marie. "Experimental Music and the Question of What a Body Can Do." In *Musical Encounters with Deleuze and Guattari*, 149–68. New York: Bloomsbury, 2017.
Thompson, Mark Christian. *Anti-music: Jazz and Racial Blackness in German Thought Between the Wars*. New York: SUNY Press, 2018.
Thoreau, Henry David. "A Telegraph Harp." In *Poems for the Millennium*. Vol. 3, edited by Jerome Rothenberg and Jeffrey C. Robinson. Los Angeles: University of California Press, 2009.
Thoreau, Henry David. *Walden*. New York: Oxford University Press, 1999.
Uexküll, Jakob von. *A Foray into the Worlds of Animals and Humans*. Translated by Joseph D. O'Neil. Minneapolis: University of Minnesota Press, 2010.
Veal, Michael. "Starship Africa." In *The Sound Studies Reader*, edited by Jonathan Sterne, 454–67. New York: Routledge, 2012.
Weiss, Joseph. "The Composer as Producer." In *The Aesthetic Ground of Critical Theory*, edited by Nathan Ross. New York: Roman and Littlefield, 2015.
Whately, Warren C. "African American Strike-Breaking from the Civil War to the New Deal." *Social Science History* 17, no. 4 (Winter, 1993): 525–58.
Wilderson III, Frank. "Afro-Pessimism and the End of Redemption." *Humanities Futures*: https://humanitiesfutures.org/papers/afro-pessimism-end-redemption/ (Last accessed July 5, 2019).

Williamson, Alastair. "New Music, Late Style: Adorno's 'Form in the New Music.'" *Music Analysis* 27, no. 2/3 (July–October 2008): 193–99.

Witkin, Robert W. *Adorno on Music*. New York: Routledge, 1998.

Žižek, Slavoj. "Against the Populist Temptation." *Critical Inquiry* 32, no. 3 (Spring 2006): 551–74.

Žižek, Slavoj. *Less than Nothing: Hegel and the Shadow of Dialectical Materialism*. New York: Verso, 2012.

Index

acceleration. *See* tempo
Adams, John   39, 88, 131
advanced music   12, 15, 23, 31–2, 39–41, 45, 49 n.135, 58, 67, 85–6, 96, 102, 111, 122, 124–5, 129
affect   xiii, 75, 79, 88, 93
affirmation   7, 44–5, 50, 82, 89–90, 100, 114, 116–17, 121, 141, 143, 147
Afro-futurism   6 n.24, 27–8, 46, 89–90
aleatory. *See* chance
Alexander, Texas   59
alienation   10, 15–16, 22–3, 39–41, 43, 53–5, 57, 66 n.76, 75, 119, 123
allegory   13, 18, 25 n.28, 47, 51, 54, 56, 63 n.60, 77, 123
Allman, Duane   29, 60, 66
Althusser, Louis   43
Amacher, Maryanne   16
Améry, Jean   47, 66, 82
amplification   xv, 11, 23, 26–7, 28, 33–7, 55, 58, 60–1, 76–7, 82–5, 87–9, 91, 104, 125, 127 n.92, 131, 138, 142
Anastasio, Trey   29
Anders, Günther   124
Anderson, Laurie   91
animal   2, 14 n.63, 16, 21–2, 31–7, 45, 50, 73, 84, 114–15, 120–1, 138, 140–1, 144, 146
anthropomorphism   13–14, 23–4, 26, 33–7, 41, 43, 48, 106
antinomy   xv, 57, 82, 94–8, 100 n.245, 120–1
antiphony. *See* call and response
arborescence   ix, 69–70
Armstrong, Louis   110
Artaud, Antonin   101
assemblage   viii n.4, ix, 13, 87–9
atonement. *See* redemption
Attali, Jacques   32
aura   19, 24, 26, 27 n.37, 29–31, 37, 45, 47, 72–3, 80, 97, 109, 114, 126, 137, 139, 147

Auschwitz   xii, 6–7, 9, 47, 79, 95, 98, 109–47
autonomous music   xiii–xiv, 27, 47, 70, 74, 95–6, 100–1, 103, 129
avant-garde   xii, 69, 94

Bach, J. S., 19, 21, 31, 34, 40, 47, 55, 66 n.74, 77, 91
Bailey, Deford   82–5, 140
Baker Jr., Houston A., 59
Baldwin, James   64, 82, 86, 103
Bang on a Can   88, 125
Baraka, Amiri   55, 57–8, 96 n.221
baroque. *See Trauerspiel*
Bartók, Béla   136
Baudelaire, Charles   36, 140
Beckett, Samuel   xi, 46–7, 64 n.67, 98, 122, 132–4, 138
becoming
  -animal   29, 31–4, 73 n.115, 84, 121, 140
  -bird   2, 15–16, 21–3, 26–8, 32, 34, 45, 63, 69–70, 141
  -child   1–2, 4–5, 8–9, 11, 15, 19, 29, 64, 72, 106, 121–3, 130–1, 134, 136, 138, 144
  -insect   15, 21, 26–8, 32–7, 128
  -molecular   15, 21, 27, 31, 34–7, 51, 60 n.44, 67, 70–1, 102, 133–4
  -music   2, 15, 38, 83
  -other   x, 10, 93
  -with   14 n.63, 32
  -woman   15, 31–2, 47
Beethoven, Ludwig van   22–6, 28, 41 n.95, 47–9, 55–6, 63, 66 n.74, 89, 91, 105, 118, 130, 138–9, 143, 145
Berg, Alban   38–9, 68
Bergson, Henri   x, 69, 71
Berry, Chuck   78
Beuys, Joseph   120
biology   3–4, 47, 50, 66
Black expressive music   28–30, 41 n.95, 57 n.29, 59, 73, 77, 83, 101 n.245

Blakey, Art   141
Blanqui, Louis Auguste   116
Bloch, Ernst   19, 43 n.107, 115
blues   xii–xiii, 28–30, 54–66, 68, 71–4,
    76–80, 82–4, 86–7, 89–92, 96–9,
    105, 107, 141
body   xi, 21, 41, 46, 70, 74–6, 99, 109,
    112, 124, 132
  without organs   14, 16, 44
Boulez, Pierre   38–9, 127 n.92
bourgeois   4, 6, 15, 23–6, 32, 42,
    49 n.135, 50, 69, 74–5, 80, 87,
    93 n.207, 94–6, 100–2, 114–15, 121,
    123, 134
Brahms, Johannes   1–18, 60, 65, 78, 134,
    143, 145
Braxton, Anthony   85–6
breath. *See* aura
Bresnick, Martin   127
Brooker, Charlie   136
Broonzy, Bill   76–8, 81, 88
Brown, James   90
Brown, Willie   62
Bruckner, Anton   142
Bryars, Gavin   127
Burbridge, Oteil   90

Cage, John   28, 43, 46, 83, 106, 139, 143
call and response   5, 16, 64–5, 85, 89, 144
camps   7, 47, 75, 98, 109–11, 116–17,
    120–1, 132–5, 141, 144
Canetti, Elias   32
capital   xii–xiii, 9, 11 n.52, 24, 37–8, 58,
    67, 73, 79, 88, 103, 111–17, 124,
    126, 128 n.93, 142
  its axiomatic, xiii, 57, 86, 93
Carlos, Wendy   91
Cascone, Kim   86
categorical imperative   95, 120–1
Chambers, Paul   85
chance   viii, 8, 34, 46, 50, 76–8, 96–100,
    107, 121, 126, 129, 134–5
Chaplin, Charlie   144
character   vii, xii, 29, 36, 44–5, 50, 59, 64,
    76–9, 82, 84, 96, 102, 111, 142
childhood. *See* becoming-child
chorus   10–11, 25–6, 41, 47–8, 50, 80,
    85, 132
class   vii, xiv, 10, 17, 49, 75, 92–3,
    94 n.208, 120

co-enactment   73, 92–3, 99, 102
Coleman, Ornette   96
Collins, Bootsy   90
colonization   54–6, 72, 100
  colonizer and colonized   54, 59, 64–6,
    71, 74–7
  decolonization   xiv n.31, 61, 65–7
color. *See* tonality
Coltrane, John   83–4, 99 n.236, 105
commodity   xiv, 10, 16, 34, 68, 74–5, 91,
    93, 96, 100, 103, 106, 139 n.130, 143
communism   10, 34, 37, 50, 118–20
constellations   viii–ix, 4, 16, 21, 35, 44,
    48, 55–6, 65, 77, 104, 111, 126, 146
control society   74–6, 79–80, 113
convention   xiii, 16, 21, 28, 34–5, 37–8,
    48, 58, 67–9, 71, 83, 93, 95, 122,
    125 n.88, 126
cosmological   xii, 3, 9, 16–17, 20–1,
    28, 44, 46–8, 88, 90, 104, 116–18,
    132–3, 139, 146
  and elemental   2, 30, 34–6, 50, 105,
    132
Cotton, Elizabeth   80–2, 88
counterpoint. *See* polyphony
criminal. *See* fugitive
critique   x, xii, xv, 12–13, 21, 35, 42,
    49–50, 55–6, 77, 81, 86–7, 92–6, 98,
    101, 111, 122, 124–5, 139
  critical theory   xiii, 120
  and rescue   38, 47, 137
culture industry   xiii, 36, 82, 91–5, 124,
    126

dance   26, 30, 61–2, 68–9, 84, 96, 130,
    145
danger   x, 34, 61, 85, 88, 130, 143
  moment of   8, 11, 78, 134
Danto, Arthur   124
Davis, Angela   57, 76
death   8, 10, 16–17, 53, 60, 62, 65, 68,
    78, 82, 95, 97, 104, 106–7, 115, 121,
    129, 131, 133, 135–7, 141–2
  drive/instinct   37, 42, 109–10, 113
debt   69, 118–19, 122
  infinite   xii, 24, 68, 111–17
decontextualization   vii, 89–90, 146
deterritorialization. *See* territorialization
dialectic   vii, x–xiii, xv, 3, 11, 14, 23,
    25–6, 30, 34, 38, 43–5, 49–50, 60–3,

68–71, 78, 87, 96, 99, 101, 106,
124–30, 142
  of enlightenment viii, 15
  image 16, 30–1, 37, 129 n.99
  of natural-history 4, 12 n.53, 13, 44,
  68, 76, 119, 128, 130
  at a standstill 11, 13
diaspora xiii, 29, 53
  African 54, 72–3, 75, 80, 95
  Jewish 6, 80
difference x–xi, 12, 14, 39, 41, 46, 49, 68,
  71, 99, 133–6
digital xv, 23, 31, 34, 70, 85, 128
Döblin, Alfred 33
domination vii, xi, xiii, xv, 3, 22, 35, 41,
  43, 45, 49–50, 79–80, 86, 97, 100,
  111–12, 123, 133, 137, 139
  of nature 7, 14 n.63, 63, 75, 109–10
Douglas, Frederick 65
Dresser, Mark 85
drum 34, 60, 71, 83–4, 89, 126, 131,
  137–8, 140–2, 146
Du Bois, W. E. B. xiii
Dumas, Henry 69

Eastman, Julius 86
echo xv, 3, 9–10, 12 n.54, 15–18, 19–20,
  24, 32, 34, 47, 50–1, 56, 58–61,
  64–6, 71–2, 76, 81, 83–4, 86, 88–9,
  92, 95, 109, 128–9, 131, 142–3, 145
ecology 21, 87–9, 129
editing 23, 31, 70 n.99
effects 29, 31, 34–6, 84, 86, 88, 101, 105,
  127, 131, 141, 143
electricity 9–10, 17, 23, 28, 32–3, 35–6,
  85, 106, 129, 132, 136, 138, 141,
  146
electroacoustic xii, 3, 9, 16, 21, 23, 27,
  36–7, 46, 55, 60, 68, 84–5, 88, 104,
  106, 119, 127–8, 142
Ellington, Duke 83, 140
Ellison, Ralph 100, 101 n.245
Eno, Brian 28
epic 24, 50, 72, 75, 77, 81, 88, 104, 138
escape xiii, 3, 7, 29, 33, 54, 58, 65,
  67–8, 73 n.115, 74 n.120, 76–7, 79,
  80 n.145, 81, 86, 110–11, 114–16,
  120, 122, 131, 137, 140–1, 147
Eshun, Kodwo 27 n.37, 29 n.46, 37,
  76 n.129, 90

exchange xi, xiii–xiv, 12 n.52, 49, 111–13
  value 94, 96, 126, 139 n.130
experience xii–xiii, 21, 40, 47, 83 n.160,
  101, 103, 134, 147
  destruction of 30–1, 40, 42 n.102,
  64 n.67, 94 n.208, 107, 138, 145
experimental xii–xiv, 21, 28, 32, 38, 46,
  55, 94, 102, 105, 107, 119, 127 n.92,
  130, 137
expression vii, xi–xii, 5, 8, 15, 34, 39–40,
  43–5, 47, 53–4, 58–9, 72, 74, 83,
  91, 93, 103–4, 112, 114, 123, 132,
  136 n.121
expropriation xiii, xv, 9, 31, 103, 118

fairytale 1, 8, 26, 104, 131
fascism 10, 15, 34, 37, 44 n.109, 50, 100,
  112, 115, 118, 121, 147
fashion. *See* convention
fate 18, 33, 54, 76–9, 81, 107, 110–11
Feldman, Morton 40
Fennesz 118
fetishism xiii, 99–103, 107, 139 n.130
film 13, 38, 69, 95, 109, 119, 125,
  127 n.92, 129, 137, 143–4, 146
Fishman, Jon 141
flow xii, xv, 11, 22–3, 32–3, 35–6, 48, 60,
  70, 75, 85, 88–90, 105, 113, 121–2,
  124, 132, 134
Floyd Jr., Samuel A., 79, 83
form vii–x, xii, 2, 16, 25, 35, 49,
  49 n.135, 57 n.29, 67, 71–4, 76,
  92–3, 97, 104, 120, 124, 126–8, 131,
  137, 143
  and content 38–41, 70, 88 n.102
Freud, Sigmund xii, 112–13, 121–3
fugitive xiv, 25, 54, 56, 86–7, 91
fugue 25–6, 55, 130

gambling 71, 76–81
General Intellect 23, 31, 118
genius 29, 48, 77, 82, 99, 103
George, Stefan 46
Gillespie, Dizzy 100
Gilroy, Paul 29 n.44, 80
Glass, Philip 127
Glissant, Édouard 59, 61, 64, 71
Godard, Jean-Luc 139, 143
Gordon, Michael xiii, 23, 104, 125–32,
  137–47

Index

Gordon, Mike   90, 118
Gould, Glenn   19–21, 27, 31, 34, 59, 131
gratitude   6–8
  Dankgesang   6, 18
guilt   xii–xiii, 25, 45, 74, 98, 118, 132, 136
  context/nexus   xii, 7, 22, 54, 60, 73 n.15, 74 n.120, 79, 81–2, 111–17, 120

happiness   6, 78, 82, 103, 115–16, 127, 140
  promise of   1, 7, 9, 11, 25
Haraway, Donna   14 n.63, 91
harmonica   29, 60, 82–4
harmony   4, 16–17, 20–1, 27, 29, 32, 41–2, 77, 79, 85, 106, 123, 137, 143
Hartman, Saidiya   61, 75–6
Hecker, Tim   118
Hegel   x, 13, 22, 45, 48, 71, 83, 86, 89, 92, 99, 110
Hendrix, Jimi   29, 126
Hilbig, Wolfgang   119, 133
history   vii, xi, 1, 3, 6–10, 13–14, 16, 17, 22–3, 26, 33–5, 38–40, 43, 45–9, 53–4, 64, 68, 71–2, 74, 81–2, 88, 95–6, 98, 103–4, 111, 115, 117, 119, 124, 126, 129, 134, 136, 139, 145–7
  historical materialism   6, 16, 137
  natural (*see* dialectic)
  prehistory   16–17, 24, 50, 56, 78, 111, 121, 125, 128, 134
Holiday, Billie   67
Honegger, Arthur   83, 140
Hood, Thomas   89
Hooker, Earl   66
Horkheimer, Max   46, 87, 98
House, Son   59, 69
humanism   23, 25, 42–4, 50
  humanity   22–3, 44 n.109, 47, 66, 115, 134, 144
  post-human   25, 84, 118

idealism   12, 33, 48, 89
ideology   xii, 3, 12, 32, 43, 50, 81, 92, 117
Ikeda, Ryoji   146
image   vii, xi, 1, 3, 6, 9, 17, 26, 47–8, 55, 64, 69, 82, 90, 107, 109, 113, 119, 129, 131, 133, 137
  of thought   x, 75

immanence   vii–ix, xii, 11, 12 n.55, 25, 27, 35, 38 n.86, 41, 42 n.102, 44, 48–9, 57, 59, 72, 76, 86, 96, 103–4, 120, 126–8, 131, 135
  critique   ix, 95
improvisation   xiii, 31, 60, 70 n.99, 76–8, 85, 88–9, 91, 96–103, 105–7, 115
Indifferenz   9, 16, 132–7, 142
insects. *See* becoming-insect
instrument/instrumentation   5, 11, 15, 20, 22–7, 32, 34–5, 37, 44, 58–61, 63, 65, 71–3, 76–7, 81, 83–6, 93, 104–5, 120, 125–8, 130–2, 141, 144–5
intensity   60, 69, 75–7, 89, 118, 124, 135
Iton, Richard   58

James, Elmore   57, 66
James, Skip   79
jazz   xii–xiii, 28, 55, 57 n.29, 58, 61, 73, 83–6, 91–2, 95–101, 117 n.45, 127, 141, 145
Jefferson, Blind Lemon   63
Joachim, Joseph   5, 78
Johnson, Blind Willie   63–9
justice   47, 50–1, 58, 64–5, 128 n.93

Kafka, Franz   7, 73–5, 106, 115–16, 121, 128 n.93
Kalhor, Kayhan   66
Kant, Immanuel   xiii, 25, 77, 83 n.160, 99, 136
Kiefer, Anselm   121
kitsch   xv n.33, 95, 104, 117 n.45, 143, 146
Kluge, Alexander   94, 130, 144, 146
Kracauer, Siegfried   49
Kraftwerk   140
Kraus, Karl   20
Kürnberger, Ferdinand   121

labor   viii, xiii, 16, 23, 27, 29, 40, 42, 50, 60, 74, 76 n.129, 80–1, 92, 103, 116–17, 120, 122, 124, 131
  dead and living   xiv, 24, 31–2, 34, 37, 65, 85, 119, 137, 139
Lang, David   125, 127
language   vii, viii n.4, x, 1, 20, 22, 41, 53–7, 71–2, 81, 119, 126, 135, 140
Lanzmann, Claude   109

law   3, 7, 9, 11, 12 n.54, 47, 65, 68, 87, 103, 109, 119, 123, 128 n.93, 137
Leibniz, Gottfried Wilhelm   90
Lem, Stanislaw   9, 15
Levi, Primo   82, 114, 133
Lewis, George   85
life   x, 3, 6–7, 22, 45, 62, 77, 79, 81–2, 97, 110–11, 113, 115–16, 121, 133
Ligeti, György   27, 131, 142–3
Lincoln, Abbey   66
line of flight   26, 98, 114–17
Little Hans   121–3, 131
locomotive. *See* train
Loli, Giulia (Mutamassik)   86, 118
López, Francisco   36, 128
Löwenthal, Leo   75
Lucier, Alvin   28, 130
Lukács, György   74
lullaby   xii, 1–2, 4, 6, 8, 11, 16, 21, 26, 36–7, 44, 59, 62, 64, 68, 102, 121–3, 134, 136

McConnel, Page   118
machine   ix, 11–12, 14 n.63, 16, 23–4, 31, 36–7, 40, 57, 63, 70 n.100, 84–6, 88 n.182, 91, 97, 121, 124–5, 127–8, 140, 147
machining the voice   xv, 15, 20, 22, 51, 59, 72, 83, 91, 105, 138
Mahler, Gustav   10, 117 n.45
Marshall, Ingram   68
Marx, Karl   xii, 3, 8, 10, 27, 43, 50, 109, 118–19
masochism   41, 60, 68, 91, 99, 111, 122, 133
material   5, 12 n.55, 13, 20, 28, 33–4, 39, 41, 43, 50, 57, 66, 70, 72, 76, 94 n.208, 104, 111–12, 116, 122–3
Maupassant, Guy de   11
meaning   7, 16–17, 22, 47, 53–4, 56–7, 83, 89, 91, 98, 110
mediation   x, 13, 16, 20, 36, 38 n.86, 67, 72, 105, 128
   and immediacy   45, 94 n.208, 95–6, 98
melody   4–5, 15, 18, 20, 22, 25 n.29, 32, 44, 56, 59, 76, 81, 83, 86, 104, 106, 122, 131, 139, 142–4, 146

memory   xiv n.30, 5–8, 11, 18, 29 n.46, 40–3, 49, 56–8, 64–7, 73, 102, 106–7, 119, 134, 136, 142, 145, 147
Merzbow   84
Messiaen, Olivier   137
metaphysics   vii, ix, xii, 6–7, 13, 17, 35, 47, 53, 55, 60, 77, 81, 83 n.160, 85, 88
microtonal   16, 21, 36, 44, 128
Middle Passage   xii, 64, 98
Mimaroğlu, İlhan   146
mimesis   ix–x, 2, 11, 14 n.63, 29, 36–7, 48 n.130, 59, 63, 66–7, 73, 82–3, 85, 87, 89, 93, 96–7, 99, 119, 135, 138, 145
minimalism   xiii, 28, 42, 88, 125–7, 137
minoritarian   61, 86, 114
minstrelsy   58, 60, 92–5, 115
modernism   xiv, 27–8, 75, 95, 101, 111, 124, 144
molecular. *See* becoming-molecular
monad   30, 104, 123, 135
more. *See* surplus
Morrison, Bill   137–8, 146
Mozart, Wolfgang Amadeus   139
Müller, Filip   109, 117
multiplicity   vii, viii n.4, xi, 75, 76 n.29, 105
   multiple-cry   11, 15, 22, 25 n.29, 41, 75, 87
Murray, Albert   61–3, 77, 79
musique informelle   35, 38, 111, 126
muteness. *See* silence
myth   vii, xii, 15, 48, 63, 82, 84, 104, 106, 115, 125, 127, 132
   as fate   33, 76–8
   as punishment   12 n.54, 110–11

naiveté   33, 85, 114–15
natural beauty   86–7
natural-history   vii, x, 1–18, 44–5, 51, 63, 65, 68, 115, 123, 128, 142
need   viii, xi, xiii–xiv, 7, 11, 21, 29 n.44, 32, 35–6, 46, 62, 71–2, 75, 78, 84–7, 94, 100 n.245, 126–7, 143
   ontological   x–xi, 111, 125
negation   xiv, 62, 69, 128, 135
negativity   44–5, 60, 76, 89, 130, 147
neurosis   112–15, 121
neutralization   33, 45, 74, 85, 91–2

Nietzsche, Friedrich   x, 11, 21, 36, 42, 46, 48, 84, 102, 111–16, 118–20, 132
nihilism   x, 114, 117
noise   10, 15, 21, 27, 32, 35–6, 38, 41, 50, 67, 76, 83–6, 89, 92, 105, 119, 127, 147
nomadism   xiv, 57, 77, 86, 92, 114–15
nonidentity   xv, 8, 13–14, 44, 46, 97, 101, 128, 134
nonintentional   vii, 22, 48, 128, 132, 140 n.132
now-time   9, 25, 107
Nurse with Wound   119
Nyman, Michael   127

object/objectivity   viii n.4, ix, xi–xiv, 7, 13, 14 n.63, 22, 24, 25 n.28, 27–8, 30–1, 35, 39, 43, 46, 48–50, 53, 74–6, 83, 94, 101, 111, 114, 120, 122, 124, 134–5
Oedipus   1, 32, 81, 83, 112–15
Oliveros, Pauline   39
ontology   xi, 13–14, 35, 111, 135
Opitz, Martin   71–2
oral. *See* vocal
Oryema, Geoffrey   66
Otte, Hans   143
overtone   xiii, 26, 28, 42, 85–6, 125, 131

Paganini, Niccolò   77
Pärt, Arvo   96
Patton, Charlie   58–61, 63, 65, 76
Penderecki, Krzysztof   47, 96, 134, 139
people   10, 21, 26, 35–6, 49–51, 76, 81, 99, 118, 123
percussion. *See* drum
physiognomy. *See* character
Pimmon   86, 127
plane of consistency   ix–x, 12 n.53, 27, 61, 68, 126
Plato   63–5, 106
play   4, 17–18, 22, 25 n.28, 30, 32–3, 36, 42, 46, 53–5, 58, 60–2, 64, 72, 83, 85, 88, 93–4, 105, 107, 121, 127–9, 132, 141–3
polyphony   20, 39–40, 42, 44, 55, 71, 87, 105
popular music   xiii–xiv, 51, 63 n.60, 73, 91, 95, 102

positivism   x, xv, 13, 47–8, 92, 94, 130, 137
Poulenc, Francis   140
Powell, Badan   77
power   9, 11, 15–16, 24, 30–1, 33, 68, 84, 87, 93 n.207, 98, 102, 114, 124, 128, 139, 145
   of false   xii, 116
practice/praxis   xiii, 7–8, 10, 33, 43–6, 50, 62, 70, 92, 96–8, 106, 117, 120, 126, 133
   pseudo   3, 50, 100, 117, 122
pragmatics   viii–ix, 46, 69, 71, 88, 99–101, 116
presentation   vii–xv, 73, 81, 128, 141
prison   17, 33, 44 n.109, 51, 54, 56, 75, 80–1, 110, 116, 123, 135, 137
private property   6, 26, 41, 65, 75, 92, 103, 139 n.130
production   xiii, 11 n.52, 19, 23–4, 27, 31, 34, 36, 38–40, 42–3, 48, 50, 57, 68, 73–4, 90–1, 93, 96, 98–102, 107, 111–12, 115, 121, 127
   desiring   xi, 49, 95, 97, 104
   forces and relations   xv, 22, 68, 87–8, 97, 101 n.245, 106, 127 n.92
   industrial   24–6, 32, 36, 60
protection. *See* security
Proust, Marcel   5, 7–8, 30, 106–7, 136
psychoanalysis. *See* Freud
Puar, Jasbir   88
public   20, 66, 73–6, 95, 101–2
Pynchon, Thomas   86

race   54, 58
   racism   43, 62, 79–80, 86, 95–6, 113
Rainey, Ma   65
Rancière, Jacques   28, 62
rationalization   9, 22, 44 n.109, 62, 79, 91
Ravel, Maurice   141
reconciliation   vii–viii, xiv, 10–11, 19, 23, 26, 28–30, 45, 47–8, 50, 65, 74, 81, 103, 105, 115, 123, 133, 136, 141, 145
redemption   viii, xii–xiv, 10, 15, 17–18, 22, 29 n.46, 33, 45, 51, 61, 67, 81, 95, 107, 112–13, 116–19, 123, 143, 146
refrain   2, 5, 11, 16, 19, 23, 30, 36, 45, 50, 71, 81, 85, 95, 104, 128, 143

Index

Reich, Steve 88, 125, 127
reification xiv, 42, 48, 70 n.99, 87, 90–1, 93, 100, 103, 110, 120, 122, 129, 134–5
remembrance. *See* memory
repetition xiii, 2, 5, 9 n.39, 11, 14, 28–9, 60, 68, 90, 99, 110–11, 122, 125, 130–2, 137–8, 140–5
representation vii, ix, 13, 68, 84, 97, 102, 121, 128, 131
rescue. *See* redemption
resignation xv, 8, 64, 98, 107, 119, 129, 140
   onward dialectic 29, 54–5, 66, 68, 77–81, 89, 92, 105, 131, 138, 141
Resnais, Alain 131
revolution 8, 10, 31, 42, 92, 93 n.207, 97, 100, 116
rhizomatics ix–x, 35, 44, 73, 90, 100, 129, 142
rhythm vii, 4, 10, 15, 24, 26, 29–31, 37–8, 49, 60–1, 71, 77, 81, 83, 88, 95, 104, 106, 128, 138–9, 141, 144
Riley, Terry 28–9, 86
ritornello. *See* refrain
Roach, Max 66
Robeson, Paul 66, 91
rock-and-roll 29, 91, 125, 146
Rockmore, Clara 131
Rossellini, Roberto 100
Rothko, Mark 40
Russell, George 38, 127
Russolo, Luigi 35
Rzewski, Frederic 97

Saariaho, Kaija 39, 85
sacrifice 16, 43, 103, 114, 116, 120
Said, Edward 92
Satie, Eric 119
scatting 59, 71–4, 82
Scelsi, Giacinto 40
Schaeffer, Pierre 28, 83
Schafer, R. Murray 36
Schelling, Friedrich 71
Schiller, Friedrich 25–6, 33 n.65, 54, 142
schizophrenia xi–xii, 35, 42, 106, 116–17, 121
Schoenberg, Arnold 37–40, 96, 122–3, 134
Schubert, Franz 33

Schumann, Robert 27
second nature 33–4, 50, 70 n.99, 80, 107, 115, 124
second reflection xi, 7, 97, 135
security 1–2, 4, 7–8, 16, 30, 50, 53, 55, 68, 79, 95, 102, 105, 120, 136
self-preservation vii, 2–3, 22, 45, 109, 114–15, 123, 129
semblance x–xiii, 3, 12 n.52, 25, 38, 44–5, 50, 62, 65, 69–70, 73, 77, 89, 115, 118, 141
   beautiful 9, 25, 80, 104
Seneca 53
sense/sensory/sensation 9, 40, 43, 49, 56, 66, 69, 88, 89 n.186, 94 n.208, 98, 100, 102, 109, 134–5, 138
   logic of 38 n.86, 93, 97, 116–17 n.45, 135 n.114
Shakespeare, William 55, 126
Shostakovich, Dmitri 63
shudder 50, 82, 102, 106, 111, 119, 134, 135 n.118, 146
Sibelius, Jean 96
silence vii, 5–6, 9, 13–14, 16–18, 20, 22, 25–6, 29, 36–7, 46–9, 50–1, 54, 56, 60–1, 63, 66–7, 78, 83, 89, 95, 98, 100, 106, 110, 122, 129, 140–1, 145
slavery xiv n.30, 6, 29, 55–6, 59, 64–5, 79, 87, 95, 98, 144
slide 58, 63–6, 69, 84, 88, 130
Smith, Kaitlyn Aurelia 118
Socrates 62, 65, 123
soloist. *See* virtuoso
song xii, xv n.33, 1–34, 37, 41, 44–5, 47, 50–1, 55, 62, 65, 67–8, 71–2, 76–7, 80–1, 83, 91, 103–4, 106, 131, 138, 141, 143–4
   bird 2, 15, 21–2, 26–8, 32, 45, 63
   farewell (*Abgesang*), 8, 10, 23–4
   folk 49, 54, 60
   full 15, 21
   solo 10–11, 21, 61, 74, 87
   sorrow (*Trauergesang*) xiii, 21–4, 33, 54–9, 69, 79, 82, 86–7, 91
sorrow (*Trauer*) xii–xiii, 5, 17, 22, 33, 44, 49–51, 53–107
soul 65, 90, 92, 106, 114–16
sovereignty 22, 31, 79, 110
space 18, 31, 35, 37, 40, 46, 65, 74, 92, 128, 133–4

smooth and striated   16, 91
spatialization   39, 43
spell   viii, xiii, 2–4, 6, 11, 15, 17–18, 33–4, 36, 40, 45, 47, 50–1, 70, 78, 82, 85, 96, 109–11, 114, 121, 141, 145
Spiegal, Laurie   68
Spinoza, Baruch   3
spirit   x, xiv–xv, 13, 22–3, 34, 41, 47, 75, 83–4, 87, 91–2, 97, 106, 112, 114–16, 136–7
spiritual   28, 50, 55, 58, 61
state   8 n.37, 49, 57, 68, 73–6, 80, 86, 89, 91–2, 98, 102, 112–13, 115, 121, 126, 133–4, 143
state of emergency   xii, 2, 89, 119, 127, 130
Stockhausen, Karlheinz   27, 38, 46, 127–8, 143
stop-time   77, 83
storytelling   16, 40, 57, 72
Strauss, Richard   118, 134, 141
Stravinsky, Igor   39, 42
structural listening   93–4
studio   19, 27, 31, 38, 70 n.99, 126, 128
style   36, 55, 81, 92, 122, 126
subject/subjectivity   xi, 10, 12–14, 22–3, 34–5, 38, 40, 47–9, 49 n.135, 53–4, 65, 71, 74, 81, 95, 119–21, 133–6, 140, 145
sublation (*Aufhebung*), 23, 104, 115, 119, 127, 136
suffering   22, 26–7, 45, 50, 66–7, 75–6, 117–18, 124, 126, 135, 137, 139, 146
Sun Ra   27–8, 86
surplus   48, 118, 124

Tchaikovsky, Pyotr Ilyich   143
technique/technology   x, 9, 11, 15–16, 20–3, 26–8, 31, 34–7, 40, 42–3, 45–6, 58, 63–4, 67, 69, 71–2, 75–6, 81, 87–9, 94, 96, 98, 106, 119, 120, 125–6, 128–31, 142, 144
  technical reproduction   xv, 20, 24, 28, 31, 37, 45, 60 n.44, 70 n.99, 71, 87–9, 97, 107, 130–1
tempo   5, 23–5, 31, 36, 63, 70–3, 84, 130, 141
territorialization   xiii, 1–2, 4, 10–11, 15, 19, 60, 121

deterritorialization   viii, x, 1–3, 10, 13, 21–2, 42, 50, 57, 68, 84, 88, 91–2, 109, 114, 139 n.130, 142–3
reterritorialization   3–4, 41, 91, 109, 115, 142
texture   9, 26, 30, 32, 38, 42, 85, 91, 104, 118, 121, 126–7, 131
theology   43, 47, 57, 64, 80, 105, 110, 117
Thoreau, Henry David   132, 140
timbre. *See* texture
time/temporality   9, 14–16, 25, 37, 39–40, 47, 49, 61, 63–7, 69–70, 73, 77, 83–4, 90, 92, 104, 107, 113, 118, 123, 134, 136, 138, 140–1, 145
  capitalist   37–8, 65
  Chronos and Aeon   125–9
  historical   17, 37–8, 49
  messianic   25, 107, 125–9, 136–7
Tobler, Georg Christoph   101
Tocqueville, Alexis de   101
tonality   xii, 5, 16, 21, 26–30, 34, 36–40, 42, 44, 46, 70, 95, 101, 119, 127 n.92, 128, 130, 138, 143
torture   6, 66–7, 81–2, 99–100, 109, 111, 117–18, 124, 133–6, 142
totality   viii, xi–xii, 4, 9, 31, 40, 44, 51, 55–6, 89, 98, 104–6, 116, 123, 145
tragedy   4, 17, 41, 54, 122
train   xiii, 24, 28–9, 31, 59, 76, 80–1, 83–4, 93, 133, 138–40, 142–3
transformation   viii, x, 2, 11, 31, 42, 61, 84, 88, 118, 145
transitoriness (*Vergänglichkeit*), 8, 10–11, 13, 15, 17–18, 29, 86, 106, 134–6
transposition   34, 67, 70 n.99, 77, 82–4, 89, 105
Trauerspiel   vii, 9, 22, 26, 53–5, 57, 71–4, 77, 79, 81
trauma   40, 49, 66–7, 121
truth-content   x, xiii–xiv, 12, 28, 30, 44, 57, 59, 71, 82, 94 n.208, 101 n.245, 102, 117, 122

Übermensch   118–20
unconscious   vii, 7, 67, 90, 97, 99, 119, 129, 131, 145, 147
utopia   xv n.33, 20, 25–6, 64, 69, 82, 104, 117, 132–3, 135–6

Varèse, Edgard 35
Verdi, Giuseppe 27, 61
Villa-Lobos, Heitor 140
virtual viii, 40, 69, 71, 104–5, 131, 135, 139 n.130
virtuoso 5, 16, 20–1, 27, 35, 37, 77, 83, 128
vitalism 13, 79, 105, 112, 115, 121
Vivaldi, Antonio 126
vocal 22–4, 34, 76–7, 81, 83–4

Wagner, Richard 26–7, 34, 61, 76, 142, 144
Walker, T-Bone 79
war vii, 2, 10, 30, 40, 88, 122, 124, 127, 129, 133, 137, 146
    machine 57, 86, 115

Waters, Muddy 60
Weber, Max 112
Webern, Anton 38–9
Werfel, Franz 72
White, Josh 91
Wilderson Jr., Frank 95
Wittgenstein, Ludwig 9
Wolf, Howlin', 59, 62
Wolfe, Julia 125
Wooten, Victor 90

Xenakis, Iannis 36, 137

Yoshihide, Otomo 118
Young, La Monte 28

Zimmer, Hans 96, 125

smooth and striated   16, 91
spatialization   39, 43
spell   viii, xiii, 2–4, 6, 11, 15, 17–18,
    33–4, 36, 40, 45, 47, 50–1, 70, 78,
    82, 85, 96, 109–11, 114, 121, 141,
    145
Spiegal, Laurie   68
Spinoza, Baruch   3
spirit   x, xiv–xv, 13, 22–3, 34, 41, 47,
    75, 83–4, 87, 91–2, 97, 106, 112,
    114–16, 136–7
  spiritual   28, 50, 55, 58, 61
state   8 n.37, 49, 57, 68, 73–6, 80, 86, 89,
    91–2, 98, 102, 112–13, 115, 121,
    126, 133–4, 143
state of emergency   xii, 2, 89, 119, 127,
    130
Stockhausen, Karlheinz   27, 38, 46,
    127–8, 143
stop-time   77, 83
storytelling   16, 40, 57, 72
Strauss, Richard   118, 134, 141
Stravinsky, Igor   39, 42
structural listening   93–4
studio   19, 27, 31, 38, 70 n.99, 126, 128
style   36, 55, 81, 92, 122, 126
subject/subjectivity   xi, 10, 12–14, 22–3,
    34–5, 38, 40, 47–9, 49 n.135, 53–4,
    65, 71, 74, 81, 95, 119–21, 133–6,
    140, 145
sublation (*Aufhebung*), 23, 104, 115, 119,
    127, 136
suffering   22, 26–7, 45, 50, 66–7, 75–6,
    117–18, 124, 126, 135, 137, 139, 146
Sun Ra   27–8, 86
surplus   48, 118, 124

Tchaikovsky, Pyotr Ilyich   143
technique/technology   x, 9, 11, 15–16,
    20–3, 26–8, 31, 34–7, 40, 42–3,
    45–6, 58, 63–4, 67, 69, 71–2, 75–6,
    81, 87–9, 94, 96, 98, 106, 119, 120,
    125–6, 128–31, 142, 144
  technical reproduction   xv, 20, 24,
    28, 31, 37, 45, 60 n.44, 70 n.99, 71,
    87–9, 97, 107, 130–1
tempo   5, 23–5, 31, 36, 63, 70–3, 84, 130,
    141
territorialization   xiii, 1–2, 4, 10–11, 15,
    19, 60, 121

deterritorialization   viii, x, 1–3, 10,
    13, 21–2, 42, 50, 57, 68, 84, 88,
    91–2, 109, 114, 139 n.130, 142–3
reterritorialization   3–4, 41, 91, 109,
    115, 142
texture   9, 26, 30, 32, 38, 42, 85, 91, 104,
    118, 121, 126–7, 131
theology   43, 47, 57, 64, 80, 105, 110,
    117
Thoreau, Henry David   132, 140
timbre. *See* texture
time/temporality   9, 14–16, 25, 37,
    39–40, 47, 49, 61, 63–7, 69–70, 73,
    77, 83–4, 90, 92, 104, 107, 113, 118,
    123, 134, 136, 138, 140–1, 145
  capitalist   37–8, 65
  Chronos and Aeon   125–9
  historical   17, 37–8, 49
  messianic   25, 107, 125–9, 136–7
Tobler, Georg Christoph   101
Tocqueville, Alexis de   101
tonality   xii, 5, 16, 21, 26–30, 34,
    36–40, 42, 44, 46, 70, 95, 101, 119,
    127 n.92, 128, 130, 138, 143
torture   6, 66–7, 81–2, 99–100, 109, 111,
    117–18, 124, 133–6, 142
totality   viii, xi–xii, 4, 9, 31, 40, 44, 51,
    55–6, 89, 98, 104–6, 116, 123,
    145
tragedy   4, 17, 41, 54, 122
train   xiii, 24, 28–9, 31, 59, 76, 80–1,
    83–4, 93, 133, 138–40, 142–3
transformation   viii, x, 2, 11, 31, 42, 61,
    84, 88, 118, 145
transitoriness (*Vergänglichkeit*), 8, 10–11,
    13, 15, 17–18, 29, 86, 106, 134–6
transposition   34, 67, 70 n.99, 77, 82–4,
    89, 105
Trauerspiel   vii, 9, 22, 26, 53–5, 57, 71–4,
    77, 79, 81
trauma   40, 49, 66–7, 121
truth-content   x, xiii–xiv, 12, 28, 30, 44,
    57, 59, 71, 82, 94 n.208, 101 n.245,
    102, 117, 122

Übermensch   118–20
unconscious   vii, 7, 67, 90, 97, 99, 119,
    129, 131, 145, 147
utopia   xv n.33, 20, 25–6, 64, 69, 82, 104,
    117, 132–3, 135–6

Varèse, Edgard 35
Verdi, Giuseppe 27, 61
Villa-Lobos, Heitor 140
virtual viii, 40, 69, 71, 104–5, 131, 135, 139 n.130
virtuoso 5, 16, 20–1, 27, 35, 37, 77, 83, 128
vitalism 13, 79, 105, 112, 115, 121
Vivaldi, Antonio 126
vocal 22–4, 34, 76–7, 81, 83–4

Wagner, Richard 26–7, 34, 61, 76, 142, 144
Walker, T-Bone 79
war vii, 2, 10, 30, 40, 88, 122, 124, 127, 129, 133, 137, 146
 machine 57, 86, 115

Waters, Muddy 60
Weber, Max 112
Webern, Anton 38–9
Werfel, Franz 72
White, Josh 91
Wilderson Jr., Frank 95
Wittgenstein, Ludwig 9
Wolf, Howlin', 59, 62
Wolfe, Julia 125
Wooten, Victor 90

Xenakis, Iannis 36, 137

Yoshihide, Otomo 118
Young, La Monte 28

Zimmer, Hans 96, 125

www.ingramcontent.com/pod-product-compliance
Lightning Source LLC
Chambersburg PA
CBHW061834300426
44115CB00013B/2374